SLOW PLANNING?
TIMESCAPES, POWER
AND DEMOCRACY

Mark Dobson and Gavin Parker

First published in Great Britain in 2025 by

Policy Press, an imprint of
Bristol University Press
University of Bristol
1-9 Old Park Hill
Bristol
BS2 8BB
UK
t: +44 (0)117 374 6645
e: bup-info@bristol.ac.uk

Details of international sales and distribution partners are available at
policy.bristoluniversitypress.co.uk

© Bristol University Press 2025

British Library Cataloguing in Publication Data
A catalogue record for this book is available from the British Library

ISBN 978-1-4473-6770-3 hardcover
ISBN 978-1-4473-6771-0 paperback
ISBN 978-1-4473-6772-7 ePub
ISBN 978-1-4473-6773-4 ePdf

The right of Mark Dobson and Gavin Parker to be identified as authors of this work has been asserted by them in accordance with the Copyright, Designs and Patents Act 1988.

All rights reserved: no part of this publication may be reproduced, stored in a retrieval system, or transmitted in any form or by any means, electronic, mechanical, photocopying, recording, or otherwise without the prior permission of Bristol University Press.

Every reasonable effort has been made to obtain permission to reproduce copyrighted material. If, however, anyone knows of an oversight, please contact the publisher.

The statements and opinions contained within this publication are solely those of the authors and not of the University of Bristol or Bristol University Press. The University of Bristol and Bristol University Press disclaim responsibility for any injury to persons or property resulting from any material published in this publication.

Bristol University Press and Policy Press work to counter discrimination on
grounds of gender, race, disability, age and sexuality.

Cover design: Lyn Davies Design
Front cover image: Getty/ Anthony Bradshaw

Contents

List of figures and tables	iv
Notes on authors	v
Acknowledgements	vi
Preface	vii
1 Time, speed and slow planning?	1
2 Time and practice in social theory	16
3 Time and participation in planning	50
4 Time and neoliberalisation in planning	90
5 Time and deliberation in planning	116
6 Time, planning and timescapes for the future	140
References	156
Index	174

List of figures and tables

Figures
3.1	Example of local housing delivery profile over time	65
3.2	London Borough of Barnet's 'Benefits of using the fast-track service'	71
3.3	Individual decision-making process	79
6.1	The orrery	147

Tables
2.1	Bourdieu's key ideas in application to planning practice and time	19
2.2	Dominant conceptions of time: linear time versus circadian time	32
2.3	Codex: key thinkers and their ideas applied to planning	47
3.1	The planning timescape in England: policy and plans examples (Examples 1–5)	56
3.2	Example LDS timetable	60
3.3	The planning timescape in England: development management examples (Examples 6–10)	67
3.4	The planning timescape in England: public participation examples (Examples 11–13)	74
3.5	Time in planning: some dimensions and factors in decisions	80
3.6	Maslow's 'five needs' hierarchy and planning practice	82
5.1	Narrower and wider conceptualisations of participation: realist versus relational and co-produced	129
5.2	Five key factors for deliberation	137

Notes on authors

Mark Dobson is Lecturer in Planning and Development at the University of Reading, UK. His PhD focused on planning reform and austerity localism.

Gavin Parker is Chair of Planning Studies at the University of Reading, UK. He is a Fellow of the Royal Town Planning Institute and a Fellow of the Academy of Social Sciences.

Acknowledgements

We wish to thank all at Policy Press, particularly Emily Watt, Anna Richardson and Dawn Preston for their support and encouragement. Our own temporal strategies have shaped the book and clearly account for the time taken in completing it. Our appreciation for the necessary tolerance, or perhaps absorption, goes to our colleagues, friends and families.

Preface

The impetus for this book stems from a growing concern over the emphasis placed on the performance of planning systems in terms of speed and efficiency – what has been termed 'project speed' in the UK. These criteria are often presented as objectives in and of themselves, that is, as the effective means to service economic growth, and feature prominently in reform agendas. While this is not a book on neoliberalisation of planning systems per se, it cannot avoid this backdrop, as this is the dominant ideological orientation informing the political economy of many Western advanced liberal democracies. That ideological framework is one that valorises speed and efficiency as means to achieve growth and, in this way, challenges the very basis of good planning.

Our focus on time goes well beyond the intellectual advent of neoliberalism ushered in by Fredrich Von Hayek and the Mont Pelerin Society in the 1930s, and as a political project beginning in 1979 with Margaret Thatcher in the UK and Ronald Reagan in the US. The role of time in supporting the construction of capitalist societies was long ago underscored by Marx, writing in the 19th century, and economic and political analyses of societies have long held a concern for the temporal dimensions of past, present and future societal conventions. This book is situated within the temporal context of a 40-year run of various neoliberal project iterations in the UK, with a focus on planning. However, it should be borne in mind that time and its regulation on the terms required by modern capitalism has a much longer history. Contemporary neoliberal approaches can be seen as a progression and intensification of a long-standing and complex relationship between political projects, cultural change, resource allocations, perceptions of risk and environmental challenges.

In presenting 'slow planning' here, we are not actually suggesting that all planning processes be slowed; instead, we draw on social theory and assertions implicit in forms of deliberative democracy to develop a potential antidote to project speed and a recalibration that can allow views to be identified, considered and debated in the planning process. Our contention is that 'proper time' should be acknowledged and woven into planning practices.

We highlight opportunities to take time in planning more seriously by unpacking time in social theory. There is a particular need for this given that any particular organisation of time orchestrated to service speed and efficiency may serve powerful economic or political interests. Such dispositions can appear to offer sufficient time to engage in planning but are choreographed, in effect, privileging timescapes. As such, our reading of time in and for planning is bound up with power, legitimation and democratic engagement. This is a starting point for evaluating how these all relate to the orientation and design of planning systems for reflective planners and involved communities to assist in producing better-quality outcomes.

1

Time, speed and slow planning?

Why planning and time?

The consideration of time in relation to planning is an obvious one: planning is critically concerned with time as an activity in creating plans and policies for the present and future. Yet, beyond such seemingly self-evident claims and understandings of the importance of time, we need to consider the concept much more deeply to appreciate the profound role time and 'timescaping' plays in structuring society, economies and politics, as well as for understanding how temporalisation shapes planning, which in turn shapes the experience of planning. Time has often been an obscure or uncritically accepted part of discourses shaping planning. As we argue here, time, in its deployment both rhetorically and practically, can have profound impacts on both planning processes and outcomes.

The starting point here is that time, as well as related words that are entangled with time, such as 'speed', 'efficiency' and 'delay', play a more significant role in economic and political discourse than may be recognised. Paradoxically, time is almost hidden from view by its ubiquity in everyday life, that is, our behaviours, relations and practices. If the arrangements and impacts of time hide in plain sight, this may be one reason why time has remained largely as a background feature or container in the planning literature and within considerations of wider professional practice. As Ewing (1972: 439) stated half a century ago: 'The utterly essential dimension of planning is time ... Yet time is the one dimension of planning that never gets discussed. It is treated as if it were a constant that everyone understands.' Only recently has more direct and critical engagement with the topic begun to emerge in planning studies.

To illustrate this point, if we take the perspective that time is merely an objective and natural part of the physical universe, then its relevance can seem very far detached from individual experience and how we encounter time. When we consider time from a social-science perspective, where time is typically viewed as socially constructed and embedded in power relations, then its role becomes much clearer in terms of how time is organised and performed through society and its institutions. In reality, time is experienced as a variety of temporalities that influence behaviour. In essence, there is not one time but multiple timings that dictate the rhythm and pace of life: economic time, political time, administrative time and so on (which are reflected in numerous instantiations: boom and bust, democratic election cycles, working hours, tax payment schedules, medical appointment slots, or the timing of a census). Therefore, treating time as singular and objective, as is often the case in popular discourse, robs understanding of its context-dependent, subjective and relational nature – and, more importantly, the power relationships involved in who decides the timings of politics, economics and society, as well as planning.

Throughout this book, we aim to demonstrate that time is not neutral or innocuous. Instead, temporal choreographies and the 'timescape' (Adam, 2004, 2008; Howlett and Goetz, 2014) play an important role in reifying and sustaining economic, political, bureaucratic and social practices. Such timing(s) can promote professional practice and public participation but, equally, can lead to exclusion from, or the subversion of, good planning. The purposes of exercising power and control, and the impact on others effected through time, are critical to this exploration.

Following Ewing (1972), the potential trap of falling into 'self-evidential' assumptions about time as a 'background' to practice may be one reason that other natural- and social-science disciplines have attended much more closely to the importance of time within their academic outputs than have planning scholars (Laurian and Inch, 2019; Hutter and Wiechmann, 2022). Raco et al (2018: 1190) have recognised the lack of research and engagement on the politicised nature of timescapes and temporalities in planning, noting that 'when addressed [these] have been dominated by simple binaries between the speed of planning and decision-making processes and project outcomes'. They argue for more research on the politics and governance of the built environment, as well as engagement with the relationships between power, resources and time.

Furthermore, Matthews (2014: 41–2) highlights that 'the varied temporalities – that is experiences of time – that come together in planning and development processes creat[e] conflict and the possibilities for consensus', and while not taking these issues on directly, he makes the case that 'debates around collaborative planning and community engagement in planning processes have not fully interrogated time in all its forms – historic time; imagined time; developers time; policy-makers time; community time'. We agree that too little attention has been paid to the multiple times shaping planning and seek to start this project in earnest.

Unpacking the myriad effects/affects of time in and for planning is a significant task (and one that cannot be achieved in a single book). The purpose of this volume is to provide a solid starting point that can act as a foundation and springboard for further research on planning and time. While we attempt to keep the relevance of planning in view throughout, this task requires taking an interdisciplinary view of time from social, economic, political and democratic theory. This necessitates opening up our reading to consider time from the broader social-sciences literature.

The main chapters in this book therefore seek to appraise wider social theorisations of time and deploy them to help consider how time has been used to shape planning. We apply such theorisation to planning to highlight the multiple temporalities at play, which form an important basis of the power relations that shape practice(s) between actors and interests in planning systems. Collectively, we see these forming what we term the 'planning timescape'.

The implications of using time as a lens for planning research are potentially far-reaching. It is beyond the scope of this book to consider all the possible permutations and applications of this perspective. Instead, we seek to sketch out the terrain by providing an overview of time in planning, as well as offering our interpretation of the role and implications of time in terms of the English planning system and helping advocate a research agenda.

Times past?

While we argue that time has not been paid sufficient critical attention in the planning literature, intellectual attention to questions of time and speed have long been recognised. Weber, in his path-breaking *The Protestant Ethic and the Spirit of Capitalism*, noted how 'the extraordinary increase in speed by which public announcements, as well as political and economic facts are transmitted exerts a steady and sharp pressure in the direction of speeding-up the tempo of administrative reaction' (Weber, 1904, quoted in Toffler, 1970: 143). Such reflections on the increasing pace of 'modern' life also underscore that 'the more complex societies have become, the more "urgently" timing problems have been posed' (Martineau, 2016: 32).

Taking a historical perspective can remind us how the modern age has required that time be mastered to organise industrial capitalist societies. It is notable that the great commentator on cities and architecture Lewis Mumford (1934), in his sweeping text *Technics and Civilisation*, considered the moral, economic and political choices that we make as a society, and recognised the temporal dimension. For Mumford, these choices have, over the past centuries, produced an industrialised machine-oriented capitalist economy. For him, time and its deployment meant that, even by the 1930s, 'the measurement of time became the timing of everyday activities, the temporal control of work activity and the rationing of time' (Mumford, 1934: 13) had become normalised. Mumford observed that 'each culture believes that every other space and time is an approximation to or perversion of the real space and time in which it lives' (Mumford, 1934: 13). In this latter point, he draws attention to alternatives and differences across cultures and groups. This highlights the way that time is aligned to particular goals and priorities, and in this way, he prefigures early work on social theories of (relational) time that we discuss in Chapter 2. Similarly, Luhmann's work on trust and power also recognised the significance of time, and noting over four decades ago that 'a theory of trust presupposes a theory of time' (1979: 12).

Returning our overview to the present day, the context in which UK planning systems currently operate has been one shaped by over 40 years of neoliberal-informed policy approaches, as overseen by successive UK governments since the late 1970s. The effects of neoliberal thought and associated policy and practice have widely been recognised to include the deregulation of state planning, the removal of strategic planning, the marketisation and commercialisation of planning, and reliance on private sector inputs (Lord and Tewdwr-Jones, 2014). This has also been characterised as presenting an 'open for business' culture (Inch, 2018) by governments that increasingly prioritise growing the economy (that is, growth) as their main political and policy platform.

It is now commonplace in political and public debate that anything perceived as being a barrier to business or growth is unnecessarily 'holding the country back' from achieving its potential. The typical targets of such narratives are often 'bureaucracy' and 'regulation'. These culprits are positioned as standing in the way of efficient and effective business. The underlying tone of appeals for deregulation and 'cutting red tape' are often tied to the need to 'get things done'. This is where the governance of time begins to overtly shape policy. Moreover, as we delineate later on, this highlights what Lazar (2019) terms 'temporal-rhetorical framings' and reflects what Nowotny (1994) calls 'chrono-technologies', where time can be highly influential in shaping political and public discourse(s), which signal measures imposed to regulate practice (the import of such concepts is discussed further in Chapter 2).

As the title of this book suggests, one of the main issues with policy that attempts to speed up processes to meet a business objective, or otherwise impose temporal privileging, can be that the importance and quality of the activity in question can be undermined and subsumed to a broader economic growth agenda. This can include sacrificing other objectives, such as inclusion, deliberation and serving the public interest (discussed in more detail later). These have become trade-offs to prioritise 'project speed', whereby politicians and policy makers have serially attempted to placate business interests by presenting 'on the hoof' policy solutions to speed up or bypass bureaucratic and/or regulatory processes. Apparently, these solutions have been offered without careful thought about their full ramifications. We observe that there has been too little consideration of what is either lost or even gained, both now and in the future, by making changes to processes or rules using deadlines, time limits or other chrono-technologies that privilege 'growth' goals.

Starting with Madanipour's (2017) distinction between three types of time that influence approaches to urbanism and that shape our cities – substantive time, relational time and intuitive time – this reading of planning and its social institutions comes closest to discussing a relational view of time:

> The emphasis on events and their relationship offers the possibility of a transition from the mechanical to a social understanding of time. Time, like space, is a social phenomenon, subject to social processes that generate its concepts, regulates its application and consolidate its meanings. If time and space are envisaged as relationships, they become subject to the stabilizing effects of social institutions. Temporality is managed through the development of social institutions, the recurrent beliefs and modes of conduct that would generate continuity and predictability, helping to manage change and control events within a stable social framework. (Madanipour, 2017: 171)

The strength of this relational perspective of time is that it can inform a rebalancing that offers the possibility of a more inclusive relationship between the multiple stakeholders and diversity of interests involved in planning. Such reflections, which move away from objective portrayals of time, mean that 'the future of the city may be opened to alternative imaginations ... While the relations may be subject to the strong and powerful forces that influence the course of events, a relational notion opens up the possibility of rethinking these arrangements' (Madanipour, 2017: 171–2). On such a view, planning is seen as a participatory and democratic forum for considering the future.

This change of perspective is nothing less than a challenge to powers that seek to control time to pursue their own ends (for example, for speed and growth). This type of critical reflection on time and how it is embedded in (seemingly natural) social institutions and cultural norms forms part of the basis of our arguments. We think that this is especially relevant to the UK, which is subject to seemingly constant government and business claims for 'reform' to better suit the needs of development and economic growth. Such pressures will be familiar across planning systems internationally, where they have been subject to more or less neoliberalised reforms.

Given the implications of the foregoing discussion, we do not seek to argue that all bureaucracy is efficient or that some regulations and rules do not become outdated and need revision, but this is not what is driving project speed. It is quite a different matter to revisit laws and policies, and/or to impose time limits or sanctions, if this is a product of an appraisal of success against the original goals and wider challenges at hand. This would be considered good reflective practice in an educated, professionalised and democratic society. Current approaches appear far less about providing detailed evidence or appraisal of existing policies and practices. Instead, the influence of powerful interests is discernible as they press for advantage to make time work for their own ends. We argue that this is a poor foundation and basis for informed policy making and for well-planned (sustainable) outcomes based on democratic checks and balances.

This approach to public policy formulation and reform is not isolated to the planning system but rather reflects a wider shift in the governance of the public sector by successive UK governments that have typically sought to apply quick fixes to complex problems. Ian Dunt (2023: 26), in his exposé of Westminster, highlights that '[t]he British political system rewards short-term tactics over long-term strategy, irrationality over reason, amateurism over seriousness, generalism over specialism and gut instinct over evidence'. Grube also emphasises that in politics, 'frenetic pace is often celebrated. It suggests enthusiasm, "grip", and a determination not to be held back by the entrenched rules of the game … But people in a hurry break things' (2022: vii–viii). We view the latest 'project speed' agenda targeting planning-system performance as just one manifestation of this broader deprofessionalisation and politicisation of governing the state's social institutions. Furthermore, such approaches to governing can become more pronounced (and fervent) within neoliberalised and populist political environments. This leads to a suspicion that policy is being based largely on intuition, ambition and ideological preferences over evidence, consultation or considered strategy.

While beyond the explicit focus on time here, it is worth recognising that the wider context of government pressure to reform planning according to political goals, such as a neoliberalist agenda, is further complicated by the way that planning issues can be used as a battleground in the so-called 'culture wars' that accompany populist rhetoric (see Parker and Dobson, 2023). These are typically characterised as disagreements about cultural and social beliefs between groups, especially between people with more conservative attitudes and those holding more progressive opinions. Such rhetoric often seeks to politicise past, present and future ideals in their favour.

We can view instances of culture wars as struggles for dominance over the values, beliefs and practices that should be accepted within a civil society, that is, to shape societal morality, which have generated and indeed necessitated polarised views. In planning, this can be seen in examples that arbitrate where rights and the environment are at stake, and end up a victim of both sides (that is, for conservatives, overstepping on individual freedoms, and for progressives, planning policy not doing enough to move beyond the status quo). We can see such cultural conflict manifest in recent debates, for example, over the urgency to achieve climate action, such as net-zero carbon emissions targets, the introduction of 15-minute neighbourhoods and low traffic zones, as well as the extension of the Ultra Low Emission Zone (ULEZ) in London.

Throughout this book, we have been mindful not to fall into the trap of criticising speed or growth in all cases; indeed, these can be laudable aims for improving a range of situations. Rather, what we seek to question here is the pursuit of speed or growth at all costs. It is not for us to say what objectives are good or bad but, rather, to assert that whatever approach is taken in deciding them, allowing time for the inclusion of stakeholders and deliberation on the range of impacts and issues involved seems wise. Without such an approach to planning, the substantive goals of public interest and sustainable development are curtailed. In short, time is needed to both reflect on existing approaches and objectives that shape the present and future, and, more critically, to consider how they compare to any alternatives.

This has led us to suggest that we need a more considered approach to questions of time in policy and practice. We use 'slow planning' as a title not to argue for a slow process but to acknowledge that planning should not be rushed or simplified. We should start from the point of 'proper time', with inclusivity, deliberation and public interest driving modalities of planning. With this in mind, we can start to think about temporality and temporalisation in relation to planning.

Planning fast and slow

In the influential book *Thinking, Fast and Slow* by Daniel Kahneman (2011), the author discusses human decision making and how we respond, or should respond, both quickly and more slowly to different situations. In that text, it is stressed how 'time does matter. ... The central fact of existence is that it is the ultimate finite resource' (Kahneman, 2011: 409). Similarly, Rosling et al (2018) argue that pressure to realise 'urgency' may block analytical thinking. These authors draw attention to how one result can be making up our minds too fast and taking action that has not been well thought through. In reality, there is always likely to be some pressure or discounting involved in how we arrive at conclusions and weigh up the foreseeable costs and benefits of time taken (that is, bounded rationality), and this conditions how we prioritise tasks and time expenditure. This pragmatism also implies that we operate in a psychological state where the boundedness of our understanding of a task or situation shapes decisions and raises several questions, including: how do we know how much time to take over any given decision?

This brings into view, on an individualised basis at least, that many forces or pressures shape our approach to work and our behaviours. Such conditions lead us to make daily judgement calls about the most effective and beneficial effort and time to deploy. The time aspect of such conditions can be understood as a 'temporally bounded' rationality, which, for Felt (2016: 182), shapes the 'temporal choreographies' that influence responsibility, citizenship and democracy – what we will explore and refer to later as 'time shaping practice'.

While human decision-making processes are complicated, the task of making judgements is often compounded within more complex disciplinary professions. This clearly applies to planning given the synoptic nature and breadth of considerations recognised as features of spatial planning (see Tewdwr-Jones, 2017). Planning itself involves many different roles and specialisms, and draws in multiple knowledge strands (see Parker and Street, 2021). As Donald Schon (1982: 353) identified 40 years ago: 'planners function variously as designers, plan makers, critics, advocates of special interests, regulators, managers, evaluators, and intermediaries. In planning as in other professions, each role tends to be associated with characteristic values, strategies, techniques, and bodies of relevant information.'

Even before this, the multidimensional nature and multidisciplinary character of planning was recognised in the UK as far back as the 1950 Shuster Report (see Presthus, 1951), and this multi-actor environment implies that time, as well as knowledge, are critical ingredients for good planning. Yet, while planning has always been a multifaceted and technical discipline, we see a growing complexity of planning as a professional activity given the increasing range and scope of challenges that require solutions in the early 21st century. Conversely, this role has often been downplayed by some governments and interest groups, and planning has been afforded less time and resources to address them.

The question of time becomes most pertinent not only when pondering over particularly complex situations or where the problem under consideration is 'wicked', which is an acknowledged feature of many planning situations (see, for example, Hartmann, 2012; Rittel and Weber, 1973), but also where some may elect to simplify the nature of the issue, render it tame and then offer a solution that (only) then appears appropriate or legitimate (Head and Alford, 2015; Wright et al, 2019). It seems clear why Schon (1982, 1983) highlighted the key role of reflection and deliberation for professional practitioners when dealing with complex issues on a regular basis. The planning profession may also require a more active or critical reflection beyond 'self-reflection'. What we mean is that self-reflection over issues and solutions almost certainly has to be accompanied by deliberation with others (indeed, we go further in arguing later that planning is by its nature participatory).

In the UK, however, planning 'performance' is measured by government primarily in terms of the speed of decision making. Thus, if time for reflection is taken as an important feature of professional practice, it is still moot whether and how planners can afford reflection in systems across practice environments that squeeze time. How one reflects and uses time for deliberation is just as important as any quantum of time, as is the question of who is involved and what knowledge is applied. These are several of the critical elements for contending with (a more inclusive and deliberative) practice, and this frames consideration of what participative dynamics are to be sustained in planning. Such issues all bear time implications, impact on different actors and affect planning and development outcomes – a situation we present later as representing the multiple temporalities of planning and that shape the planning timescape.

While the pursuit of growth through speed, efficiency and certainty has long been legitimised by UK governments and urged by powerful land and development interests, 'project speed' and its underpinning attacks on planning have become increasingly febrile (see Chapter 4). In this context, there is concern that such political rhetoric and associated timescaping will impair planning, erode public confidence, promote exclusionary practice and deliver unsustainable outcomes if these are viewed as acceptable 'collateral damage' in the drive for speed to service a growth agenda.

Placing these debates aside momentarily, suspicions about the quality of decisions, how (wicked) planning challenges are understood and how solutions are arrived at abound. Is there something that we should recognise and reflect on about the importance of time in making decisions in planning? Can time pressure sometimes be a positive force in 'concentrating minds'? Some might say that overthinking undermines planning, as it should be a stage preceding delivery or action, as well as facilitate action rather than unreasonably delay it. If not appropriate to the task, though, what mistakes, oversights or exclusions may be compounded by time pressure? As Hartmann (2012) observes, accepting 'just-viable' options may ultimately be deemed acceptable on these grounds, leading to accepted normative states that have not been open to scrutiny or wider deliberation. In reality, we just do not know enough about how such a calculus is made. Conversely, if 'fast' planning is acceptable, then what credentials justify it or provide the criteria against which to judge it? What is the (presumed) relationship between speed and quality? That is to say, we need to critically reflect on the fast and slow of planning.

Time is also important for setting the parameters of debate and action in planning. Its use as a means of control and facilitation is more than simply a 'container' of events (Hutter and Wiechmann, 2022). Multiple temporalities can be viewed most clearly between key participants in the process (such as landowners, developers, politicians and councillors, local authority planners, and diverse community members), as well as in the different emphases placed on land-use mapping, participation and decision making across different international planning systems, and when considering possible end states or other normative goals.

This brings into view the dilemma of time taken in planning, where balancing speed/delay against time needed to prepare and think is likely to be difficult. While recognising the complexities of planning, it is true that careful thought does not guarantee optimal outcome(s). Rather, adept judgement and the smart use of system design and resources is also needed. Recognition that when decisions are made, they are imperfect is a reality. And when they are found to be so, can we at least say that 'best efforts' were made? We might ask that they pass tests other than simply a speed test, perhaps deliberation over the decision and possible alternatives has been undertaken, such that those affected can understand the (value) judgements at hand, and so transparency becomes a servant to this goal. Moreover, a clearer and more systematic approach to different planning tasks, projects or issues needs to be kept in view.

Closer consideration of the range of elements and issues incorporated by modern planners and planning systems reveals the possibility that different issues, policies or decisions need more or less time, more or less resource, and, it follows, more or less input. The deployment of resources influences the assessment of 'time' needed. As such, some tasks may be expedited by putting more people onto the job or spending money on outsourcing tasks, or indeed by extending the bounds of co-production to ensure knowledge and understanding are brokered effectively. In this sense, a lack of time to complete a particular task can, in some circumstances, be counteracted by an increased deployment of other resources. This highlights some of the time asymmetries found in planning given the uneven distribution of time, money and knowledge resources across interested parties. Time is not the only factor to be reckoned with, but the criticality of timeliness, or, as we go on to discuss, 'proper time', can play an important part in relation to a specific task or issue.

Questions of what is at stake and how time-critical a decision or a policy is provoke reflection on any blanket presumption, or uniform prescription, about the time needed in planning. The specific element of planning (that is, the issue or stage), the knowledge required, the skills held and the need to involve others are other factors. How time is apportioned and 'needed' in planning has had too little attention, particularly in relation to system design and to sustaining the operating principles that underpin a given system. This leads to our consideration of the role of time *in* planning and *for* planning.

As we go on to discuss across the following chapters, the way that planning is organised and shaped by time can be viewed as producing a timescape that has been socially and politically constructed and contested. Abram and Weszkalnys (2011: 3) emphasise the multiple 'possibilities that time offers space'. If time is disciplined to the extent that studies of neoliberal planning lead us to believe, then what implications are there for practice and, indeed, for how planning is actually done? What relations of production are maintained, and, for instance, what are the actual costs involved in the 'black box' of local plan production? This follows calls that planners, in both research and practice, 'need to explicitly explore what it means to collectively and inclusively muddle through the various temporalities involved in plan making and urban change' (Laurian and Inch, 2019: 278).

We cannot take on all that this implies here, but such concerns have been manifest across many aspects of life and activity. Movements relating to slow food, slow tourism and slow living (see Honoré, 2005; Slow Movement, 2017) have been joined by wider attempts to urge 'slow cities', 'where decision-making times allow time for proper democratic and judicial-technical oversight of development processes' (Raco et al, 2018: 1180). These separate but related movements reflect a groundswell against 'fast' practice, particularly in response to concerns over the impacts of social acceleration and living in a 'high-speed society' (Rosa, 2010, 2013). We see this in so-called '24/7 capitalism', rolling news cycles and constantly updating social media feeds. This context is also likely to impact on the level of (cognitive) attention or focus that is paid to any particular activity or event, given the potential for 'information overload' and 'burnout' within increasingly complex and fast-paced societies, as well as the clock time expended on them.

Decisions over the timings of society are also deeply political, for example, how long children must stay in school education for, how long the working week is and when people get to retire, to name a few. We can see political moves to realign time and its availability, for instance, in efforts to 'extend' working lives by removing the need to retire from work or raising the pensionable age, in effect, boosting time into the economy. These have all changed as societies and social institutions have developed (that is, they are socially constructed under prevailing cultures).

Cautionary voices and deliberately oppositional movements have highlighted the use of time as a strategic resource and help indicate the importance of time in planning and for planning better. As we discuss in Chapter 2, the control of time shapes the future and critically makes practice. For example, different speeds of process and decision making can act to create new opportunities for investors and developers who operate with shorter- or longer-term outlooks and business models, as well as to perform or enable other social groups. As it stands, commercial and financial discourses can crowd out and even completely corrode other substantive aims of planning. In this context, participation or apparently deliberative activity can too easily become manipulative or superficial, resulting in even further public distrust in planning actors and institutions. Laurian and Inch (2019: 278) suggest that when powerful interests attempt control through time, this can also be challenged by using time:

> Extending the call for 'slow cities' and 'slow building', 'slow planning' can be a selective tactic for accommodating multiple temporalities and concerns, tempering the negative impacts of urban development processes dominated by financial rates of returns or the preferred pacing of dominant actors. ... Selective deceleration tactics could aim to set aside time to stimulate thinking about the now and the future by making time slow down or stand still.

Similarly, Weber (2015) argues for a 'slow urbanism', which allows time for proper democratic and technical oversight of development, as well as the introduction of new forms of regulation that underpin this mode. In parallel with such calls, the focus here hinges on a question about what time and space there is for deliberation in planning, both for professional planners and for other actors with a stake in planning outcomes. To unpack this, we have chosen to focus largely on the procedural elements of the English planning system timescape (as set out in Chapter 3).

Our contention is that good planning takes time, but that is not necessarily the same thing as abandoning clock time or condoning 'delay'. What is needed is more open discussion about the 'right timing' or, as we highlight throughout the book, 'proper time' in planning. This is where the resources and values of those involved are aligned with the time needed to plan well. At its best, we argue that a 'slower' planning – a play on the truer meaning of 'deliberative' – can provide a public interest planning where the calibration between key interests is both fairer and likely to produce better outcomes. This does not mean necessarily slower in terms of simple linear or clock time but, rather, that the sensibility and modalities of planning need to keep the impacts of time choreographies and temporal governance in sight and, as a consequence, use time better.

Our advocacy for 'slow planning' therefore pivots on arguing for quality processes and outcomes of planning within any given time period. On this reading, it is the deployment and utilisation of time that is key rather than the duration of activities or 'events' (see Adkins, 2009; see also Chapter 2). This is a critical difference that can highlight various attempts to manage and control time, and helps reveal how the exercise of power features in the use of time in planning and by and across different interests in planning. In this respect, we anticipate the criticism that simply 'allowing more time' for the planning process will solve all planning problems as crude and unrealistic. Time is one resource constraint or risk among many that create practical challenges, along with funding, staffing, knowledge and skills, and political cycles, to name but a few. Yet, appeals to speed can be crude and unrealistic where they misunderstand or ignore the realities of, or proper times for, planning issues.

As such, the premise of the discussion is to assert that 'planning' (that is, the planning field) needs to understand and communicate its own 'proper time(s)'. This should be recognised in the plural because different actors, tasks, projects or processes may need more or less time and resources. Simplistic attempts to 'speed up' planning run the risk of impairing the quality of the activity, curtailing deliberation and impacting on the ability to discharge a professional role. It is also likely to diminish the ability of the less powerful, informed or resourced to engage effectively in the system. Therefore, one of the main arguments put forward here is that a clear 'principle-based' and appropriately deliberative planning system is necessary in a democratic system and pluralist society. This is where considerations of speed and the 'control of time' (Adam, 2004) cannot be allowed to overwhelm or discipline actors' behaviours through the use of discourses of efficiency, certainty, delivery and growth. It is lamentable that these have become the dominant logics under a neoliberalised (and increasingly commercialised) planning system.

As we will discuss throughout the book, planning systems and practices have increasingly come under pressure to be faster, be more efficient and avoid delay under neoliberal policy environments. In the UK, the latest iteration of this discourse is 'project speed', forming a central part of the agenda to reform planning to better serve these goals (as covered in Chapter 4). While timely planning plays its part in facilitating these objectives, planning and its performance should not be measured by speed alone. Instead, decoupling from the speed imperative can enable a better planning that also keeps in view public accountability, inclusivity, deliberation, synoptic thinking and consideration of strategic (spatial) planning aims.

Structure of the book

In order to take some of the issues and concerns expressed as part of this introduction to planning and time further, the book is organised around a series of key themes and ideas relating both to theorisations of time and to key aims and objectives associated with (spatial) planning. We deploy ideas of timescapes/timescaping and proper time to frame the exploration of the (multiple) temporalities of planning and the political endeavour that we label 'project speed'. Across this theorisation, we keep in view a set of normative ideals around which planning may be reasonably coalesced; not least, these are inclusivity, public interest and sustainable development.

To do this, we use the English planning system as a case in point to highlight the effects/affects of attempts to chrono-synchronise, or 'timescape', planning tools, processes and participants in service of a dominant economic growth agenda. Many of the issues and approaches raised around plan making, decision making and public participation will have a wider resonance with, and relevance for, planning systems and practices internationally.

This first chapter has provided an initial grounding for the rationale, aims and scope of the book. It has also indicated why this topic area should be embraced and absorbed, and how this is useful for providing a deeper understanding of time *in* practice and the impact of time *on* practice.

The deeper exposition of time and practice as conceptualised in the wider social sciences is set out in Chapter 2, where a theoretical understanding of time as both a social construct and a technology of power is highlighted. The chapter develops a lens through which to examine time in planning and draws on a range of theorists' work, notably, Pierre Bourdieu, Barbara Adam, Helga Nowotny and Nomi Lazar, whose ideas are presented as key in highlighting the operation of power, political strategy and the relationship of time to practice (and vice versa).

Taking the rich set of ideas covered in Chapter 2, Chapter 3 discusses examples taken from across the English planning system where time has been used to orchestrate planning practice in various ways, what we characterise as a 'timescaping' and 'chrono-synchronisation' project. This serves to indicate the (intended and unintended) inclusionary and exclusionary work of political time in relation to the key stakeholders and tools used in planning practice. As a response, we develop the argument that planning as an activity is inherently participatory and that, as a consequence, participation cannot be separated from professional planning practice.

While leading up to and linking the planning timescape to politics and political time, Chapter 4 features a discussion of planning and the role of time in a neoliberalised policy environment. This outlines the idea of 'project speed', used to focus attention on the political project of reforming planning in the English case. The past decade or so has seen concerted efforts to orient the planning timescape such that it is not necessarily in service of good planning, nor supporting democratic accountability, but is aligned instead to primarily achieve growth. We view the reforms promoted by waves of neoliberalisation and project speed over a longer period as attempts to control the present and future on the terms most agreeable to a narrow constituency. This provides the groundwork for considering more normative goals of planning.

Chapter 5 then considers the role of time, public interest and deliberative democracy in relation to how planning inputs are managed. Particularly, we indicate the implications and linkages across time as a resource, the aims of planning, and the processes and tools available to foster proper time for planning. Care to sustain appropriate deliberative practices are, we argue, linked to the act of planning itself (as a participatory undertaking) rather than isolated as an adjunct to public engagement. In essence, we make a case that enabling deliberation is an important component of good planning, and this is particularly pertinent as attempts to come closer to legitimising planning in the public interest are still an actively debated question.

Chapter 6 summarises the main arguments of the book and argues for a more reflective planning and practice that takes time more seriously. We contend that to effect this requires a rethinking of normative principles and overall goals, as well as, it follows, a reshaping of the timescape(s) of planning in order to fashion proper time(s). This assemblage will be one where the central tenets of inclusion, deliberation and public interest feature as firm design principles for planning systems, processes and practices. We also rehearse a research agenda towards the end of the chapter in which understanding time in and for planning can be further developed.

Chapter 2 begins by setting out a review of how time has been treated in social theory. It outlines how time and temporalisation shape practice, particularly how time orients practice in the service of political goals, and where theories of time span the disciplines of economics, politics and sociology, holding far-reaching implications as a consequence.

2

Time and practice in social theory

Time as a framework for planning

As we outlined in Chapter 1, the overall rationale for the book is to draw attention to the frequent use and impact of time-related rhetoric and measures. These reinforce particular policies and reforms, and serve to organise planning activity. The discursive use of time is often linked to politically inspired claims that planning systems are immersed in 'red tape' and act as a delay to important economic activity. It is clear that such rhetoric has become pervasive in neoliberal contexts, and efforts are made to assert speed as an unquestioned good.

Successive UK governments have bemoaned the slow pace of the planning system, particularly in England, and the claimed impact this has on growth and development. Amid a number of UK politicians over time, Robert Jenrick, then Secretary of State (SoS) at the Ministry of Housing, Communities and Local Government (MHCLG)[1] and person responsible for planning, claimed in 2020 to want to make planning 'more efficient, effective and equitable' and create 'a significantly simpler, faster and more predictable system' (MHCLG, 2020: 8). This aspiration was reinforced with further temporal cues by then Prime Minister Boris Johnson, arguing for a planning system that 'is simpler, clearer and quicker to navigate, delivering results in weeks and months rather than years and decades' (MHCLG, 2020: 6). Such exhortations have become commonplace, and appeals to make planning faster and more efficient to better support growth form the crux of numerous planning reforms aimed at fixing alleged system failings (discussed further in Chapter 4 in relation to the neoliberal and related political appeals to project speed).

Given the initial explanation setting out why time is so important to consider in relation to planning, we now examine time as a social construct and political tool. We review how time has been theorised in the social

---

[1] The government department responsible for planning in England has undergone numerous name changes, and in the time periods focused on in this book, three labels have been applied: the 'Department for Communities and Local Government' (DCLG), the 'Ministry of Housing, Communities and Local Government' (MHCLG) and the 'Department for Levelling-Up, Housing and Communities' (DLUHC).

sciences, drawing on key thinkers who emphasise, among other things, the role of time in shaping social and institutional practices (Section 1), capitalist economic systems (Section 2), interpersonal power relations (Section 3) and political strategies (Section 4). This sets out the framework for analysis and provides both an insight into, and a guide to understanding, how timescapes structure planning. By considering how the use and organisation of time structures how planning is practised and who is involved, the recognition that planning itself produces futures is brought into view. This theorisation is applied later to the planning system in England as a case in point in Chapter 3, and key theoretical ideas are used specifically to examine the way time is organised and deployed (discussed throughout the book).

The theoretical treatment of time set out here draws primarily on the collective work of Pierre Bourdieu, Barbara Adam, Helga Nowotny and Nomi Lazar, along with other prominent social theorists. Overall, we are drawn by Bourdieu's (2000) assertion that time makes practice and this relationship realises temporalisation; that is to say, practice makes time and, reflexively, time shapes practice. This is a key idea here, and the constituent elements of time theory outlined in the following provide the conceptual framework and analytical tools to understand time as practice and its role in the exercise of power and in forms of control both in and of planning. The implications of these and the relationship to the tools used in practice are unpacked later. Here, we first present why time is so important and demonstrate the utility of theory to assess planning practices.

How we deal with time and the impact of temporal strategies on the practice of planning should be recognised and reflected upon more carefully rather than assuming that 'speeding up' or 'slowing down' is the main issue at stake. This brings into view how the deployment of knowledge and resources to address (planning) issues acts to fold and extend time, compress or extend the duration of activity, or set relative prioritisations in practice. Planning processes may take longer or not depending on a range of contributory factors and may be consciously and unconsciously given more attention or be criticised, reflecting power/knowledge tensions. This also means that temporalities are presented and experienced differently, and priorities in and of time are varied. The implication, of course, is that individual 'social' time is relative and constructed from within particular discourses and interplays of power. For our purposes, how resources (including clock time) are applied to planning tasks has important practical and distributional consequences. Where structural intervention, deliberate deregulatory efforts or the maintenance of dominant norms feature strongly, they can be linked to questions about how time is used and how other resources are expended in planning.

The following review of the import of Bourdieu's ideas to planning practice and considerations of time is followed by a closer inspection of time in modern societies, specifically in relation to implications for planning and, most notably, via the work of Adam, Nowotny and Lazar. Together, these elements lead us towards an appreciation of the different timescapes and multiple temporalities involved in planning practice, which form the focus of the final section in this chapter.

Section 1: Pierre Bourdieu – time and practice

The contribution of the sociologist Pierre Bourdieu's work on practice and the role of time forms a significant high-level basis for our consideration of time in planning. From Bourdieu's work, we approach power and time through the lens of his comprehensive 'theory of society', sometimes referred to, perhaps a little narrowly, as social field theory, whereby power is culturally and symbolically created and constantly (re)legitimised through practices shaped by agency and structure(s). Some have characterised his work as no less than traversing the ground between 'an anthropology of everyday life and a social critique of politics, political dynamics, and the possibilities for social change' (Shenkin and Coulson, 2007: 301). As we apply it here, Bourdieu's ideas may be reframed and deployed as a means to critique the dynamics and assumptions found in planning practice, and to consider possibilities for change.

Our view of practice, as highlighted here, pivots on questions about how those with an interest in the field of planning are enabled to participate in knowledge generation and decision making, as well as to examine how, as part of that interactive process, time is one of the factors that organises the social relations of planning practice. One element or outcome of this chapter, and subsequent application, is to highlight how engagement and deliberation is practised and how deliberation qua participation is practice (or at least a substantive element of it). Time to plan clearly becomes critical to practice and essential to inclusive practice.

Bourdieu makes four related contributions to how time influences behaviour and vice versa, and these key ideas help outline our discussion of time and its relationship to planning practice and the 'field of planning'. This is where the relations of power act to shape behaviour and filter new practice. Bourdieu's theoretical vision also attempts to explain how key elements of 'habitus', 'field' and 'capital' have the potential to be dynamic and act to shape change. Important for our focus, and for planning more expansively, is his assertion that practice is not something *in* time but, rather, that *practice makes time* (Bourdieu, 2000: 207; see also Table 2.1). As we will expand on later, this sets up a dynamic relationship of temporalisation, where time and practice influence each other.

Bourdieu: the key ideas

It is notable that the application of Bourdieu's ideas has received only limited application to planning, albeit with some notable exceptions (see Howe and

Table 2.1: Bourdieu's key ideas in application to planning practice and time

Concept	Explanation	Application to planning and time
Field	Bourdieu views social fields as semi-autonomous human constructions with their own bounded set of beliefs that rationalise the rules of behaviour. Each field has its own distinct 'logic of practice'. Collectives of people occupy multiple social fields (economic, political, education and so on) at a time, and this common social space is termed the 'field of power'. The actors operating within a field are positioned in relation to their (positive or negative) economic and cultural capital, and these differences create social 'distinction'. Crucially, the social field of power is uneven, as those with (pre-existing) particular forms of capital are advantaged and are best placed to accumulate more capital for personal advancement. Therefore, fields are hierarchised where dominant agents and institutions have considerable power to shape behaviour within them, making them antagonistic and 'sites of struggle' (Thomson, 2012).	The idea of field helps with our focus on the planning field and time in that: 'While the game that is played in fields has no ultimate winner, it is an unending game, and this always has the potential for change at any time. ... The issue of temporality and particularity does imply ... that new field analyses are always required' (Thomson, 2012: 76–8). For example, some planning reforms (such as project speed) are political attempts by those with power to (re)shape the logic of practice to suit a power/control agenda and are contested by other participants who have such change imposed on them.
Habitus	Bourdieu explains habitus as a property of actors that is both a 'structured and structuring structure' (cited in Maton, 2012, p 50). Habitus is structured by an individual's past experiences and structuring in that it shapes one's present and future practices. Together, this structure comprises 'dispositions' (see later). Crucially, the habitus cannot be separated from the 'field' (see earlier) in which it is situated, that is to say, it is a 'relational construct' of social behaviour. As Maton (2012: 51) clarifies: 'habitus focuses on our ways of acting, feeling, thinking and being. It captures how we carry within us our history, how we bring this history into our present circumstances, and how we then make choices to act in certain ways and not others.'	Habitus is the link between an actor's past, present and future, and therefore has a clear temporal dimension. It is an active and evolving relational process between the individual and the social world they inhabit, that is to say, the 'dialectic of the internalization of externality and the externalization of internality' (Bourdieu, 1977: 72). The creation of a 'new' sociological eye allows an actor to re-evaluate their own (past, present and future) habitus (and reflect on how the field rules and doxa have developed over time). The individual recognition and reflection on the position of participants in planning within such temporal power relations is a key first step for reclaiming proper time in planning practice.

(continued)

Table 2.1: Bourdieu's key ideas in application to planning practice and time (continued)

Concept	Explanation	Application to planning and time
Practice	For Bourdieu, 'practices' are the result of the 'unconscious relationship' between the habitus, the capital held and the field one is operating in. This relationship is summarised as: [(habitus)(capital)] + field = practice. Bringing the preceding concepts together, we can understand this relationship as follows: 'one's practice results from relations between one's dispositions (habitus) and one's position in a field (capital), within the current state of play of that social arena (field). ... Thus, to understand practices we need to understand both the evolving fields within which actors are situated and the evolving habituses which those actors bring to their social fields of practice' (Maton, 2012: 50–2).	An individual's habitus, capital and field are all subject to temporal changes that (re)shape their social context internally or externally, and are therefore time sensitive. The dimension of time highlights how practice can change when habitus, field and capital relations shift within the field of power. These changes can be viewed when law and policy is introduced or reformed that shift practice(s).
Doxa	Doxa are the shared unquestioned (pre-reflective) opinions that determine 'natural' practices and attitudes, which have become so ingrained within their social field of practice that they form 'a set of fundamental beliefs which does not even need to be asserted in the form of an explicit, self-conscious dogma' (Bourdieu, 2000: 16). In other words, 'what is essential goes without saying because it comes without saying' (Bourdieu, 1977: 165). Essentially, doxa highlights the social arbitrariness of unquestioned shared beliefs within a field that shape, maintain and reproduce power relations. That is to highlight 'the misrecognition of forms of social arbitrariness which creates the unformulated, non-discursive, yet internalized and practical recognition of that same social arbitrariness', and to 'make explicit the forms of misrecognized symbolic power (that is, doxa) that underpin the implicit logic of practice, expectations and relations of those operating in these fields' (Deer, 2012: 114–17).	Doxa highlights Bourdieu's concern that reflection on existing rules is mediated by the day-to-day experiences of established practices, which stifles what is implicit and taken for granted (that is, a focus on *what is* rather than *why it is* within a social field). This may be seen as actors within a field not having the time or space to 'radically identify and question the unthought categories of thought' (Deer, 2012: 125). This can be seen in planning where certain conventions and deadlines have become so ingrained that they are not consciously questioned, for example, that minor applications should be processed in eight weeks and major applications in 13 weeks.

Table 2.1: Bourdieu's key ideas in application to planning practice and time (continued)

Concept	Explanation	Application to planning and time
Capital	Bourdieu identified four forms of capital: • economic (money and assets); • cultural (for example, forms of knowledge; taste, aesthetic and cultural preferences; and language, narrative and voice); • social (for example, affiliations and networks; and family, religious and cultural heritage); and • symbolic (things that stand for all of the other forms of capital) and can be 'exchanged' in other fields (see Thomson, 2012: 67).	These forms of capital shape what options are available to actors when positioning themselves within a field. They are linked with habitus (how one sees their place in the social world) and *illusio* in terms of strategy (see later). These forms of capital are not necessarily stable over time and can be gained or lost. It is typical that investors and developers have various forms and combinations of capital available to them to pursue their strategy than do public authority planners or local communities.
Disposition	Closely related to the concept of habitus is that of 'disposition', which, for Bourdieu, is crucial for bringing together the ideas of structure and agency: 'It expresses first the result of an organising action, with a meaning close to that of words such as structure; it also designates a way of being, a habitual state (especially of the body) and, in particular, a predisposition, tendency, propensity or inclination' (Bourdieu, 1977: 214). The *Oxford Dictionary* (2022) helps in defining a particularised set of dispositions as 'a person's inherent qualities of mind and character', and the relationship of these traits to the wider field in which they operate as 'the way in which something is placed or arranged, especially in relation to other things'.	Dispositions are durable in that they last over time, but they are not fixed and so are also transposable when situated within different social fields. As with habitus, dispositions can become activated (as durable or transposable) when relationally situated within different fields of action. As such they have both a temporal and spatial dimension of being. Dispositions can be seen in political views on the role of planning, particularly as held by neoliberal politicians inclined to speed/growth.
Hysteresis	Hysteresis represents a change or disruption between habitus and field, as well as its consequences over time experienced at the personal level, in other words, when actors' 'dispositions [are] out of line with the field and with the "collective expectations" which are constitutive of normality' (Bourdieu, 2000: 160).	'When hysteresis occurs, new opportunities are created by altered field structures. However, there is a high level of risk associated with hysteresis, since for a time at least, field struggles take place in the context of an unknown future. The outcomes of field change can therefore be loss of position, power and wealth because of the revaluation of symbolic capitals and sources of legitimacy' (Hardy, 2012: 144).

(continued)

Table 2.1: Bourdieu's key ideas in application to planning practice and time (continued)

Concept	Explanation	Application to planning and time
	'The essential features of hysteresis have been shown: the mismatch between habitus and field, and the time dimension associated with it ... [and] as a thinking tool, [it] provides explicit links between the objective nature of systemic change (field transformation) and the subjective character of an individual response to that change (altered habitus)' (Hardy, 2012: 144). Conflict or resistance to change (also linked to 'symbolic violence') can be experienced as disciplining of a recognised discord between the individual's habitus or their assumptions about the arbitrary cultural doxa that conflict with existing practice.	This shapes how individuals may be shaped through Bourdieu's pedagogic action, where they learn quickly or more slowly the 'rules of the game', what Clegg (1989) labels 'the standing conditions'. Changes to the national policy expectations or resources afforded to planners can result in a hysteresis between their professional values or motivations and the need to enact actions that go against these in practice, leading to internal conflict over their role.
Illusio	*Illusio* are the techniques operating to enable the interests of members in the field to gain advantage or symbolic capital and create accepted doxa and the behaviour/dispositions that support useful conditions.	The use of political time to shape the planning system and planners is effected to suit a particular interest and/or group or individual operating in a social field.
Reflexivity	Reflexivity is seen in structure–agency or habitus–field interactions that lead to dispositional adjustment – more particularly, this is one factor that regulates change. Actors reflect and adjust based on an assessment of their interest and position in the field to develop a renewed gaze.	Actors in planning require time to adjust based on assessment of how policy and other factors require them to assume new practices or adjust existing ones.

Langdon, 2002; Hillier and Rooksby, 2005; Shin, 2013; Abram, 2014). Bourdieu helps us consider the structure–agency dynamics of social fields and the doxa, or cultures and dispositions, that sustain them in planning (see Gunder and Hillier, 2016; Mace, 2016). Shin (2013: 268) argues that Bourdieu's work can 'help planners strategically participate in urban planning and politics. ... By identifying the stakeholders who have alternative logics of practice (habitus) and interests (capitals) across diverse social sectors, planners might be better able to effectively mobilize.' We go further and highlight not only how Bourdieu's overall set of interrelated ideas help understand planning processes and outcomes but also specifically how time and its control plays a key role. Bourdieu's work helps us to conceive how actors behave and how time figures in behaviour or outcomes (see, for example, Bourdieu, 1977, 1998).

In his later work, Bourdieu (2000: 228) is explicit about the importance of time and how 'temporal power is a power to perpetuate or transform the distribution of the various forms of capital'. Even in his early material, such as his *Outline of a Theory of Practice* (Bourdieu, 1977), Bourdieu argued that people come to understand temporal parameters, such as pace, duration, frequency or repetition, when they enact them regularly.

Bourdieu theorises different capital forms as key 'resources' that people hold or aim to accumulate or exchange, and through other concepts, such as *illusio*, he helps explain how individuals position and strategise to further their interest in the field. Given the richness of his canon and multiplicity of ideas presented in this section, Table 2.1 provides an overview, with the right-hand column of the table indicating how each concept may apply to planning and time. It is notable that the elements set out are interactive, and this requires us to recognise how they impact on each other recursively.

Habitus, field and capital

Bourdieu's overall contribution to modern social theory is most apparent in his formulation of the now widely applied framing concepts of 'field', 'habitus' and practice, as well as forms of 'capital'. Bourdieu uses these terms to outline a methodological framework for exploring behaviour as reflections of actual and potential power relations. The constructs of 'field' and 'habitus', and how these act to structure practice, are accompanied by other concepts that help explain how and why practice manifests in social space. Critically, those ideas cover how continuities, challenges and change are accounted for over time. Together, these attempt to show how and why actors reproduce or adjust particular social behaviours in and through space and time.

One of the most prominent of Bourdieu's ideas is habitus: the set of beliefs and attitudes that the individual has come to accept as normal and acceptable. Habitus has been described as 'necessity internalised and converted into a disposition that generates meaningful practices' (Bourdieu, 1984: 170). Habitus signals a complex of enduring dispositions that humans acquire over the course of socialisation. Habitus also manifests itself in particular ways of comprehending and classifying social phenomena, shaping preferences, and through self-presentation. It reflects what individuals believe to be important based on their values vis-a-vis the field(s) within which they operate, including how they calibrate time. The understandings and behaviours of local planners, community members and developers in relation to their ideals and the planning system are likely to feature some common assumptions in this regard, as well as some critical differences. These are explained by Bourdieu by recourse to different field conditions and competing or dissonant cultural norms.

In utilising habitus to describe the individual's learned behaviour and disposition, Bourdieu argues that this 'semi-durable' state of being acts to guide and organise how we think and behave. This commences through a process of inculcation or 'apprenticeship' learning, which begins in childhood. This learning process is intertwined with time because, as Rifkin (1987: 56) points out, 'Every culture inculcates its newest members by way of an elaborate and often complex process of temporal entrainment'. We learn that certain ways of doing and being are rendered normal or acceptable through a disciplining and learning process. Individuals come to understand that there is gain from compliance or via considered brokerage through various forms of strategising. The individual disposition is learned and internalised. In a professional setting, this apprenticeship involves learning the rules of the game (that is, the field), and this process continues throughout work and other life experience. The individual habitus may jar with the field conditions, and a conflict known as 'hysteresis' may be experienced, resulting in an individual conforming or resisting the practice field and/or field adjustments occurring as part of a critical 'reflexivity' (Adkins, 2004, 2009).

Bourdieu describes society as an arena within which complex 'communities' of agents engage through various 'fields'. Discussion of the field looms large in Bourdieuian thinking, a social field is a structured system with a logic of social positions that are occupied either by individuals or by institutions. Bourdieu (1992) defines fields as systems of social positions, structured internally in terms of power relationships. On this view, all forms of social engagement can be assessed as action geared towards practical functions and strategies of capital accumulation or transubstantiation (exchange). Behaviour may be understood in terms of particular logics of practice. In essence, this refers to action to maintain or enhance interest. It is also an arena within which struggles take place. Change and the individual are viewed less in terms of types of time 'pressures' involved; rather, how the dynamics of the 'field' can be transformed over time and how time is part of the field conditions that structure behaviour are considered. This is reflected in asymmetrical relationships between social agents, who constantly manoeuvre and struggle over limited resources:

> Each social field of practice (including society as a whole) can be understood as a competitive game or 'field of struggles' in which actors strategically improvise in their quest to maximize their positions. Actors do not arrive in a field fully armed with god-like knowledge of the state of play, the positions, beliefs and aptitudes of other actors, or the full consequences of their actions. Rather, they enjoy a particular point of view on proceedings based on their positions, and they come to acquire a sense of the tempo, rhythms and unwritten rules of the game through time and experience. (Maton, 2012: 53)

Field helps us understand how individuals are influenced by power relations that are mediated and inculcated via the habitus, the field culture (the doxa), the stakes involved and the individual's resources (capital) and 'position' in a given field (Bourdieu and Wacquant, 1992). Entry into a field also implies a tacit acceptance or accommodation of the rules of that field, including temporal norms. There is an implicit assumption of some degree of autonomy with regard to the external environment, which again stresses its powers of enforcement (that is, self-regulation and policing by dominant actors). However, this concept also requires attentiveness to reflexivity and the 'management' of gradual change or discord (via 'symbolic violence' and 'hysteresis', as discussed later), as well as accepting that external change can act to destabilise the practices of the field.

Conflict is likely and change is possible in Bourdieu's world view, but the field tends to sustain particular accepted ways of doing 'practice' unless a powerful realignment occurs to alter this, or less apparent or individually significant iterations are gradually absorbed over time. What is important is how the extant rules of the field act to shape behaviour and how changes wrought from beyond the field can alter a field. The critical point for us in this exploration of time (and deliberation) in planning is how a 'reset' of the planning field geared to allowing 'proper time' for planning activity can be aided by an understanding of field dynamics. This point indicates how the theoretical analysis can help to realise positive change and, at the same time, how deliberate institutional changes to the temporalities of planning shift practice (as explored in later chapters). Generating a better understanding of why and how time has been organised, as well as the effect this has on society generally, though critically in the planning field specifically, underpins this particular exploration of time and planning.

Given our concern for practices of good planning and attendant questions over inclusivity, deliberation and public interest, Hayward (2004: 13) argues that Bourdieu's work poses challenges for deliberative theory and the practice of deliberative democracy:

> habitus is embodied and enduring, because the norms and the standards that fields institutionalise often elude conscious awareness, and because actors tend to misrecognise the work that doxa perform, by the Bourdieuian view, the solutions proposed by friendly critics of deliberative democracy – changing habits, changing norms, and supporting multiple deliberative fora – are insufficient to challenge the cultural inequalities that function to undermine deliberative democratic equality.

This critical set of issues are considered further in Chapter 5 when discussing deliberative planning; however, the spectre of these challenges is raised here to highlight the linkages between Bourdieu's work, questions of time and deliberation in planning, and the structural issues involved in rendering planning practice more equitable and inclusive.

Considering how individuals structure their behaviour both in context (field) and in time is made more recognisably useful because Bourdieu was explicitly concerned with questions of time as part of his theorisation of the social world. In Bourdieu's later work, the question of how practice changes is confronted. That work reflects an attempt to answer critics who had claimed that his earlier work was structurally deterministic in asserting that 'practice results from relations between one's disposition (habitus) and one's position in a field (capital), within the current state of play of that social arena (field)' (Maton, 2012: 51). Clearly, influences from beyond a field can prompt change.

Doxa, illusio and hysteresis

Field conditions are generally sustained through a dominant culture, or 'doxa'. In essence, these shape the accepted behaviours of the field and, as a socialised culture, reflect practices and dispositions. Time influences capital transfer and deployment. In this situation, practitioners do not question the link between performance and speed within the planning process because this is seen as 'self-evident', or commonsensical within the doxa of established practice (Bourdieu, 2000: 97). In planning practice and its institutions, 'clock time' has become firmly embedded and 'common sense' acceptance influences action via 'performance' measured in terms of speed and efficiency.

If there is a mismatch between the individual's habitus and the dispositions required in a field, a hysteresis effect can manifest: 'as a result of the hysteresis effect ... practices are always liable to incur negative sanctions when the environment with which they are objectively confronted is too distant from that in which they are objectively fitted' (Bourdieu and Passeron, 1977: 78). Through a mix of reflexive adjustment and Bourdieu's 'symbolic violence', such dissonances are capable of resolution given that symbolic violence reflects a form of norm imposition and can manifest observably or as an internalised adjustment.

In Bourdieu's later work, the idea of *illusio* (or strategising in the field) highlights the more strategic behaviour of actors and how different interests are maintained or pursued. This is reflected in the way that practices are conducted (and the time associated with them). *Illusio* explains how change and positioning in fields can be brokered and figured. Building on this framing, Widin (2010) presents three key aspects of how *illusio* is reflected in terms of how different groups orient themselves to particular interests (noting that the interests of some will tend to dominate others). Dominant individuals or groups may obscure their interests using a variety of tactics; therefore, the 'stakes' that players pursue (beyond rhetorical declarations about the objects valued) help explain why actors behave as they do. The concept draws attention to where and how dominant actors can regulate and control a field as a means of normalising behaviours.

While this explanation may not spell out the significance of *illusio* fully, we can parse this in terms of how *illusio*, as the pursuit of interest and the stakes calculated, is constituted by those objects that carry symbolic capital and are therefore considered of value in the field. It follows that particular actions or outcomes hold 'value' in the field of practice, that is, planning practice. Some actors will behave to preserve pre-existing aspects of field practices and others to change it; for example, some actors might see benefit in accepting a new time limit for a particular activity, while others may not and will seek to resist it. This gives a glimpse of the useful application of a relational analysis of practice through time and helps explain why and how temporal choreographies could be deployed or resisted by actors.

Bourdieu and time

This brief high-level overview leads us to consider more specifically how Bourdieu's work helps us understand the relationship and effects of time on practice. First, we can say that time and its use is linked to power. This is fundamental to helping to explain why time is managed, manipulated, calculated and 'transacted'. In Bourdieu's (1977: 143) conceptualisation, he argues that 'time derives its efficacy from the state of the structure of relations within which it comes into play'. Such relations involve strategies of giving or withholding time, as well as compartmentalising time with any associated limits and deadlines, which reflect power.

Bourdieu (2000: 206) goes further in asserting that 'practice [is] temporalization', meaning that practice organises or 'makes' time. This places the consideration of time as a critical factor in discussing practice. He argues both that time is constituted in practice and that (as earlier) while practice does not take place *in* time, practices *make* time. This critical point is deliberately repeated here and brings into view the question of how time is used as a tool in exerting power and how practices are organised to deliver on particular (planning) priorities and accepted aims, both in and of time.

The inculcation of priorities via time usage highlights potential tensions in processes and tasks where time apportionment clashes with the previously accepted bounds of normal practice, or any limits on individual capacities, such as resources, knowledge or social capital. As we examine in Section 2, Barbara Adam's work delves more deeply into how time has been organised and deployed to effect control, with squeezes or 'time binds' forming only one element of the control of time. Toffler (1970: 42), in his work, writing in parallel to Bourdieu's early outputs, appears to be coincident in his view of time and practice, highlighting that 'responses to time are culturally conditioned … knowledge is taught in subtle, informal and often unconscious ways'. From this perspective, Toffler (1970: 44) reasons that 'a great deal of human behaviour is motivated by attraction or antagonism toward the pace of life enforced on the individual by the society or group within which he is embedded'.

Given the relationship of time to power, the Foucauldian treatment of power therefore lends itself here too. When one compares Bourdieu's framework of ideas with governmentality and technologies of control through time, as well as other means of disciplining, they are clearly congruent. One of the key contributions relevant here is the attention drawn to the disciplining of behaviour and the use of power and time to govern conduct. Accepted techniques of disciplining society to maximise 'efficiency' include using time more intensely. This reflects one aspect of self-regulation and the imagination of what is both acceptable and normalised. Time becomes a means to help achieve particular outcomes in a field, variously fostering or discouraging collaboration, efficiency, de-risking, the achievement of particular targets or other objectives, and indeed some achievements over others. Time organisation, orchestration or synchronisation form an element of the technologies of performance through which behaviour can be measured and governed 'from above' (Rose and Miller, 1992). As we highlight later, the form and application of specific chrono-technologies cut across the dynamics of both performance and agency, or what is done, how, when and by whom.

The relevance of Bourdieu's work to practice has been examined by Atkinson (2019), who discusses four elements of temporal experience recognisable in the Bourdieuian canon. These are, first, the general temporal structure of consciousness, which acts to shape how past, present and future possibilities are reckoned. Atkinson indicates linkage to planning in his depiction of time consciousness, where attitudes towards the future are something to be colonised, which is 'characteristic of the spirit of capitalism: the projection or forecasting of possibilities, the actual positing of the future [is] ... something to be considered and mastered' (Atkinson, 2019: 953). In this way, plans create the future, or at least orient future decisions and provide some certainty for capital. Delay or lack of programming of the future is likely to be unsatisfactory, and particular knowledges and capital forms applied in the field will act to constrain and enable particular actions. These shape future strategies as more or less possible and more or less certain.

The second aspect of Bourdieu's theory of practice and time dimension is 'field rhythm', which involves the question of timings in and of fields, or their flow and pace – a consideration that is conditioned by the relative position of a group or individual in a field. The way that the field itself is subject to change and consolidation can create tension between new and pre-existing actors and stipulations, or guidance from beyond the field will be harmonious or dissonant.

A third aspect of field culture is that of established 'markers' in time and their role in shaping change (for example, meeting cycles, elections and the associated speeding up and slowing of activity in the field to accommodate or otherwise meet such markers). These may be used to frustrate change or be shifted to accommodate or enable alternatives. Stipulations over, for example, local plan timings or other deadlines are clear exemplars here, as are relaxations or special dispensations, such as extensions of time (EoTs), which we discuss in Chapter 3.

Overall, the field involves the imposition of 'schedules', where timings are imposed on practice. The grandest example in this category, which acts to organise this, is the application of clock time itself. More granularly, this idea revolves around how interventions are accepted in the field of practice and act to alter the temporal organisation of the field. Typically, where new schedules, deadlines or other stipulations are applied. All of these factors impact not only established actors (that is, professional planners) but also people who are not formally recognised as actors in the planning field. This has clear import when considering the array of individuals, groups and interests in planning, their relative position in the field, and their ability to adopt the field rhythm, align with markers and schedules, shape policy, and otherwise inform decisions.

The fourth aspect of Bourdieu's work specifically relating to time links to the question of how time is 'squeezed', often recognised under the label of 'time binds'. This brings into question how the quantum of tasks and limits on time frames alter behaviour and practice. This has received significant attention, not least because of work intensification and technological change, which have tended to exacerbate time squeezes. Southerton (2003) explains that experiences of time squeeze raise consciousness of a need to manage time, which can easily fall foul of the contexts in which people are operating. Responses can affect whether or not practices are able to be performed in preplanned or rigid temporal routines. In this context, people develop what has been termed a 'temporal strategy' to cope with the various calls on their time and conform to the needs of field practice. In this way, Bourdieu's view that practice makes time becomes clearer, in that how people operate will speed up, slow down or 'fold' time.

The culture or doxa prevailing in a field encourages coping strategies or tactics, as outlined by Hochschild (2005), where individuals create their own temporal strategy combinations involving 'absorption', 'enduring', 'delegation', 'deferring' or 'resisting' behaviours. Those that engage actively with time pressure, for example, those who compress activity and commit more of themselves, form part of the first group who will absorb such pressure. The next strategy is enduring such pressure, typically achieved by pushing other commitments or needs to a more marginal position. Then there are those who have the wherewithal to delegate by passing activity onto others. In planning practice, this may also reflect, to a degree, the outsourcing phenomena (see Slade et al, 2019). A further strategy is deferral, where matters are delayed or otherwise reorganised. Lastly, a strategy of resistance is where impositions are met with opposition, such as rules designed to deflect time binds (for example, clocking off punctually or not reading emails after a certain time). All of these temporal strategies are a product of internalising competing pressures, standing or anticipating potential gains. Critically, they help bring into focus and make clearer the relationship to how time 'makes' practice.

Synthesis: time for Bourdieu

Together, the elements expressed in this section present a view of the key relationships between time and practice, and develop from and operate within a meta-theorisation of field theory. How and why actors behave as they do is an integral part of Bourdieu's work. Time is clearly not the only factor, and such ideas that both include and focus in on time can help to explain how planners come to accept normalised behaviours within their practice 'field' and respond as part of efforts to create conditions for particular uses of time. The way that time is divided, allocated and measured, as well as the meaning and values attached to time and its use, reflect not only 'choices' but also how power shapes the use of time and acts to narrow or otherwise direct choices. How the use of time is measured and valued therefore becomes critical to our lived experience and, ultimately, the quantum and quality of time we spend on different activities and associations. How, when and where we deploy time may in turn reflect our standing in terms of capital forms (for example, symbolic, cultural and social).

We now move on to consider the idea of the time economy, where timekeeping moves into the practice of time rationing as part of modern exchange relations, which render time 'a resource that has to be handled economically' (Adam, 1995: 87). This is where (work) time is not only quantified and parcelled but also monetised (for example, through worker 'time sheets' or client 'billable hours'). This leads into a consideration of time in conditions of capitalist economic relations and how the organisation and control of time is critical to efficiency. The key nostrum presented through Bourdieu's work that time is constituted in practice highlights why we should be interested in how the organisation of practices 'make' time. Section 2 emphasises the needs of a socio-economic system that seeks to deploy time to discipline practice and the structuring dialectic of temporalisation that exists between practice and time.

Section 2: Barbara Adam – time and capitalism

The deployment of clock time often serves to subordinate the practices of daily life, and as modern society developed, the burdens of organisation and administration grew, and the assembling of practices via the regulation of time became dominant. E.P. Thomson (1993: 356), in citing Bourdieu's work, referred to the clock as the 'devil's mill'. The apparent hegemony of clock time has been the subject of challenge in favour of alternatives, such as 'event time' (Adkins, 2009), or expanded to accept different rhythms, for example, in aligning practice to other environmental and cultural considerations. As we will contend, these are particularly germane as the need for alternative futures are brought into question. These require different ways of thinking and doing, and potentially an 'opening' of the planning field. This involves closer examination of time-practice assumptions and arrangements.

While Bourdieu assists in placing time into the wider dynamics of social fields of practice, social theorists have engaged with questions of time in more detail. Within the social sciences and related disciplines, there has been considerable attention paid to how time is regulated and shapes modern society, not least emanating from critical Marxist and postmodernist theory. A particular focus for such theorists as Barbara Adam has been how time has been shaped and used within capitalist societies, and the implications for practice more specifically. Following the insights of Bourdieu, how economic time makes practice, as labour becomes increasingly tied to the timing(s) most conducive to capital and investment, is explored. We can view these ideas as part of the origins of achieving growth through appeals to greater efficiency and performance, as well as characterising the rhetoric that associates planning with 'delay' (such as the neoliberal perspective and project speed agenda discussed in Chapter 4).

Adam (2004: 69–70) considers the way that time has been organised over a long period of socio-economic development and recognises the distinction and incompatibilities between (inter)subjective experiences of time and objective expressions of time in social systems:

> [I]n everyday life, the relative temporality of past, present and future and the objective time of calendars and clocks are not chosen on an either-or basis. Rather, they coexist, interpenetrate and mutually implicate each other. We move between those temporal worlds with great agility, giving little thought to the matter and are unperturbed by their conceptual and logical incompatibility. We construct them from the position of the present and accomplish their smooth integration in daily social practice. ... With the taken-for-granted dominance of clock time ... understanding can be achieved only by considering the social relations of time, that is, people's involvement with time through particular practices and technologies.

In her discussion of time in modern and pre-modern societies, Adam (1990, 1995, 2004) usefully set out some key differences in conceptualising time, indicating, for example, linear versus cyclical time and how these are reflected in dominant views, as well as competing conceptualisations, of time. Table 2.2 expresses these differences and provides an indication of how competing times and alternatives could impact on, and find expression in, reimagined planning practice and associated timescapes.

To demonstrate this, Adam highlights five key elements, labelled as the '5Cs' of industrial time: time 'creation' (clock time), 'commodification', 'compression', 'colonisation' and 'control', where 'the quest for control is to a large extent about obtaining dominion over time for economic gain and social advantage' (Adam, 2004: 123–4). This forms a key motif here, where we argue that it is not speed per se that governments and developers want from planning but, rather, the 'control' of planning, according to whichever tempo or timings best suit the(ir) political-economic agenda.

Table 2.2: Dominant conceptions of time: linear time versus circadian time

Dominant time	Alternative time	Implications for planning and planners
Linear	Circadian (cyclical)	Rolling programme of 'planning' – thinking forwards, deliberating and acting in advance.
Clock based	Task or event based	Moving away from (artificially) fitting a task to a predetermined deadline but, rather, shaping the time needed to fit the implications of the task and/or innovating across the factors/resources needed.
Quantitative	Qualitative	Types of knowledge and understanding shift – methods and types of inputs alter to reflect methods of evidencing that are more deliberative.
Calendar based	Nature based	Similar to linear and circadian (as earlier) but recognising issues and needs that are seasonal rather than predefined, and shaping planning events and practices that suit a diverse range of people.
Diachronic	Synchronic	Recognising multiple times and ability to operate in and across times. Holding parallel events and ensuring liaison across boundaries are related to synchronicity.
Set time	'Proper time'	Lack of understanding of the specific needs of a task or process, or of other actors' rhythms. Instead of applying a standardised amount of time across a wide set of actions (for example, a planning decision within eight weeks), proper time is mindful of actor capacities and urgency of issues – it is relational not static.
Target based	Needs based	Shifts from need to targets – or, more pertinently, the opposite reflects a more nuanced appreciation of what plans and policies direct change at scale and across forms and functions, for example, instead of housing 'targets', reorient to housing 'needs', with attendant shifts in the time dimension.

Source: Based on Adam (1995: 29–30; 2004) and Nowotny (1994), with additions from the authors

Adam (2008) deploys the term 'timescape' to embrace a number of constituent factors that together form the assembly of time-related features that influence behaviour (or practice). These include time frames, temporality, timing, tempo, duration, sequence and temporal modalities (that is, past, present and future). The timescape includes both time-related rules and temporal regularities (or what Martineau (2016: 36) refers to as the 'social time regime' that reflects the 'politico-institutional forms taken by social time relations'). Drawing on Adam's work, we focus centrally on the planning timescape to frame our examination of time in and for planning throughout the subsequent chapters.

Clock time: creating the conditions for capital

The five elements of Adam's deconstruction of time in capitalist societies pivot on the way that time has been socially constructed and regarded in terms of 'exchange value' to underpin modes of production and consumption. Clock time developed as a critical element of the organising structure of early mercantile and industrialised capitalist societies. In discussing this, Adam (2004) highlights that the relationship between time and money was historically kept distinct because, in the Christian tradition, it was held that the selling of time for profit was sinful (that is, because 'time belonged not to individuals but to God'). This meant that under such conditions, there was little motive for measuring time accurately beyond the perception of natural rhythms/seasons. The action or practice of lending money for a rate of interest (then labelled 'usury') was legitimated in the late mediaeval period. This effectively 'set time free for trade, to be allocated, sold and controlled' (Adam, 2004: 126), and since then, other technologies have developed to enable its measurement and apportionments, as well as assist in structuring economic interactions. This moral repositioning and the means to create clock time has had profound socio-economic implications:

> When 'time is money' then time costs money and time makes money because the economic practice of charging interest means that capital has a built-in clock that is constantly ticking away. Every second, minute and hour, every day, month and year brings profit on the invested sum of money. Equally, every day, month and year that money is borrowed has to be paid for in interest. (Adam, 2004: 126–7)

Capitalist societies, which intrinsically value profit and growth as a social goal, may encourage narratives of 'urgency' to become embedded. Where time is not spent in pursuit of profit (that is, 'productive' time), it is seen as wasted or counterproductive: 'Thus, when time is money, speed becomes an absolute and unassailable imperative for business. At the same time, when speed is equated with efficiency, then time compression and intensification of processes seem inevitable' (Adam, 2004: 39). This has critical implications for planning systems operating within capitalist economies, particularly when subjected to forms of neoliberalisation.

Clock time has become so embedded in society that it has become unconsciously naturalised. Unpacking the reasons for applying and enabling this approach to time and its consequences is instructive: 'Universally rationalized and sectioned, decontextualized abstract time is thus a precondition for calculable actions geared towards the appropriation of a controllable and controlled future. Clock time as the material expression of this time had become naturalized to a point of being seen as time per se' (Adam, 2004: 44). The implications of the socialisation of clock time cannot be underestimated in terms of its influence on the New Public Management (NPM) approaches and neoliberal political discourses that have been applied to planning. This has some quite profound implications, not only for society in general terms but also for *how* we undertake planning as an activity and potentially on *what* we plan for under these conditions. That is to say, we now typically conflate clock time as normal and 'natural'. Not only has clock time become 'time' but its use as a means to control behaviour has also become routinised. The implication is that because of the accepted naturalisation of clock time as time itself, we rarely consider alternative ways of organising activity or the differential impact of time on various actors, that is, the multiple temporalities of life and the dynamics of specific places and issues. As Martineau (2016: 46) explains, 'social time relations in capitalist societies are dominated by clock time: capitalist clock-time occupies a *hegemonic* position in the hierarchy of temporalities that form capitalist social time relations, alienating, subordinating, colonising, absorbing and/or marginalising other conceptions and practices of time'.

A feature of clock time and related appeals to speed/efficiency is the use of 'crisis' narratives that stress the need for immediate action and the use of urgency as a means to push through policy changes quickly (on the 'shock doctrine', see Naomi Klein, 2007). This question of time being used to press for urgency has important ramifications for planning practice in terms of how we think, let alone how we plan. Rosling et al (2018: 227–8) argues that the deploying of urgency in calls to action 'make[s] us stressed, amplifies our other instincts and makes them harder to control, blocks us from thinking analytically, tempts us to make up our mind too fast, and encourages us to take drastic actions that we haven't thought through'. Those authors claim this instinct is 'almost never true. It's almost never that urgent, and it's almost never an either/or (scenario)' (Rosling et al, 2018: 228).

If we step into planning and development practice to stress the point, there is a view within the land and development industry that planning is not a 'productive' stage but, rather, a 'delay' to the activities or 'flow' of mobilising land, capital, resources and labour for production. The market perspective therefore views planning as merely a risk to development, where time is equated to 'money' (or 'return delayed' and 'costs increased') and is therefore wrapped up with a wider view of state regulation as a barrier to the supply and production of development. Some of the dissonance created lies in the question of the control of timings, revealing that it is not necessarily speed or delay that is important here but certainty. We argue later that the control of (planning) time is seen as a means to deliver certainty by developers and national politicians.

Adam (2004: 127) warns that clock time is not neutral and unbiased in its effects; instead, 'we need to ask whose time is valuable to whom and whether or not the value involved can and should be translated into money'. We might therefore restate in this vein that planning has value, though not only to capitalist systems or calculus. It has value in numerous other ways, as the Royal Town Planning Institute (RTPI) has been keen to highlight in respect of enabling development, let alone other roles in securing public goods:

> Planning is critical to providing clarity and confidence for investments by markets so that they are able to deliver good development. Planning can improve the quantity and quality of land for development, ready land for construction (for example, by treating contaminated land), resolve ownership constraints (where there are many different owners), and bring forward investment by ensuring that the right infrastructure (such as transport and public amenities) are in place. (Adams et al, 2016: 1)

This explanation focuses on planning and development, while more comprehensive defences include Klosterman's (1985) still-influential article, which cites a range of positive ways in which planning either adds value or protects goods and resources that have clear value and that protect against 'negative externalities' and 'market failure' (for more expansive discussions of value and values in planning, see Campbell, 2002; Adams and Watkins, 2014; Adams et al, 2016).

Commodification of time: equating time with money

The second of Adam's key facets of modern time is its commodification. The ability to abstract and quantify time is a prerequisite to rendering 'time' available to exchange and commodifying labour inputs. That is to say, time is constructed in capitalist societies as a unit to be bought and sold. As Chancellor (2022: 28–30) explains, 'Interest represents the time value of money' which 'lies at the heart of valuation'. Similarly, Odell (2023) notes how the corporate clock has come to dominate modern life, where time has become equated with money, and argues for reclaiming a more humane relationship with time. From the hegemonic position of landowners, developers and investors, time is therefore a means to generate capital rather than to serve social need or organise activities that do not directly present themselves as means to make time-capital gains.

A rather crude or simplistic economic reading would assert that planning activity should seek to ensure that time is being used productively in relation to costs and profits. This is effectively 'project speed' thinking. This perspective views time purely as a resource and unit of exchange. Of course, such arguments do not consider that (clock) time applied is not the same thing as time efficiency, nor how different forms of economic, social and environmental 'value' are created or maintained through planning activity. The definitional parameters of efficiency (in time and scope), as well as of planning itself, become sites of struggle, as the control of such definitions helps justify different courses of action or political programmes.

Alternative modalities and aims service a set of wider social and environmental functions, or can be linked to the democratic use of time to enable inclusivity and deliberation. This pivots around determining 'public interest', and such a counterposition to the time-as-commodity view is likely to be in conflict with capital accumulation. We can also see effects on knowledge production and use where commodification has occurred. Time (and money or opportunity costs) to develop or to source knowledge and expertise is incurred where communities either have to invest capital in the purchase of expertise (such as planning consultant inputs) or make their own time investment to develop the knowledge and skills to participate within the planning system (such as through community or neighbourhood planning).

Time compression: making time efficient

The ability to create and commodify time typically involves the compression of time and veers towards tropes of speed and efficiency. The drive to compress derives from time-cost concerns that the ability to produce or complete a task, process or product more quickly either saves money or is otherwise seen to be made more efficient and potentially increase outputs. This view places emphasis on the ability to compress time in the interests of efficiency and, for that reason, the means to effectively control speed. It is likely that time compression will only benefit some, while measures may also be targeted at certain groups or activity.

Neoliberal discourses tend to conceptualise planning 'risk' in relation to the speed and certainty of the land-use plan allocation and permission process for a particular development, not a wider conceptualisation of (long-term) risk, such as the social and environmental impacts of economic activities or the deferred costs and risks associated with short-termist thinking and resource (over)use. This is a frame that only reckons on the time and risk being prioritised, resulting in the immediate interests of capital being preferred over competing and future interests:

> Capitalism is distinct in its relationship to the future whether this be in its systems of credit and interest, insurance or financial trading. ... The

economy therefore operates in the sphere between present and future with a view to using the future to secure the present. To achieve that task, it borrows from the future to finance the present. The radical present orientation is demonstrated at its fiercest in the discounting of the future ... [where] the value of the future is calculated with reference to the use and extractive value it holds for the present ... be this in economics, science or politics, makes parasitic use of the future – our own and that of successor generations. (Adam, 2004: 141–2)

It is clear that some development practices wilfully ignore future 'negative externalities' in exchange for economic or political gains in the present (such as using fossil fuels that contribute to climate change, building poorly designed structures, attempting to gain permission to build on flood zones and so on). Yet, one of the strongest justifications for planning activity is that the future is protected in the present by considering a range of stakeholders and interests, and through appeals to sustainable development and long-term thinking. Yet, this role raises possible temporal clashes that can pit the interest of the present against the future.

Colonisation of time: regulating behaviour in time

The fourth aspect that Adam draws our attention to is that of the colonisation of time, referring to how time may be used to organise and regulate particular activity. This parallels Bourdieu's observations set out in the first section on time shaping the 'field of practice' and vice versa. Adam differentiates between how colonisation *with* time may be accompanied by colonisation *of* time. In the former, colonisation *with* time or using time is now largely unquestioned and accepted, and refers to time as an 'imperative that unfolds through a range of policy initiatives with time-bound outputs and expectations' (Datta, 2019: 397). In this way, all involved in a given activity will be expected to adhere to clock time and associated deadlines and other strictures. This also imposes the same standard on all-comers, regardless of the resources, information or other capitals that are necessary to enable the effective use of that time.

Conversely, the idea of colonisation *of* time refers to a long-run effort to override the limitations of time, to the extent that we now hardly notice, for example, that work that could only be done in the daylight or in warm weather in the past can instead now be performed throughout the day or year, or in different locations. This also represents a decontextualisation of time, such as that evident in the time efficiencies offered by technology and the partnering of the intent to colonise with time and associated time bounding. This form of colonisation effectively serves to abstract time from setting, process and outcome (although see Elias, 1992 for a critique of the dualism between 'natural' time and 'social' time that creates a false nature–society divide and obscures their fundamental relationship). A task can now be discussed in days and hours, and in global terms, rather than what precisely is involved, when it is best to do something, where and how it may be done well. When assessed together with colonisation *with* time the overall impact is to allow preset and standard time limits to be imposed. These can be insisted upon regardless of natural or other resource-related constraints. Although, as we discuss in later chapters, such efforts can often run into difficulties and necessitate accommodations, exceptions or parallel times to fit with the realities of, or practical obstacles to, working *with* and *in* time in practice, such arrangements are unlikely to alter the default or underlying colonisation.

In planning, this aspect of temporal regulation can be seen where preset time to reach decisions on planning applications can be avoided through the use of alternative arrangements. As we show in Chapter 3, particular interests have been given dispensation to broker agreements, for example, through the use of EoTs or planning performance agreements (PPAs), which effectively allow for a brokerage of time to occur and act to suspend prior temporal and resource stipulations. However, as research indicates, such attempts could simply involve a reshaping of the contours of time pressure given that 'PPA derived funding could add undue pressure to the decision-making environment' (RTPI and Arup, 2018: 33). Indeed, Adam warns us of unintended consequences of time control.

Control of time: the end game

Lastly, Adam places control of time as the overarching feature that reflects the aim of power, being found across all of the '5Cs'. In essence, all the elements are being orchestrated or assembled together to produce a time-control effect. Adam argues that this temporal choreography acts to fashion a 'timescape', where time creation, commodification, compression and colonisation are operating together in and on space. How such elements are brought together and orchestrated within a timescape may also be labelled 'chrono-synchronisation' (the 'timing of time') and reflects how particular governance projects make use of temporal strategies to justify action, inform policy and align actor practices.

In our view, there is a clear linkage with Bourdieu's conceptualisation of time and its role in organising societal relations and Adam's account of the role of capitalist economic relations in promoting efficiency through time. As we explain, the regulation of time through clock time impacts on how a field is regulated, how particular dispositions are shaped and orchestrated, and the measures that force the pace of activity. Bourdieu's identification of time squeezing and time scheduling meshes well with Adam's (2004: 145) commentary on the way that time has been organised in capitalist societies:

> Time frames and timing, temporality and tempo, time point, duration and succession have all become subject to control, that is, to speeding

up and slowing down, to rearrangement of sequence and order, to evening out and accentuating of peaks and troughs. The variable, rhythmic times of life are regulated and disciplined to conform to uniform, invariable temporal patterns.

Planning is equally performed through the time limits set as norms of the field, that is, the 'planning timescape', and influenced by governments and other statutory or industry stakeholders that hold legal or financial power. Adam also warns us of the limits and problems associated with such efforts to control time/practice:

> The pursuit of temporal control confronts us with the (im)possibility of the task, tempers the industrial hubris. When so much control fails and converts intended actions into unintended consequences, there is a need to (re)consider ... [and] take stock of the way we approach finitude and the temporal limits to human being. Despite the very clear imperative, however, the reflective turn is unlikely to come from science or politics ... [where] powerful agendas ... are potent disincentives to reflection. (Adam, 2004: 147)

This reading of social time indicates that change is most likely to come from conflict and insurgency, the hysteresis that Bourdieu delineates, where 'Instantaneity and absolute connectivity expose the fault lines of the logic and confront users with entirely new temporal limits and possibilities that require the restructuring of socio-economic relations', and where the 'social relations of time are central to this revision and renewal' (Adam, 2004: 148).

Controlling time is an important part of efforts to control socio-economic life and corresponds to Bourdieu's concern with time making practice and Adam's scrutiny of how time organises practice according to economic and capitalist logics that become naturalised (and akin to doxa). By way of concluding this section, we can perceive that, together, a range of tools and techniques that involve all 5Cs require that the device of 'clock time is used to regulate and rationalise the pace and seasonality of organisms and beings, social activities and institutions' (Adam, 2004: 145). Taken together, the timescape can effect significant control in planning. In Bourdieu's work, the conditions and habitus of participants in the field are critically shaped by the timescape, and the way that actors endorse or challenge temporal strategies holds clear implications for social practice generally and planning practices specifically.

In considering Adam's work and applying it spatially, Schwanen and Kwan (2012) provide a summary of Adam's theorisation of time by highlighting how time is intricately linked to space and matter. They identify seven structural features of time and the temporal:

Time frame pertains to boundedness, beginning and end, and scale or unit (as in moment, year, life time, or epoch), whilst temporality is about process, change, ageing, irreversibility, and directionality ... timing refers to synchronisation, coordination, and what the ancient Greeks called kairos – the 'right' time. Tempo refers directly to movement and thus to pace, rate of change, and velocity; duration to extent and distance in time as well as to instantaneity; and sequence to succession, priority, and simultaneity. Finally, the temporal modalities consist in past, present, and future and thus bring into focus memory, path dependency, expectations, and affects/emotions. (Schwanen and Kwan, 2012: 2043)

The work on time by Southerton and Tomlinson (2005) also acts to essentialise aspects of Bourdieu's and Adam's thinking. Southerton and Tomlinson conclude that three key mechanisms are associated with the relationship between practices and time: first, the amount or volume of time deployed; second, its use and organisation with other actors and tasks (that is, coordination); and, third, what is given over to a particular practice (that is, resource allocation and what time is used for). They also suggest that multiple experiences of time (that is, substantive, temporal disorganisation and temporal density) indicate how a move beyond one-dimensional interpretations of time (and feelings of lack of time or 'time squeeze') can help account for the relationship between social practices and their conduct within the temporalities of daily and professional life.

When considering time in such a context, the effect *on* time and how perceptions of time influence behaviour *in* time become of concern to planning theorists (Friedman, 1990; Adam, 1995). Time (limits) can concentrate the mind, but they can also lead to pressured decisions, to conservatism or towards insular behaviours. Such measures may also act to reorient resources to shape (or possibly stifle) innovation. As such, there is no automatic assumption that speed and deadlines are intrinsically bad or good here; rather, we wish to highlight that how time is presented and responded to surely affects planning and its different interests.

Section 3: Helga Nowotny – time and power

Sections 1 and 2 have reviewed, respectively, Bourdieu's and Adam's work with reference to time and practice, as well as (economic) time within capitalist societies. We now add to this by examining the import of Helga Nowotny's work, which hinges on how power and different interests perceive 'proper time', or *eigenzeit*. In this central nostrum of her work, Nowotny (1994: 4) argues that 'proper time' in social situations may be comprehended as follows: 'proper time stands for a constellation of beliefs regarding future, past and present ... it stands for the totality of a person's or group's ideas and experiences of time'; moreover, 'commercial, industrial, political and ideological interest groups have their own proper times ... all these proper times are in ceaseless conflict or, more precisely, the persons and groups maintaining those proper times are'. Along with Bourdieu's practice and Adam's timescape, proper time forms a core idea explored and applied through the assessment of planning in later chapters (see also Table 2.3).

Nowotny is not the only social scientist to have recognised the significance of time and its use in relation to power. As Dean (1994: 173) argues:

> time and space and their mutual enwrapping are constitutive elements in the practices of government and technologies of power ... it is extremely fruitful to analyze how practices of power, rule and government, organize and co-ordinate activities in time and space ... temporalities intersect to compose the always transient and difficult form of the present, a present for particular cultural groups.

Given such claimed import of time for power relations, attempts to mediate between interests is also an attempt to reconcile time(s) – or what Rifkin (1987: 13) terms the 'battle[s] over time values'. While the former mediatory role is a widely accepted one for professional planners, this latter understanding of the time dimension is less well recognised but critical. Nowotny demonstrates not only that power is mediated and enacted through time but also that we should both consider the multiple temporalities of different actors and reflect on the ones that prevail. In other words, having concern for what Hassan (2009: 49) describes within 'empires of speed' as the 'hierarchy of temporal rhythms' which underpin the 'dominant timescapes' over 'subsidiary temporalities'.

The question of multiple temporalities underlines how participation (whether in politics, business or planning) is likely to be on the terms of those inviting it and to suit their own time given that time may be linked with or withheld from any negotiation of the terms of engagement. We discuss the implications of recognising the multiple temporalities of planning further when considering the inclusionary/exclusionary potential of time for participation in planning in Chapter 3 and consequences for 'public interest' and democratic deliberation in Chapter 5.

Johnson and Johnson (2021: 217) recognise the different ways participants experience time and space. They theorise this via the construct of 'coeval rhetorical temporalities', a concept that attempts to account for multiple and possibly conflictual human and non-human experiences of time and space. They argue that modernisation has invited tropes of efficiency and control, and they see possibilities in the recognition of human and non-human as coeval. They invoke the idea of *kairos* as timeliness and argue for a deeper foundation in and correspondence to events in order to shape and focus our attention, such that 'Kairos jumps and slows down, omits long periods and dwells on others' (Czarniawska, 2004: 775).

An elaboration of *kairos* as 'the right time and due measure' offers a foundation for understanding how (un)ethical action produces both space and time. This is in contradistinction to *chronos* and its emphasis on time as objective and quantifiable (that is, corresponding to clock time), and this distinction led Nowotny to stress chrono-technologies, where time is politicised though its use in shaping policy. Similarly, Kinneavy's (1986) perspective of an ethical, emplaced *kairos* highlights how overlapping senses of time produce a politics of space that becomes critical for successful political projects.

Such ideas about multiple experiences of time raise questions regarding differences between groups: what and whose temporalities prevail, and what are the implications? The key idea of 'proper time' and how it relates to the quality of planning practice and its credentials might help to organise and service better outcomes in the built and natural environment and for social good. Yet, power determines what is considered as the proper time and goals for all actors.

As Nowotny (1994: 105) argues: 'in the analysis of the conflicts over time … it becomes clear that time represents a central dimension of power which manifests itself in the systems of time that dictate priorities and speeds, beginning and end, content and form of the activities to be performed in time'. In this way, Nowotny alerts us to proper time, defined by the relative experience and differentials between various actors. Proper time is a relative construct, and it is therefore defined by difference and draws particular attention towards the multiplicity of 'proper time', not only for both individuals and groups but also for actions, processes and decision making. Equally, the duration and use of time is identified by Adkins (2009), who argues in this way that proper time aligns with 'event' time – organised to approach the task or issue in qualitative terms. Such perspectives reject any singular imposition of time for all places and activities.

Given that different actors will take or deem certain amounts or measures of time as appropriate to events or tasks, they may demand variances, claim precedent or seek flexibility. So, prosaically, what is the 'proper time' for determining a planning application? What is the proper time for a consultation and for examining and thinking about evidence? What is the proper time for planning from the perspective of a developer whose world view is dominated by risk and return, or a national politician who wants to showcase good performance figures?

Particular choreographies may imply or assert a qualitatively or normatively better use of time – linked to some idealisation of time practice. Clearly, we should be concerned with power as it is exercised to enable, discount and control times, but there appears a lack of concern over the impact of timescapes on different interests and individuals. We see how power operates through time in politics and policy making by creating a vision for an often idealised future. Such political work implies the presentation of a '*uchronia*', where all the problems of the present can be solved by particular timescaping geared towards a claimed better future:

> Uchronias, like utopias before them, have a central social function to fulfil: they contain proposed solutions to particular unsolved problems in society. ... The uchronia which only demands more time does not escape the quantitative logic of money and its accumulation. Money and time remain substitutable, but the general money preference will predominate even when more time is demanded. (Nowotny, 1994: 139)

Uchronia is a notional timescape that tilts towards some particular future that needs to be achieved. It is rarely, if ever, spoken of explicitly; instead, attempts to choreograph and sculpt time imply some ideal time – perhaps for some, this is actually instantaneity. For planning, this presents an incompatibility, yet neoliberal reforms to planning attempt to orient the planning timescape to align with a political agenda (that is, the 'project speed' discussed in Chapter 4) that has to accept less than the perfect fix. This is clearly seen in the repeated claims that a 'faster' and more 'efficient' planning system will lead to more growth, as well as in the compromises and concessions apparent in policy. The problem with this is that there is still a central conceit that sustains this narrative, that is, that growth equates to social progress and improves everyone's quality of life ('the rising tide that lifts all boats'). Powerful interests can then deploy temporal rhetoric, implicitly underpinned by idealised temporalities and/or the imaginary zenith of uchronia, to assert that the timing that works in the best interest for all is *their* proper time(scape). As we discuss later, especially when making the case for planning reform.

To better understand how temporal narratives are constructed, we now move on to consider the political use of time as a legitimation tactic for political regimes. These discourses tend to justify present actions for the good of the future or, indeed, push risk into the future.

Section 4: Nomi Lazar – time and politics

The political sciences have been alive to the aspects of time that influence policy and are used to organise practices. Over 50 years ago, Wallis (1970) drew attention to the regulation, synchronisation and allocation of time by politics as a form of 'chronopolitics'. More recently, Lazar (2019) has considered the political construction of time and how political strategies are enacted through temporal-rhetorical framings and 'time talk' in order to produce, maintain or challenge political legitimacy (particularly in moments of crisis). In doing so, Lazar draws attention to 'the ways temporal frames generate meaning and to the ways temporal structures work to naturalize or denaturalize what is socially and politically constructed [which] generates a range of analytical tools useful for understanding political behavior' (2019: 211). From this perspective, how time is theorised, that is, what concepts are accepted and applied to political action, acts to shape practice and works to shape both what and how we 'know' the future (Strassheim, 2016). Such work highlights that time is political, and political time is useful because of the power relations that can be enacted through the control of time (that is, that political time makes practice). In a similar vein, Standing (2023) also highlights how '[t]ime has always been political' and that, 'throughout history, how we use our time has been defined and controlled by the powerful', leading to calls for a new politics of time based on collective action and 'commoning'.

More broadly, several important texts, such as Pierson's (2004) *Politics in Time* and Pollitt's (2008) *Time, Policy, Management*, have also reasserted time studies in the fields of politics and public administration. Strassheim (2016: 153) noted how political time had gained increasing attention in the literature from the 1990s and had 'reached the centre of policy debates' by the 2010s. He explains that the analysis of political time reveals how policy *by* time and *in* time influence both 'spaces of experience', that is, what we consider relevant, and 'horizons of expectation', or what we think is possible or desirable (Strassheim, 2016). Such work brings into focus how political and democratic institutions 'define repertoires of more or less acceptable courses of action that will leave considerable scope for the strategic and tactical choices of purposeful actors' (Scharpf, 1997: 42). Linz (1998: 34) even goes so far as to contend that 'time and timing ... are the essence of the democratic process'.

Leverage over time is an important source of power and means of control over present and/or future agendas. Time influences and has had influence on institutional arrangements, where these involve 'a system of rules that structure the courses of actions that a set of actors may chose', and such rules may be formal or consist of 'social norms that actors will generally respect and whose violation will be sanctioned by loss of reputation, social disapproval, withdrawal of cooperation and rewards, or even ostracism' (Scharpf, 1997: 38).

Lazar's account highlights the political work that can be enacted through the control of time. She demonstrates how, historically, calendars and clocks have been strategically created, used or reformed by political leaders to change 'the shape of time to frame their political present' (Lazar, 2019: 1). Indeed, attempts to change calendars and clocks are more than an eccentric technical exercise; rather, they represent political strategies to establish or maintain legitimacy through 'time talk' and temporal framing:

> It is commonplace that political actors invoke historical events to justify their political endeavours, but here they invoke not just events but the place of these events in shaped time, their sequence and synchrony,

and their meaning not only for the present but for the future. ... In the toolbox of legitimation strategies and tactics, a leader will find a variety of means to shape and reshape time. (Lazar, 2019: 3)

Time talk involves narratives and storytelling that give meanings to actions and events. This is done not to remember what happened in the past but to construct a new perspective of why the past is meaningful for creating the (desired) future. This political work is done through 'means of "rereading" the past in light of a future-serving interpretation of the present' (Lazar, 2019: 5). This temporal-rhetorical framing allows political leaders and powerful interests to define both the problem and the solution in one encompassing narrative of the situation. In other words, the past and future are both given meaning in the political present and can be constructed to serve different political agendas. As Zielonka (2023: 137–8) notes: '[t]he past is politicians' favourite solution for addressing the future. ... To address the future, you need strategy and resources, but to address the past you only need rhetorical skills.'

In the political narrative of UK planning systems, this can be seen in appeals to them being 'antiquated' and 'outdated', which then sets up the proposed reforms that will solve the problems via greater 'speed', 'efficiency' and 'growth'. The political narrative of planning in relation to time and 'delay' is very powerful in neoliberal discourse, and using the planning system as a scapegoat for wider societal challenges is a useful corollary. There is no considered government strategy or allocated resources to create a planning system better suited and equipped to address future priorities and challenges, only appeals to the need for further neoliberalisation to bring the system 'up to date' as justification for political action.

Astute political leaders can connect people to agendas bigger than themselves, knowing that these may be rendered more durable through carefully constructed narratives about how the past, present and future shape the identification and nature of the problem that needs to be solved. It is also where 'values' can be exposed and indicates how value judgements become key in deciding how we use our time collectively as a society, how these are justified in pursuit of particular ends and how specific practices and technologies are deployed to realise them.

Political time, as an institution, a resource and a constraint on actors in decision making, is discussed by Howlett and Goetz (2014: 477), who summarise the concept of 'political time' by referring to the specific historical-temporal location in which a phenomenon, such as a policy, exists and highlighting the significance of such effects as policy legacies, sequencing and trajectories on current political actors. Goetz and Meyer-Sahling (2009) identify both a politics and a policy dimension of political time. The politics dimension is concerned with the rules relating to timing, sequencing, speed and duration in decision making. Whereas the policy dimension is about temporal policy features, such as the distribution of the costs and benefits of major policies in time. Strassheim (2016) discusses how a main mode of political action is temporal manipulation and how, for example, the introduction of urgency and 'burning flags' are used to progress debates and move reforms in a desired direction. Conversely, intentional delay is discussed by Pollitt (2008) and Parker and Street (2015) as where 'modulation' tactics are deployed. Taken together, we can say that political time refers to the diverse range of rules, norms, conventions and understandings that serve as a resource and constraint for political institutions and actors. These affect many aspects of political and policy-making behaviour, such as the timing of decision making and the processes involved in making public policy.

Lazar (2019: 212) highlights how paying attention to contrasting political frames may clarify what's at stake in certain kinds of political engagement because 'approaches to politics framed in opposing temporalities structure how a political problem is understood and what will count as a solution'. Bastian also notes the relative lack of attention paid to 'the role of time in attaining political and/or social goals' (2014: 154). While Zahariadis (2013) contends that temporal manipulations, such as imposed deadlines, are not neutral but political devices that could lead to anti-democratic outcomes with exclusionary potential. This precipitates Lazar (2019: 212) to pose the question: 'might direct engagement with diverse temporal frames facilitate mutual understanding? Even if such understanding is not possible, the engagement might clarify why.'

This gets us closer to considering the political dimension (as well as the power dimension) involved in the multiple temporalities of planning practice. Such ideas connect the use of temporal power/control and political time to democratic questions of inclusion, deliberation and public interest, as well as the substantive aims of planning explored later in Chapters 3, 4 and 5.

Conclusion: timescapes and temporalities in planning

This chapter has provided an overview of how time has been studied and conceptualised from different critical perspectives across a range of diverse disciplines and literatures within social theory. Drawing on the key thinkers presented here, we have categorised our reading of time in relation to practice, capitalism, power and politics. The purpose of this review and discussion of key ideas is to help to create a framework to analyse the multiple temporalities and attendant temporal relations seen via contemporary planning practices in England, which may also be applied elsewhere to examine the prevailing timescapes in other national planning systems globally.

This required providing: first, a high-level theory of society and practice, drawing in Pierre Bourdieu's canon; second, the role and work of economic time in capitalism, as featured in the work of Barbara Adam; third, the power relations that govern what is considered 'proper time' for an activity or process, which stresses relationality, as set out in Helga Nowotny's analysis of time in modern society; and, lastly, the deployment of political time and associated manipulation and legitimation tactics highlighted by Nomi Lazar. While recognising that this is not an exhaustive literature review of the many and varied treatments of time in social theory (a significant task in itself), the purpose of selecting these key thinkers and their particular set of concepts and ideas was to warn that time is anything but neutral or merely a background to practice; rather, it is a resource and powerful tool to perform actors in certain ways. Such theorisations can thus illuminate how the planning field has developed a particular set of practices that need to be revealed and reassessed.

A key contribution here, as drawn from the literature, is that time is important in the disciplining of behaviour and the use of power to govern conduct in planning practice. Table 2.3 sets out a synopsis of the key ideas presented here and some indicative implications for planning.

This overview has laid the groundwork for our reading of the import of time in and for planning. We now bring these related strands of social theory together under the encompassing concept of planning 'timescapes'

Table 2.3: Codex: key thinkers and their ideas applied to planning

Key thinker	Key concept(s)	Interpretation and import for planning
Bourdieu	• *Practice* (constituted by, among other things, habitus, field, capital, *illusio*, doxa, hysteresis and so on)	Time makes practice, that is, time is not neutral in practice but, rather, constitutive of individual behaviour(s) and institutional culture norms, and therefore bound with everyday practice.
Adam	• *Timescape* • *5Cs and control of time*	Time control elements that can and do shape the planning timescape as a means to control time and hence system processes and outcomes.
Nowotny	• *Proper time* • *Multiple temporalities* • *Chrono-technologies* • *Uchronia*	No single time but multiple times for different planning actors and the power relations that attempt to embed and align one set of timings to planning practice. Instead, proper time is 'inclusive time' in planning that acknowledges multiple temporalities and the different interests at stake.
Lazar	• *Temporal-rhetorical framing and time talk*	Time mobilised and deployed using temporal narratives to justify certain courses of political action or policy.
Others	• *Political time* (Howlett and Goetz, 2014; Strassheim, 2016) • *Temporal choreography* (Felt, 2016) • *Temporal strategies* (Hochschild, 2005)	Neoliberal discourses of speed/efficiency and growth influence and are propagated by political time, which seeks to reform planning to better suit these goals (for example, project speed). This requires performing actors' behaviour according to the dominant timing, which can be responded to variously using different strategies and tactics.

as an analytical frame for evaluating the multiple temporalities of different planning actors, processes and their outcomes in practice. In essence, we view the timescape as the sum effect/affect of the temporal strategies present in a particularised context. Together, these produce a specific temporal-spatial practice field. We argue that the way in which planning timescape(s) are produced and maintained, as well as challenged, requires close attention, and using social theory to explore the dynamics of planning practice helps unpack this complex of institutional arrangements, conventions, tactics and assumptions. In this way, a better understanding of how time shapes planning processes and affects those impacted by outcomes may be generated, and how alternatives may be opened up and brokered may be considered.

This question of alternatives is salient because a number of time-related factors that influence actor behaviour include the temporal modalities that are part of the conditions of actual planning practice, which involve imposed time frames, duration, timings, tempo and sequencing. The latter relates to the order of events in time and highlights the 'choreographies' involved (Felt, 2016), that is, how these are orchestrated and fitted together. The planning timescape includes both time-related rules and temporal regularities, and is subject to change and contestation. As a result, timescapes shift and are understood unevenly. The planning timescape is thus bound up with dominant cultures, power, knowledge and institutional framing(s). These multiple elements combine and will suit or be mastered by some and be unsuitable or difficult for others (what we discuss later as the inclusionary and exclusionary potentials of timescaping), and are particularly relevant when considering the opportunities for, and impacts upon, participation in planning.

For the individual, the timescape is experienced as that which applies and is reckoned with by a particular actor in the present. However, it is clear that experience of time is also dynamic, variegated and amorphous. Drawing on Bourdieu, we can view the timescape as the structuring field of planning practice that not only seeks to perform actors in certain ways, such as towards speed and growth under neoliberal discourses, but can also be modified or challenged by individuals in various ways by using a range of strategies and tactics, for example, 'absorption', 'enduring', 'delegation', 'deferring' or 'resisting', as outlined by Hochschild (2005).

In considering the role of timescapes in attempting to govern individual behaviour/practice, we also need to pay attention to Nowotny's (1994: 147–8) warning of the tendency for institutional power to alienate actors from time:

> The frequent use of the term 'time', as if time possessed an independent existence, is connected not least with the fact that time in social facilities and institutions becomes relatively independent of individuals. ... It is this alienation of time, occurring through its concentration within institutions, which reacts as something external, is felt to be

a constraint, and can be used as an instrument of power ... who has to wait, how long, what for and how, can serve as an indicator of the value which time — whose time? — is given within an organisation. ... Power, exercised by central authorities, establishes itself over space and time. Territorially established rule was followed by the temporal kind.

When the timescape is viewed from the relational and multiple temporalities of planning, the critical question is that of control: who and on what basis time is controlled or attempts are made to effect control. We see that the particular arrangements of the timescape instil normative views that shape thought and action, and interventions in time allocation and deployment alter relations, making more or less possible particular ideas, means and practices.

In relation to planning, Lennon and Tubridy (2022: 10) highlight that 'time operates as a mechanic process that organises a particular constellation of relations between objects, ideas, people and actions to mould realities grounded in ontological and epistemological standpoints'. In that light, the existing planning timescape in England (which we review in Chapter 3) involves a complex set of multiple institutional arrangements, including those specific to planning law, through regulations, and enacted through practices that together make up the planning 'system' and in turn shape planning aims, behaviours, processes and outcomes. We view such multiple temporalities in planning as exhibiting a tension between economic (market) time, political (ideological) time, democratic (deliberative) time and procedural (bureaucratic) time. Together, these multiple temporalities intermesh and overlap, or, more pointedly, they can clash in practice.

In closing this chapter, we seek to emphasise that considering the composition of the planning timescape in England is not merely an esoteric academic exercise undertaken only for the purpose of knowledge generation but a more pragmatic endeavour to lay bare the role of time in creating the current temporalities shaping the planning system and experience of practice. We see that thinking through proper time as 'inclusive time' may well be a precondition of just planning and an aid to enhanced deliberative planning practice that works for all. Thus, consideration of the way that time impacts on all interests in planning is needed. This comes with a recognition that imperfection is a given, so let it be imperfection despite or as a product of deliberation. While there seems little point calling for a simplistic 'slow it all down' approach to planning systems, what we go on to urge is that if time and its organisation in planning is better understood and enables proper deliberation, then better planning relations and outcomes are likely. The critical point for us lies in the contention that the exploration of time (and deliberation) in planning could provoke a 'reset' of the planning field, geared to allowing 'proper time' for planning activity. It is to this task that the subsequent chapters of the book now turn.

3

Time and participation in planning

Planning as participatory

Chapter 2 presented our review of the social theory of time in relation to the four central themes of practice, capitalism, power and politics, as well as associated key concepts. The theory and framework presented in Chapter 2 have assisted in setting out how social theorists have recognised the role of time, particularly how its organisation and control has shaped practice. This body of work indicates the range of considerations and elements that have been identified as relevant to the organisation of time and how actors use time. A central argument here is that time is bound up with power and, moreover, that power is inherently relational, operating between the participants in planning and others affected by planning and development outcomes. This view incorporates the power relations inherent in Nowotny's (1994) perspective of the multiple temporalities of actors as applied to Adam's (2004) idea of the timescape.

In seeking to highlight the operation of power through time and the impact this has on different actors in planning, this chapter outlines the motifs of inclusion, deliberation and public interest, which are explored throughout the rest of the book. We view these as core elements for shaping 'proper time' in planning and practice, which serve as normative anchor points. We now show where and how time is observably a dynamic part of spatial governance, acting to police and alter relations and outcomes affected by planning. The theme of recasting the term 'participation' is relevant here as a widened view of who and what is actually constitutive of planning practice becomes more accepted. This becomes ever more apparent given the multiple actors involved in shaping planning and how timescaping impacts on these interests in various and unequal ways. While we deliberately circumvent questions of wider agency in planning, it is relevant to observe that the boundaries of who is planning are being reconceptualised, as Briassoulis (2023: 77) highlights, 'the spectrum of who/what are the planners and their roles [have broadened] and shared across sectors'. This intimates the shared endeavour that planning now entails (see Parker and Street, 2021). While it is not possible to provide a full exposition of time in relation to all actors/actants involved in planning, we highlight four key participant 'user' groupings to demonstrate the experience of planning timescapes: (1) public sector planners, (2) developers, (3) politicians and (4) local communities.

We include some reflections on the planning timescape expressed by users in practice in order to illustrate some of the key points developed here.

The key actor groups have different expectations and preferences of the planning process and outcome. They have agendas, priorities and knowledge that can be used to manipulate time or influence its use. They demand different things of time (in planning) and face pressures from different sources. As Abram (2014) argued, planning and its temporalities involve doubt, contestation and mediation, while Thousand et al (2006) also noted that varying perceptions of time shape the trajectory of relationships and influence of (planning) practice. Reflecting on the different actors, albeit briefly at first, helps reveal the contestation of the control of time and where this friction (or Bourdieu's 'hysteresis') becomes part of the means to promote views, or pursue particular interests.

Public sector planners

Professional planners operating in the public (local authority) sector are critical to the operation of institutionalised planning. In the UK, there is a common distinction between policy planners, who focus on evidence gathering, policy writing and plan making, and development management (DM) planners, who work on negotiating and determining planning proposals. Each group has influence and is enmeshed in a variety of time-limited or -controlled aspects of planning practice (see Tables 3.1, 3.3 and 3.4 later).

As more (and increasingly complex) requirements are placed on professional planners, often faced with reduced resources, a practice squeeze (which also involves an expansion of work) has been accompanied by a time squeeze (that is, a reduction of time allowances). A consequence of this has been for some planning officers in England to feel 'ground-down, overworked, depressed ... undervalued and unsupported' (Kurland, 2023).

As we depict, efforts to standardise and render planning more certain for the public, as well as for the development industry, appear to rest on simple time metrics (often emphasising speed) rather than asking, for example: how *well* are participants exploring the issues? Are they asking the right questions? Are they working with stakeholders? Are planners talking and working with the community? Are they listening? Are they reviewing what has worked and what has not? Are they being open, transparent and honest? Are they sharing and discussing the challenges, opportunities and information they are using to help them make decisions? The following quote from a local authority planner provides a flavour of the situation:

> 'What does the government want us to achieve out of this [performance] treadmill? Is it quality outcomes? ... Or, is it just stacked-up decisions

that were in time? The fact that proper engagement does take time if it's going to be quality, if it's going to be valued, if we're going to change the perception and make sure that people feel involved. They've got a voice, and that is all areas of society as well. So, how do we reach the groups that don't generally engage … if the planning system is not valid and it's seen as a creature of statute, well, what's the point in it? … Time pressure being expectation and perception, that it means different things to different people. It's subjective. Delay as a concept is subjective. You could frame something as delay, or you could frame something as engagement and collaboration.' (Local Authority Planner 'A')

The quote highlights one planner's concern that performance measures focusing on speed and 'delay' can force out good planning. They share the view that attempts to go beyond simply reaching a decision quickly should be reasserted, such that the views and interests of the stakeholders involved are represented, and competing interests can be balanced:

'That's what planning does: it balances [competing interests], and that takes time. If you do that properly, that takes time. And I think the kind of obsession with making things quicker and faster means that actually some of the quality is lost from the process. When I started [in planning], it was more about getting schemes and proposals, and trying to improve them and to work with an applicant to make things better. And increasingly, that's where you get extension of time notices and all the other mechanisms, the focus on time means that you're focusing less on quality, in my view, very often. So, it's understanding that, kind of, balance between, you know, the opportunity for engagement and being part of the process; but if you are part of the process, it may mean that the process is longer.' (Local Authority Planner 'B')

Developers

The development industry has a need to engage with planning matters and routinely orchestrate larger development proposals that are likely to take significant effort, resources and actors to assemble. In particular, the sequencing of suppliers, contractors and the 'pipeline' of delivery is complex, with timings contingent on numerous factors. This context means that many developers will tend to have a concern for (clock) time and its impact on the costs of borrowing and their bottom-line profit. As a result, developers are typically seen to want planning to be quicker and less uncertain, and this is a significant cue for 'project speed', which derives from a wish to have more control over planning processes (that is, more control over economic time).

Such control is a response to risk as well as profitability. As the following excerpt from research looking at planning risk and development states:

> [the] financial cost of risk is highest before planning permission is obtained and declines thereafter. Increasing certainty in the earliest stages of the development process would have the greatest benefits. However, delays and the need to revisit planning permissions are also seen as extremely costly, especially on large sites. Accordingly, developers include the probability of such problems and their cost into the returns they require. (De Magalhaes et al, 2018: 5)

Thus, speed alone is not the aim; instead, mastery of process is the prime goal. Part of that focus involves a desire for greater predictability of the process, which, in turn, can be achieved, in part, through greater control of time in planning (and over other stages of the development process). We can see the overarching concern for certainty expressed in the following developer views:

> 'Through that planning determination process, the [development] viability is under threat, other things have changed, funding has perhaps changed, and you need the council to come with you at a pace on that. And, frankly, they're not able to necessarily support that change. ... Whereas obviously, over time, the risk is increasing. Because the fundamental point for us is always, and our discussions with the local authorities are, we need certainty, as much certainty as we can is what drives the business to be able to make decisions.' (Housing Developer 'A')

> 'The uncertainty for us means it's very hard to plan; and you think you are planning, you are doing the right thing, and then something else hits you, a change of policy, a change of attitude, a change of politics, and you have to change direction and respond to that. That lack of certainty makes a big difference.' (Housing Developer 'B')

Pathways to achieve greater certainty do not necessarily involve deregulation or the cutting of all 'red tape' but, rather, the organisation of regulation and timings that suit. We might term this 'blue tape': a regulatory environment that seeks to support/stabilise the dynamics of the development process given the complexity and attendant uncertainty of the outside world.

Politicians – national and local

Politicians play a significant role in setting policy agendas and influencing and making decisions. The categorisation should be split into (at least) two main groups: national and local. For national politicians, variations of a wider neoliberal-informed policy approach have dominated many administrations' rhetoric about planning practice since the 1980s (see also Chapter 4). In the UK, all too often, planning is charged with creating 'delay' and speed is conflated with servicing developer interest and growth. However, as discussed earlier, such assertions have been found to be faulty because the main issues are those of uncertainty and lack of control. For local politicians and local authority elected members, their relationship with planning and time is somewhat more nuanced: they may welcome delay or, more specifically, time suspensions. Some examples include when there is local contention over a proposed major site or scheme, reviewing greenbelt designation for release, or where other planning matters, such as local plan production, interfere with local electoral cycles and campaigning (though all these issues can and do play out at the national political level as well).

It is also worth recognising how time considerations feature across planning ideas and their politics. Some prominent chrono-oriented ideas have been in vogue that conjoin time and space, such as the 15-minute city or 20-minute neighbourhood (see Charbgoo and Mareggi, 2020; Stanley and Hansen, 2020). Without dissecting those ideas here, such time markers themselves support cultures of speed or, indeed, provoke responses about the arbitrary limits of time on freedom. This notion may seem far-fetched, but just that reaction was elicited from one politician in the UK, the MP Nick Fletcher (2023), who called for a parliamentary debate on the 'international socialist concept of so-called 15-minute cities and 20-minute neighbourhoods'. Time in its relationship both to actor's interests and to space clearly carries political import, and planning can become weaponised in the 'culture wars' (see Parker and Dobson, 2023).

Local communities

Local community members play an important role in variously informing, challenging and supporting professional planners and politicians in local plan production or in the shaping of planning permissions at the local level. Community engagement can often be viewed as a tick-box exercise or an additional 'nice to have' for planners and developers, and there have been calls for greater public involvement in the UK and elsewhere for some time. Indeed, long-running debates over the form, extent and timing of participation in planning shape some of our considerations in the following (as also set out in Chapter 5). Given that planning and proper time shape the practical possibilities for planning policy, process and outcome, it is notable that local populations are typically not directly involved in planning beyond assigned consultation periods or where they can present their views at public meetings or in planning committees (see Table 3.4). In some areas, communities have become directly involved in plan making through neighbourhood planning in England (see Parker et al, 2019).

These brief introductions lead us into an exploration of specific instances and expressions of time and its management in planning, centring on the 'How is time used?' question as a substantive element of inquiry into the deployment of time in planning practice. This is partnered by our concern over the effects/affects of time in planning and how the timescape impacts on the practices of different actors with an interest in planning.

The planning timescape in practice

We argued in Chapter 2 that time impacts variably upon the different participants (that is, the four key user groups identified earlier) and that the use of time in planning can be used to include and exclude people by privileging or ignoring the capacities of certain actors in the system. The main stages and tools that form the planning timescape that actors operate within are outlined (see also Tables 3.1, 3.3 and 3.4 later), before we move on to illustrate the effect/affect of time on processes and participants. To do this, we consider a number of examples of how time has been shaping practice across English planning. This is not an attempt to map out the planning timescape in its entirety but, rather, it is intended to provide a snapshot of a range of practice examples from across the different stages and tools of planning practice where chrono-technologies are apparent, but also subject to change.

Four main timescaping tactics – speeding up, slowing down, the 'suspension' of time and setting actions 'off the clock' – are identifiable across 13 examples of planning measures operating across the main stages of planning. These are presented later in Tables 3.1, 3.3 and 3.4 and grouped into three sections in order to highlight the different aspects of planning activity: (1) policy and plans, (2) development management and (3) community involvement. We then discuss these examples more fully, linking them to their context and to theory. It is clear that the elements highlighted feature substantive time management, notwithstanding other factors that also play a role in shaping behaviours (for example, resources, attitudes, knowledge and interpretation).

Plans and policy making

In England, local planning authorities (LPAs) must prepare a local (development) plan, which sets out the planning policies to be used to determine planning applications within their area over a set time frame, typically being a 15-year plan period. The plan-making process must consider the present and future needs of the local economy, environment and society, and attempt to balance them by fully involving everyone who has an interest in the document and its implications. During these planning

Table 3.1: The planning timescape in England: policy and plans examples (Examples 1–5)

Planning example	Relation to time	Implication for practice	Type of strategy	Link to theoretical treatment of time and practice	Impact on other actors (that is, winners/losers)
Example 1: 30-month local plan production	Squeezed and 'front-loaded' local plan-making process	Reduced time for consultation, evidence collection and stakeholder engagement	Speeding-up process	Political time/multiple temporalities – government attempts to speed up the plan-making process to better support development and growth by placing the needs of development time over technical planning time and time for democratic participation	Government concern that lack of (up-to-date) local plan creates risk and uncertainty over the land allocated for development locally and the policy framework used to determine planning permission for schemes, thus imposing a new time limit for the production of local plans within 30 months
Example 2: Plan start time	Strategic/political timing	(Political) Control of start points as control of time of planning	'Right timing'	Political time/temporal choreography – announcing a specific official start point but where much work needs to be undertaken prior to this in order to meet the 30-month deadline or favour, for example, election cycles	(Local) Politicians benefit as they choose politically propitious schedule
Example 3: Plan monitoring and delivery	Means of keeping account of a plan over time in relation to targets	Need to produce authorities' monitoring report (AMR) giving information on extent that planning policies are being successfully achieved and to measure performance against programme set out in LDS	Performance management	Political time – focus on ensuring delivery is maintained across the plan period	Impact on LPA for releasing sites/granting permission in order to keep up with timing and quantum of planned development (for example, five-year land supply)
Example 4: Five-year land supply	Converting the quantum of housing need calculated for a local area into a housing temporality	Need to demonstrate an up-to-date Five-year land supply or else be open to speculative/unplanned housing development	Quantification of planning where numbers become the arbiter of good planning for housing	Temporal-rhetorical framing/crisis politics – need to meet the national housing figure to resolve the 'housing crisis'	Pressure on LPA and enabling developers to propose other sites where delivery is not sustained
Example 5: Back-ending housing delivery	Pushing delivery of housing later into the plan delivery period	Allocating delivery of lowest number of units of overall housing need figure at the start of plan period	Pushing into the future/deferring decisions – suspending and delaying of delivery	Political time/temporal choreography – manage political and community resistance to development	Eases political tension over housebuilding locally

policy stages, there are several notable time measures that have been applied or contemplated. Five instances that were conceived to speed up and introduce certainty into the plan-making system in England, or have otherwise been devised to suit a particular actor group, are set out in the following (see Table 3.1). These help to highlight the way that planning policies and plans are affected by timescaping, and offer an insight into the way that time is used as a proxy for system efficiency. They are largely directed towards the performance of the LPA. We can view these as instances of political time making and attempted temporal control over the plan-making process.

Example 1: The 30-month local plan proposal (2021–23)

This first example has been a source of considerable debate since the 2020 *Planning for the Future* white paper (MHCLG, 2020) on planning reform in England, which set out the government's expectation that local plans should be produced within 30 months (it should be noted that, at the time of writing, the proposal was on the drawing board, but it had provoked widespread discussion about its practicality and impacts). This temporal policy objective centres on the aspiration of the UK government to expedite and render more certain the production of local plans in England. Criticisms of the existing plan-making approach have largely focused on the patchwork and/or absence of 'up-to-date' plans across England. The imperative handed to civil servants was to design the production of a local plan in 30 months, with the aim to create a tightly drawn process and provide a framework for an expedited plan-making window.

The new policy objective of 30 months was prompted by the claims by some actors that local plans in England were 'taking too long'. The SoS at the time of the 2020 white paper, Robert Jenrick (2020), claimed: 'Local building plans were supposed to help councils and their residents deliver more homes in their area. Yet they take on average 7 years to agree in the form of lengthy and absurdly complex documents and accompanying policies – understandable only to the lawyers who feast upon every word.' This sentiment avoids any explanation for delay or why plans were taking longer than central government would otherwise like to see them being produced; yet, there is an implicit judgement that the time taken and constitutive elements of the plan-making process are either unnecessary and/or mismanaged.

As a result, the argument was that plan production should take no longer than 30 months from early evidence gathering and visioning to the plan becoming adopted policy locally. This would require the setting of progress points measured temporally and adherence to pre-existing plan timetables. The LPA would publicise the distinct stages of the plan-production process to fit the model. LPAs would need to work closely with the Planning

Inspectorate (PINS) and other bodies to achieve this time frame. Progress was to be 'saved' at key stages so that work would not be lost if a setback, or other change or delay, occurred, reflecting an attempt at 'time banking'.

The 30-month local plan-making proposal provoked the following response from the parliamentary select committee that assessed the government's proposals:

> The Government should extend the 30-month timeframe for the initial production of Local Plans as it is too short for creating new plans from scratch. The Government must ensure that statutory consultees have time to comment on Local Plans. The Government should consider a staggered roll-out of the new types of Local Plans across the country. It should be permissible and straightforward to undertake quick updates of Local Plans every two years, including with appropriate time for public consultation. (House of Commons Housing, Communities and Local Government Committee, 2021, para 45, pp 26–7)

The select committee response features at least three elements of time/timing in their proposal, which were to question (1) the duration, (2) the use of time and (3) the relationship between plan timings and other actors' time and resource capacities. Despite such pushback, the government response was as follows:

> The Government does not accept the recommendation to extend the 30-month timeframe to produce new local plans. Currently only 41% of England's local authorities have a local plan that was adopted in the last five years; meaning there are swathes of the country where the public have little confidence in where development is going to happen. (DLUHC, 2022a: para 12)

Rather than adopting a cyclical approach to absorb and learn from ongoing changes and the impact on the deliberation and evidence behind a local plan, the proposed process was to instead conform to preset timings and involve start dates that did not necessarily equate with local circumstances. Of course, having a programmatic approach may be desirable, but imposing arbitrary (political) timings reflects only one option available to regulators.

In late 2022 and again in the summer of 2023, the UK government revised their proposed approach and opted to formally keep a 30-month period but added a 'tooling-up' period in advance of the 30-month stopwatch and decided to work with a select number of LPAs to pilot the approach in order to ensure that the process would be feasible for others. However, debates over public involvement were provoked, which saw the initial idea to remove consultation in later stages (notably, in individual planning applications) abandoned after political backlash. In response to this point, the Local Government Association (LGA, 2021) stated:

> Local democratic oversight and community engagement are critical factors in ensuring trust and transparency in planning decisions and all aspects of the planning system. We are concerned that the proposed shortened timeframes for Local Plan engagement would lead to a loss of local democracy, with councillors and communities being cut out of the process and a reduced ability to have a say on individual planning applications.

The example demonstrates the government privileging speed of production over concerns for inclusion and deliberation in plan making. The emphasis on speed places burdens or time binds on others, including the PINS and statutory consultees. The prospect of many local plans all operating on the same strict timeline, with many starting at once, might overwhelm the capacity of such bodies and introduce new delays. In this way, we can see the multiple temporalities of actors that need to be considered and embedded within local plan making, beyond and apart from the capacity of LPAs to meet such time frames.

Example 2: Plan start times and the 'local development scheme'

This instance of time in planning concerns when a local plan is (formally) commenced. In England, the timetable for the production of local plans have been left to the discretion of each LPA. For each plan, a timetable for the stages of production is also produced, known as the local development scheme (LDS) (see Table 3.2). While the start time of the plan can be controlled by local politicians, it is also true that actual progress or tempo may also be delayed as a result of other external factors, notably, policy change at the national level, responses by statutory consultees, the receipt of elements of the evidence base and so on. This means that subsequent plan timings are somewhat contingent on unanticipated factors, as well as deliberate delay, which can together impact on the actual (clock) time taken.

The previous instance of the 30-month plan is connected, as the LDS is a timetable created by the LPA. It has some autonomy over the process, as it sets the schedule (in England, this is required under the Planning and Compulsory Purchase Act 2004). The LDS must specify:

> the development plan documents (i.e. local plans) which, when prepared, will comprise part of the development plan for the area. Local planning authorities are encouraged to include details of other documents which form (or will form) part of the development plan

Table 3.2: Example LDS timetable

Stage/timing (indicative months)	Aug 17	Sept 17	Oct 17	Nov 17	Dec 17	Jan 18	Feb 18	Mar 18	Apr 18	May 18	June 18	July 18	Aug 18	Sept 18	Oct 18	Nov 18	Dec 18	Jan 19	Feb 19	Mar 19	Apr 19	May 19
Evidence studies/planning preparation/stakeholder engagement	X	X	X	X	X	X	X	X	X	X												
Publication/pre-submission consultation (Reg 19)											P	P										
Process consultation representations													X	X								
Submission to secretary of state (Reg 22)															X							
Examination (Regs 22/23) (including hearings)																O	O	O				
Examination (post-hearing processes), including inspector's report to council) (fact check)																		O				
Inspector's final report																			O			
Preparation of plan adoption documentation																					X	
Adoption																						X

Note: Key: X = Eastleigh Borough Council timings; P = public consultation periods; O = PINS process

Source: Based on Eastleigh Borough Council (2017)

for the area, such as Neighbourhood Plans. The Local Development Scheme must be made available publicly and kept up-to-date. It is important that local communities and interested parties can keep track of progress. Local planning authorities should publish their Local Development Scheme on their website. ... Up-to-date and accessible reporting on the Local Development Scheme in an Authority's Monitoring Report is an important way in which authorities can keep communities informed of plan making activity. (NPPG, 2019: para 003)

Table 3.2 is an example of the published schedule of a local plan (the LDS for Eastleigh Borough Council, Hampshire), which indicates the stages involved in plan making set against a monthly timeline. This creates a framework for plan making organised by time and stage through its production.

While the example of Eastleigh reflects an effort to depict the time frame of local plan progress, we can note that the eventual Eastleigh Local Plan was completed in April 2022 (and compare that date to the estimated adoption month of May 2019). The reasons for the 'delay' of almost three years is rarely discussed but will include local and national elections, suspension periods, changes of administration, and alteration to national policy, which can all serve to suspend or set back the process. Planners working on local plans regard this as quite usual, and more detailed research on delay seems desirable:

'I think in terms of speeding things up, I don't think it's just as simple as saying, "We will do local plans in 30 months." I think we need some real thought about how that will work in practice; and the answer to me isn't about setting a specific time frame. It's about solving some of those issues, such as: what evidence is required; how we address the challenges from people who object to the plan, for whatever reason; how we, kind of, put the local authority in the driving seat a bit more on plan making. Because, often, there isn't a right or wrong answer. But, obviously, people whose sites aren't included have strong objections and seem to have a lot of power to delay examinations and to put pressure on local authorities to collect increasingly more evidence, which delays the process. So, I think the solution is about looking at the problems and addressing those, and that will naturally speed up plan making, rather than just setting an arbitrary 30-month time frame.' (Local Authority Planner 'C')

The creation of such a timetable also sets up the basis or benchmark for 'delay' – a form of idealised time. This reflects an attempt to impose technocratic policy making *in* time (Howard, 2005; Strassheim, 2016). Actors will use the scheme timeline as the basis for their expectations, and the timings may of themselves influence actors and structure practice, for example, to hurry or squeeze activity, with the limited public consultation allocations in Table 3.2 also being noted. These schedules reflect the wider ensemble of efforts to provide more certainty and transparency in plan making and policy at the local scale. Aspirational timings cannot account for the wide range of factors that will produce 'delay', and, indeed, it is worth noting that the Eastleigh timetable had been adhered to up to and including submission of the plan in October 2018.

Example 3: Plan monitoring and delivery

The previous examples relate to timings for plan making and the duration and tempo of production. This example highlights time in plan monitoring and delivery, most notably, the authorities' monitoring report (AMR) (formerly known as the 'annual monitoring report') and annual position statement. The AMR is published each year and contains information on the progress of local plan documents and the extent to which planning policies are being successfully achieved. This is a means to measure performance against the programme set out in the LDS. The annual position statement is a document prepared by the local planning authority in consultation with developers and others who have an impact on delivery. The statement also sets out the housing land supply position on 1 April each year (see Example 4). These tools involve assessing plan delivery over time, and particular targets are applied to manage the performance of the LPA.

The framing of a plan or its notional 'lifespan' is typically measured in years, with the lifespan subject to different speeds and deliverables associated with policy areas, notably, housing delivery. National Planning Policy typically sets out time frames for a local plan: 'strategic policies should be prepared over a minimum 15-year period and a local planning authority should be planning for the full plan period. Policies age at different rates according to local circumstances and a plan does not become out-of-date automatically after 5 years' (NPPG, 2019: para 064). This time horizon is somewhat undermined by the (then) five-year land-supply stipulation given that the plan becomes weakened if delivery is not maintained. In effect, this acts to vary the strength of policy over time; the plan is given political support nationally under the 'plan-led system' but is contingent on delivery. This highlights control exercised nationally over local authority performance and the role that monitoring reports and delivery targets play in shaping practice. It also contains the idea of 'differential rates' or the 'ageing' of local plans, which imply alternative time (see Table 2.2).

Example 4: Five-year land-supply requirement (until December 2023)

The fourth example is the requirement for LPAs to demonstrate that they have an up-to-date 'five-year land supply' for housing development (as mentioned in Example 3). This is characterised as 'a supply of specific deliverable sites sufficient to provide 5 years' worth of housing (and appropriate buffer) against a housing requirement set out in adopted strategic policies, or against a local housing need figure' (NPPG, 2019, para 002). This requirement was introduced in 2014 and is an attempt to equate a quantum of development with the timing of such development. Each LPA has to demonstrate to central government that they can assure a 'pipeline' of development sites through an adopted plan or by using an annual position statement (see Example 3) that shows numbers against time.

The calculation of the five-year housing land supply presented for scrutiny at the local plan examination also includes the idea of 'the deliverability' of sites. If a local authority cannot demonstrate a five-year housing land supply in their local plan, the appointed planning inspector will be able to recommend modifications to the plan to ensure that it does identify a five-year housing land supply. Furthermore, where a local planning authority cannot demonstrate a five-year supply, including any appropriate buffer, during the life of the plan, then the 'presumption in favour of sustainable development' applies, effectively meaning that in housing terms, the LPA has much less control over what sites are developed (thus undermining the 'plan-led' approach to local development and applications potentially being more speculative in nature). As one LPA planner observed:

> 'Massive delays in plan making mean that we are in a difficult position in terms of five-year housing land supply ... the ability to have a continually up-to-date local plan is massively impacted by the amount of time it takes to do that [work] ... The impacts of the delay are potentially no five-year housing land supply, potentially more speculative applications. Although that doesn't really happen in [local authority] because we're very much a brownfield authority, where I was previously, as soon as you didn't have a five-year housing land supply, you would be hit with lots of speculative greenfield applications.' (Local Authority Planner 'D')

In 2022–23, this requirement was under review. Many observers had viewed it as an unfair test for local authorities who were not actually in a position to control the timing of development given that delivery is largely dependent on private sector housing developers and subject to other economic and political factors. A careful assessment from the Planning Advisory Service (PAS) for England is suggestive of the difficulties:

> 5-yr housing land supply, is an embedded part of the planning system. However actually forecasting the when and how delivery will occur

can be challenging and relies on both analysing planning data and engagement with developers & housebuilders. The end result might be a single figure of X-yrs supply however the processes to get to that figure requires a lot of work by councils. (PAS, 2023a)

This example shows how 'political time' has been reified to a set time horizon by setting and enforcing a form of clepsydra (or hourglass) approach, where time is used as a means to measure and police the flow of housing delivery. Example 5 presents one LPA response to this scenario, where 'moving time' around is used as a tactic to ease difficulties in the early delivery of housing targets.

Example 5: Back-ending of the housing delivery pipeline

Given the pressure to deliver housing placed on local authorities in England and the wider imposition of targets for housing, accompanying time frames have been imposed to facilitate such delivery (for example, the five-year land supply and the hourglass approach explained in Example 4). A response on the part of some LPAs has been to organise or forecast the phasing of housing delivery unevenly across the lifespan of the local plan. This example is an instance of punctuation, that is, a deliberate modelling of action *by* time, where temporal manipulation is deployed. This is manifest in the example shown by arranging housing numbers per year across the plan period and typically plotting low unit numbers at the start of a plan period and anticipating higher delivery numbers later. This appears to be an attempt to smooth any immediate tensions over new development locally and push the bulk of delivery into the future.

This temporal strategy bids to convince other actors not only that the rate and flow of delivery will be uneven over time but also that the requisite quantum will be delivered over the full period. Figure 3.1 shows the anticipated housing numbers in Guildford Borough, Surrey, over the period of a local plan, with an uneven and 'back-ended' flow of envisaged housing apparent across time. The ascending line in Figure 3.1 highlights the 'under-delivery' in the early plan period and then a later projected 'over-delivery' of housing numbers against time.

This projection is manifest largely due to political tension over housebuilding locally. The attempt to defer housing avoids censure from national government (for example, via failure to 'pass' the housing delivery test [see DLUHC, 2022b]) and placates local concerns over development by pushing the greatest delivery into the future. As such, it can be seen as a form of temporal choreography to counter national government timescaping measures.

All five of the examples presented in these first policy and plan examples highlight that the existing timescape of local plan making has become dominated by the speed and timing of delivery. As we argue in Chapter 4,

Figure 3.1: Example of local housing delivery profile over time

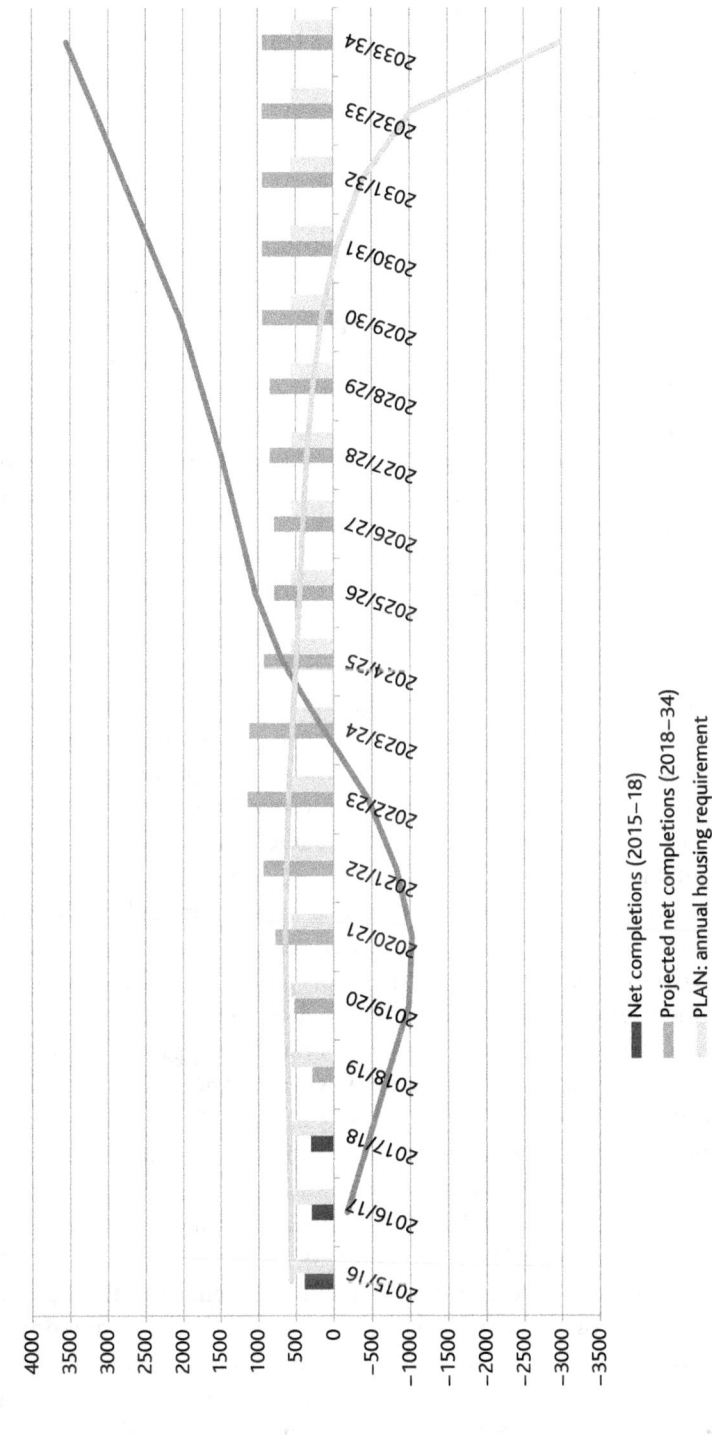

Source: Guildford Borough Council (2019: 265–6)

project speed demonstrates a partial view of the role of planning and plan making, which involves far more than the delivery of housing and contends with many other issues that need to be reflected through plans and local policy, not least ensuring the provision of public infrastructure and services, sustainable transport, employment opportunities, environmental protection, and so on.

Development management

The next set of examples concerns the development management stage of planning (see Table 3.3), when individual planning applications are assessed on a case-by-case basis against the local plan policies (and other 'material' considerations) to determine whether they should be granted permission, deferred or refused. It is at this determination stage that specific development scheme proposals are in question and require stakeholder inputs, as well as the exercise of professional judgement. The use of time here can have a significant impact on how the scheme is assessed, what inputs are received from different actors and the overall decision.

Example 6: Pre-application advice – 'pre-apps'

We begin by highlighting planning pre-application discussions, or 'pre-apps' (see Parker et al, 2022). We highlight how some activity is shifted 'off the clock' given that pre-apps are where advice is requested on a proposed development scheme before the official submission of a planning application. Discussions are therefore held to highlight any issues upfront that may otherwise cause problems further down the line in a formal application.

This is an informal and optional stage of the planning process, undertaken before the official submission of a planning application and hence before the eight- or 13-week determination period (see Example 9). Pre-apps are entered into voluntarily to shape a proposal, with the intention of 'saving' time later on in the process, where disagreements or the refusal of permission could entail delay or add other costs. Pre-apps may be regarded as pushing planning activity (and the time expended) not only 'off the clock' but also out of view. A clear indication of this dynamic lies in the claimed benefits of pre-apps, where overt features of time consideration have been stated, for example: 'Establishing a better understanding of timescales and administrative processes'; and 'Early engagement to reduce or prevent delays at the determination stage' (DCLG, 2009: 4).

Pre-apps highlight where planning activity is being pushed upstream beyond the hourglass or clepsydra of decision times. It becomes questionable whether this reduces time to make decisions or simply obscures time expenditure. The rationale usually put forward is that pre-apps can expedite a decision in the subsequent formal time period allowed for a decision.

Table 3.3: The planning timescape in England: development management examples (Examples 6–10)

Planning example	Relation to time	Implication for practice	Type of strategy	Link to theoretical treatment of time and practice	Impact on other actors (that is, winners/losers)
Example 6: Pre-apps	Front-load negotiations before submission of formal planning application	Extension of process prior to official submission for planning	'Off the clock' but helps make the public sector input time chargeable	5Cs/commercialisation of time	Enables developers to save time later by enabling a smoother application determination
Example 7: PPAs	Agreeing to suspending time limits for specific projects	Exception to general rules/timings that seek to create a mutual tailored tempo/duration	Slowing down by pushing planning activity 'off the clock'	5Cs/control of time and possibility for commercialisation of process	Disguises the time and resources involved, and opens up a market in public sector advice
Example 8: Fast-tracking	Agreeing to speed up/bypass elements of planning application testing where specific thresholds have been met and/or for an additional fee	Fast Track Route, such as in the London Plan, where proposals that meet the 35% affordable housing threshold do not need to submit detailed viability information; fast-track planning application process by paying additional fees, such as Brentford and Luton Councils	Speeding up process	Temporal choreography – developer incentivisation to be either policy compliant or pay for a faster service; local authority commercialisation to offer additional faster service over their traditional processing	Ability to progress through the planning permission process faster than the typical statutory process
Example 9: Determination deadlines	Setting standardised time frame for decisions – eight or 13 weeks for minor and major applications, respectively	Some LPAs issue 'EoTs' – time extensions where there is a specific need/agreement for a more bespoke timescale (linking conceptually with PPAs)	Performance management	5Cs/control of time	Pressure on LPAs to meet statutory determination periods/decision-making delays
Example 10: Call-ins of planning cases by SoS	Removes decision from LPAs to national level to be determined by the SoS	Suspension or lifting out of the time frame for decision making	Slowing down	Political time – national government removes local determination right and operates on its own decision-making timescale	LPA and developer have to await a decision from the SoS

67

Pre-apps focus inputs of time in a form of 'front-loading' of planning discussions between the developer and the LPA. Iterations made may avoid 'political and public risk further down the line, when such disruptions are more costly/harmful to a development scheme and thereby provide greater development certainty' (Parker et al, 2022: 72).

The developer motives for engaging in a pre-app include establishing a critical level of certainty in the planning process, so that they can make their own calculations and manage their risk profile. Thus, negotiating over the various requirements necessary to secure approval before formally submitting a planning application has proven popular (though caveated to where such additional service can be effectively resourced by the LPA). Research has shown that LPAs in England produce somewhere in the order of 10–15 per cent of their planning service income from pre-app fees, and the wider involvement of the public and local politicians in pre-apps has not been realised (Parker et al, 2022). This is despite 'a strong presumption that ... there will be formal pre-application discussions involving, where appropriate, all relevant parties, including elected members, statutory consultees and representatives of the local community' (Killian and Pretty, 2008: 10). The use of pre-apps by developers and LPAs to 'clear time' represents a good example of 'times in policymaking' (Strassheim, 2016), where deliberation and discussion are afforded to assist a later stage of policy *in* time, and where the implicit promise of time saved is, for some, the promise of money saved.

Example 7: Planning performance agreements

Killian and Pretty's (2008) review in the UK included recommendations to extend the use of 'planning performance agreements' (PPAs). Typically, these have been deployed where a major development is being conceived and the approach to dealing with advice and adherence to standardised timings can be problematic (see also Example 9). In response, bespoke arrangements can be made for the scheme if the main parties agree.

Through a PPA, a developer will agree to pay for suitable arrangements from the LPA, this can include buying out the time of a particular planning officer and effectively lifting the development into its own time frame, that is, suspending the standard determination periods. It also enables a more open discursive approach, aligning to Strassheim's (2016) distinction of policy *by* time and *in* time. This also benefits the LPA, not only because they receive some additional income but also because it relieves the time pressure for determination. The relevant recommendation in Killian and Pretty's (2008: 22) report places timetabling at the centre of PPAs:

> Government should further encourage the use of Planning Performance Agreements (PPAs) for major developments by making it clear that a

proportionate approach to PPAs is acceptable. Thus for smaller and less complex schemes, a much simpler approach to a PPA, centred around an agreed timetable, may be all that is required.

This may be seen as an example of enabling a form of 'proper time' arrangements for the two main protagonists by allowing a negotiated approach that better suits each participant's needs and resources. It is less clear how the public or local community are served through PPAs (Austin, 2011). It could be argued that a better outcome is enabled that can service a more teleologically discerned public interest. Notably, however, little research has been conducted on PPA use and operation (but see Bristow, 2008; PAS, 2023b).

Example 8: 'Fast-tracking' proposals that deliver affordable housing in London

As part of a wider business drive towards an improved customer service orientation, some LPAs have adopted the technique of creating fast-track planning services. This serves as a means of generating extra business revenue and entails paying a fee for preferential treatment that offers the prospect of time savings. This is an interesting shift because within project management more widely, the term 'fast-track' is used to notate instances where more resources are deployed so that tasks can be performed in parallel rather than in sequence. Several instances of how fast-tracking is being offered by English LPAs are set out in the following.

The first example dates from 2018, when the Greater London Authority (GLA) took the decision to allow developers to bypass the provision of detailed viability assessment information if they undertook to deliver policy-compliant levels of affordable housing (arguably, this is what they should have been doing anyway). The trade-off was a 'fast-track' channel to planning permission. This was justified on the basis that:

> Under the Threshold Approach, development proposals that provide 35 per cent affordable housing and 50 per cent on public and industrial land ... and that meet tenure, affordability and other relevant requirements, can follow the Fast Track Route. The Fast Track Route enables developments to progress without the need to submit detailed viability information and without late viability review mechanisms which re-assess viability at an advanced stage of the development process. The Mayor strongly encourages applicants to follow the Fast Track Route which has provided greater certainty to the market, sped up the planning process, and has helped to increase the level of affordable housing secured in new developments. (GLA, 2018)

This 'threshold' approach reflects how policy compliance may be used as a tool to offer a planning short cut: a form of deregulation with a time component used to incentivise adherence to policy goals. This is interesting because it represents the use of time as a resource being deployed by the local authority to perform developers and an attempt to set up a range of time incentives within the plan-led approach.

The use of a fast-track planning service can be understood in relation to the commercialisation of local authority planning. Time can be used to generate additional revenue and as a means to reduce resource constraints. In January 2023, the London Borough of Barnet produced a document entitled 'Pre-application & fast-track guidance notes and fees schedule' (see also Figure 3.2), which stated that:

> We can fast-track all types of planning applications and pre-application planning advice request – giving you guaranteed timescales and allowing you to begin work on your project more quickly. When choosing any of the fast-track services, we guarantee to contact you and provide advice from an experienced planner within an accelerated timescale. While the service does not impact on whether planning permission is granted, you will receive a quicker decision on your application. (Barnet Council, 2023: 3)

Similarly, Surrey Heath Borough Council also announced a 'fast-track' option for planning permissions in 2023, as well as for pre-applications: 'the fast-track planning service will speed up the process for people who opt for this service, providing applicants with a decision in just five weeks, compared with the standard eight weeks' (Surrey Heath Borough Council, 2023).

We can view this as part of Adam's 5Cs, where time is equated with money and, hence, the 'value' to planning applicants is to receive a faster response to their proposal. Despite the different motivations for LPAs to incentivise policy compliance or capture additional revenues, they both sit somewhat incongruously with the formal determination periods that have been imposed on LPAs from central government. These are ostensibly to ensure that timely decisions use a standardised approach. What the fast-track example shows is the use of time 'saved' as a means to negotiate other benefits – it effectively barters time against cost.

Example 9: Determination times for planning applications and 'extensions of time'

The most obvious and apparent (as well as perhaps most significant) set of time limits imposed on LPAs are the deadlines set to determine planning applications. In England, the stipulations placed on LPAs have been iterated

Figure 3.2: London Borough of Barnet's 'Benefits of using the fast-track service'

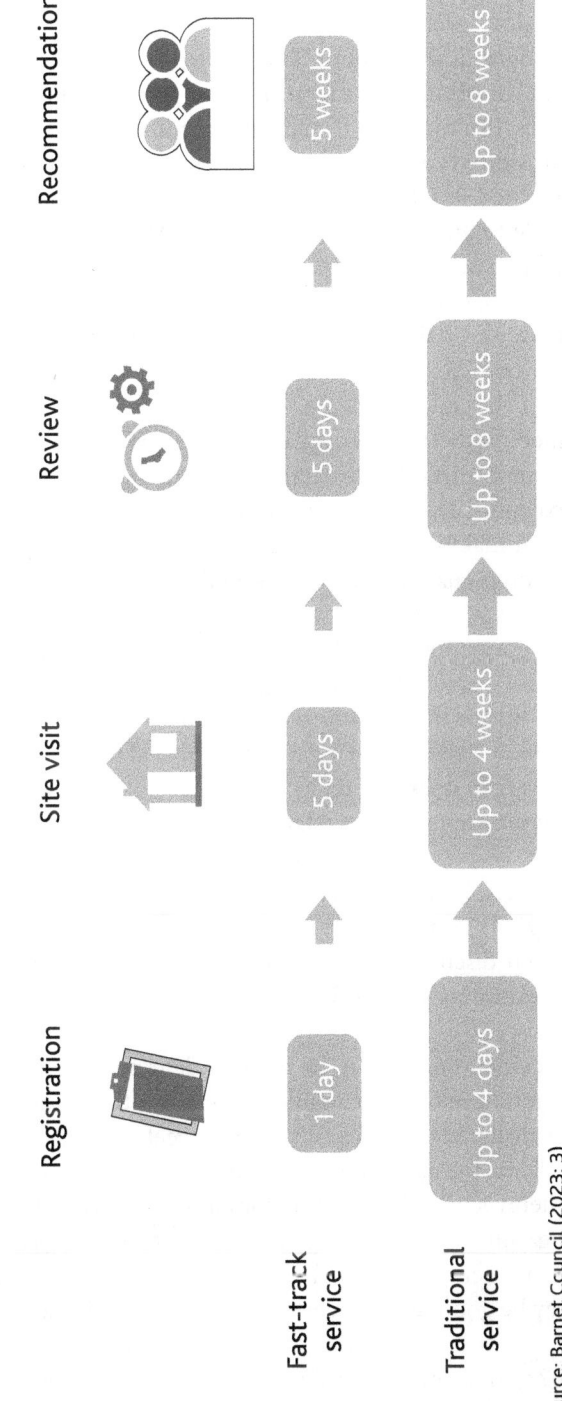

Source: Barnet Council (2023: 3)

on several occasions, leading to time limits to reach a decision, either eight weeks for smaller planning applications or a 13-week time frame for larger and major development proposals.

In England, set times to determine planning cases have been a long-term feature. Booth (2003) identifies time-limit arrangements as being in place since the Planning Act 1932, and according to Clifford (2016), this approach was reasserted and embedded following the 1975 Dobry Report. Yet, as we highlighted in Chapter 1, the scope, scale and complexity of planning has expanded significantly since that time. As Booth (2020: 41) asserts: 'It need hardly be said that since those time limits were introduced, the scale of the task has changed out of all recognition and a simple failure to observe an eight-week or thirteen-week period for processing planning applications cannot be other than the crudest measure of efficiency.'

As of the autumn of 2022, a third time period for determination was retained, with 16 weeks for those cases requiring an environmental impact assessment (EIA). As we detail later, even those parameters have been subject to exceptions and gaming. This application of a clepsydra to planning decision making was added to in 2014, when the UK government set out a 'planning guarantee', which stated:

> the government's policy [is] that no application should spend more than a year with decision-makers, including any appeal. In practice this means that planning applications should be decided in no more than 26 weeks, allowing a similar period for any appeal. The planning guarantee does not replace the statutory time limits for determining planning applications. (DCLG, 2014: para 002)

Conversely, there are examples where agreements known as 'extensions of time' (EoTs) can be agreed between parties (again, a variation on the PPA approach discussed in Example 7). The PAS (2022) for England explains such extensions as follows:

> agreements to extend the time for determination can be made for both major development applications and other applications that would normally be determined within 8 weeks ... extensions of time should really be the exception and efforts made to meet the statutory timescale wherever possible ... for complex proposals, when pre-application engagement has not happened or when unforeseen issues or the need for amendment arise through the course of considering the application, there may be good reasons why the application will take longer to determine.

In 2023, in reviewing planning performance arrangements and planning fees in England, the Department of Levelling Up, Housing and Communities

(DLUHC, 2023: paras 49–50), the renamed ministry responsible for planning in England, also stated:

> Extension of time agreements are useful in exceptional circumstances to allow additional time for unforeseen issues to be resolved to the benefit of all parties. However, the reasons should be legitimate. Currently, extension of time agreements do not count against a local planning authority's performance figures for speed of decision-making and therefore can mask instances where local planning authorities are not determining applications within the required statutory periods ... We understand that the existing metrics and the use of extension of time agreements do not adequately reflect performance of planning departments or the experience of customers.

By 2013, the UK government had conceded that reasons for delay could be produced variously: 'We accept that parties other than the local planning authority can be a cause of delay – but such circumstances again point to the need for bespoke timetables to be agreed between the parties where justified' (DCLG, 2013: para 36). We can see that this is not just a case of speeding up or slowing down planning determination in a crude sense; however, also visible is the way that 'proper time' re-emerges in the guise of an exception – itself necessitated by attempts to impose arbitrary clock time.

Example 10: 'Calling in' of planning cases

The planning application process in England can follow several routes, but some planning applications may be 'called in' by central government to consider the development proposal. The decision making is therefore removed from the local authority level. In such cases, the SoS has the power to direct the local planning authority to refer an application to them for decision. This power is typically only used if the planning issues are considered to be of 'more than local importance', and the SoS 'will normally only do this if the application conflicts with national policy in important ways, or is nationally significant' (see DLUHC, 2019).

While a call-in means the decision is taken at the national level, it also highlights a clear expression of political time, where a suspension or lifting out of the time frame for 'normal' decision making is operated. In this situation, a specific timetable to progress that application will be published by the PINS or central government. As the PINS (2022: para 1.4.2) states: 'Keeping to the timetable is fundamental to an efficient and fair called-in applications service and we expect everyone to comply with them.' Notably, this approach extends time discipline to all parties rather than only the LPA. Moreover, when using call-in powers, it is usual that an inquiry will be held. This is a deployment

Table 3.4: The planning timescape in England: public participation examples (Examples 11–13)

Planning example	Relation to time	Implication for practice	Type of strategy	Link to theoretical treatment of time and practice	Impact on other actors (that is, winners/losers)
Example 11: Speaking rights	Timed slot for public to speak in planning committee meetings	Bounded time for input into the panel	Delimiting boxing/containing time	Temporal choreography	Provides a time window for input, sequenced within a timed process
Example 12: Consultation periods	Set period for 28 days, or other arrangements with set deadlines	Renewed time frame if new information arises	Delimiting/boxing/containing time	Temporal choreography	Provides a time window for input, sequenced within a timed process
Example 13: Community-led and neighbourhood planning	No time limit because dealing with self-selecting volunteers, but issues with sequencing alongside council process of local plan production	Can create new statutory planning document and policies for neighbourhood area that form part of the council LDS	Community time in planning used to support national goals for housing delivery and growth	Political time – undertaken to exert greater control over local planning agenda	Significant open-ended time and resource commitment for volunteers with no guarantee of success

of proper timing: 'We will take account of the estimates we receive from the applicant and the local planning authority and our own experience when we set the likely length of the inquiry. Once set we will normally expect the length of the inquiry to stay within the agreed timetable' (PINS, 2022: para B.2.3).

What these five examples of planning determination highlight is that speeding up or suspending decision making tailors planning practice to the specific case and the proper time required rather than adhering to standardised time limits.

Limits on community involvement in planning

The third group of examples is presented to highlight time use and management in relation to public involvement in planning, covering time-limited speaking rights, consultation periods and community-led planning. Table 3.4 introduces this subset of examples.

Example 11: Speaking rights at planning committees

Planning committees are public meetings where evidence is presented and representations are made to the elected local councillors on that committee. This forms a means of deciding whether planning applications should be approved or rejected and/or whether any appropriate conditions or other obligations are required. This is a straightforward example of time rationing, where those wishing to make a representation to a local planning committee will be restricted to a short time limit. Typically, those speaking in support or to voice concerns or opposition to a proposal will be given a speaking slot of a few minutes each.

The following is the policy from Wycombe District, Buckinghamshire, outlining the approach they take:

> An overall total of 3 minutes is allowed for objections to be made to the Committee on an application. This time limit is for all objectors in total, not 3 minutes each. However, a further 3 minutes is allowed for a representative of the Parish/Town Council where it has objected. (Wycombe District Council, no date: 2)

Their policy allows time graduation, depending on who is speaking, but is also standardised regardless of the complexity or importance of the case being considered or the content of a representation.

The main logic here is one of efficiency, as planning committees consider numerous cases at each meeting and therefore ration time based on an assumption that key points of support or objection should be able to be rehearsed in this time frame. Additionally, it is expected that representations will also have been made in writing to the LPA during the consultation period (see Example 12). This reflects decision making *by* time, that is, organising evidence to fit the time allowed.

Example 12: Consultation periods

Consultation periods are the set times for inputs to be prepared and received by either central or local government on policy proposals, draft plans and other planning documents, or indeed individual planning applications and appeals. Here, we highlight the consultation arrangements for a planning application, whereby 21 days is usually given for interested parties to comment.

When a local planning authority receives a planning application, they validate it and 'start the clock' on the determination period (see Example 9) and on the period declared for parties to comment on the application. Where an amendment to the application is made, it is left to the LPA whether a new period of consultation of 21 days should be commenced. If such a process is not followed, then, in effect, the actual period of time for consultees (namely, the public) to consider a revised application is shortened. The LPA will be under pressure to act in a 'timely' manner, and, as such, they may well not extend or reset the consultation period clock. Clearly, there could be scope for exclusion in such circumstances where the speed of decision making is prioritised.

Example 13: Community-led planning

A final category that highlights a wider question about time management in planning is where communities are active in plan-making processes. In England, the only instance of experimentation with formal community-led plan making is neighbourhood planning (see Parker et al, 2019). This example is instructive because time management cuts across all of the categories discussed earlier and sets up a clear differential between local plans and neighbourhood plans. This goes beyond mechanisms to suspend or make exceptions in time.

Table 3.4 highlights neighbourhood planning as an example where separate and parallel activity is tolerated and time limits are not specified (though neighbourhood plans form part of the statutory planning system). Instead, the voluntaristic nature of neighbourhood planning requires that the government does not impose deadlines for their creation. Instead, plan making is allowed to run to its own temporal span. Might this be considered an instance of proper timing? Or, does it actually and also highlight the inefficiencies of planning processes that are not carefully managed? Some have indeed argued that the process should either be simplified or that timelines be agreed and adhered to by participants.

While neighbourhood plan production is not time limited, the lifespan of the forums that are empowered to produce a plan are (and some stages of neighbourhood plan production do reflect the type of limits discussed in Example 12). Once established formally, a neighbourhood forum is granted a five-year operating period, implying that the neighbourhood plan should be completed within that time. The critical difference between neighbourhood planning and local plan making is who is leading it. For neighbourhood plans, it is voluntary, and no time limits are imposed because the aim of the enabling Localism Act 2011 is to induce and mobilise citizens as planning volunteers. This highlights the differential treatment that can be afforded to those who appear in service to growth, as neighbourhood plans can only plan for more and not less development, effectively only allowing for more control over the types and locations. The growth imperative runs in parallel to the 'speed' logic that may otherwise cut across the combined localist-growth aims of neighbourhood planning (see Wargent and Parker, 2018; see also Chapter 4).

Participation, people and time in planning

The examples that we have compiled from the English planning system reflect the exercise of power, sometimes with clear political motivations, using deadlines, time limits or other delimitations based on clock time. What we draw from this is evidence of a rolling and programmatic process of timescaping the planning system. Planning reforms can lead to a variety of responses, and the different reaction types set out by Hochschild (2005), that is, 'absorption', 'enduring', 'delegation', 'deferring' or 'resisting', provide a good base for further study. In Chapter 4, we set out a range of time-related examples that have been introduced over a considerable period, with commentators pointing to 1979 as a key date, with the election of Margaret Thatcher, as that administration embarked on what many regard as the first 'wave' of neoliberal or New Right-inspired planning reforms in the UK. Yet, before we assess the recent politics of time and planning, we first consider how timescaping can impact on people and how they participate in planning.

The previous section mapped out examples of the main stages and tools of planning practice in England, indicating where time is apparent in its limiting, rationing or suspension of clock time. This provides a time-oriented overview of the structure and features of the English planning timescape through which actors engage in the system. As we have shown, the timescape plays a part in shaping engagement and the possibilities of inclusive and 'proper' planning. To probe further, we turn towards recent attention to *phronesis* in planning as being instructive in relation to individual experience of planning as a process (see Flyvbjerg, 2004; Gunder, 2010; Briassoulis, 2023). This area of planning theory explores *phronesis* as the rational faculty to make 'the right decision for the right reason at the right time' – albeit under particular or constrained circumstances. Briassoulis (2023: 60) positions *phronesis* as a condition and process involving 'knowledge of the particulars of a case', and argues that this situatedness complements technical and epistemological knowledge forms.

Such viewpoints emphasise the richer composite role that context and place play, as well as the influence of practices, processes, power, values, discourses and structure–agency interactions in achieving good planning. That is to say, the application of *phronesis* can help conceive of timescapes that enable the benefits of those composite factors to be realised from the individual's perspective and contrasts and complements how time shapes practice.

Flyvbjerg (2001, 2004) claims that early philosophical treatments of *phronesis* did not consider power issues, and as a result, he has argued instead for a 'progressive *phronesis*', which contends with power alongside values and context. The approach argues that both an analytical/positive view (that is, how decisions are made) and a normative view (that is, how decisions should have been made) need to be kept in mind. This implicitly involves questions of time and its organisation for deliberation and reflection. Attempts to critically reflect and re-theorise the planning process using *phronesis* involve, according to Briassoulis (2023), the key stages of assessing a planning problem: (1) assess in context, (2) exercise deliberation and (3) make judgements over choices.

Sophisticated reflections about the ontological and epistemological basis for reaching 'good planning' outcomes accept how time impacts on planning and 'planners', widely defined, and reflects the socially constructed and open character of plans. This highlights that time is an important factor in developing knowledges and understandings necessary to develop '*phronimos*', that is, the substantive grasp of *phronesis*. This is best explained as the assembly of knowledges and understandings that enable, sustain and enhance good planning. Figure 3.3 portrays the range of factors that Briassoulis (2023) contends are implicated in *phronetic* planning and for the individual decision-making process.

What the representation in Figure 3.3 sets out in relation to the key actors involved is that their disposition and the combination of knowledges required are both complex and different. Despite temporalities being absent from the figure, we draw from this how time deployment – the timescape – can have numerous consequences at stages of the individual's response to planning questions. Such an observation echoes the interrelationships found between time practice/practice time that are present in Bourdieu's work. Table 3.5 provides a simplified representation of practice, speed, deliberation and measurement taken together, and indicates how individuals will consider each facet against questions of priority/importance, resources (both available or implied), knowledge implications, considerations of accountability and different options or solutions.

Figure 3.3: Individual decision-making process

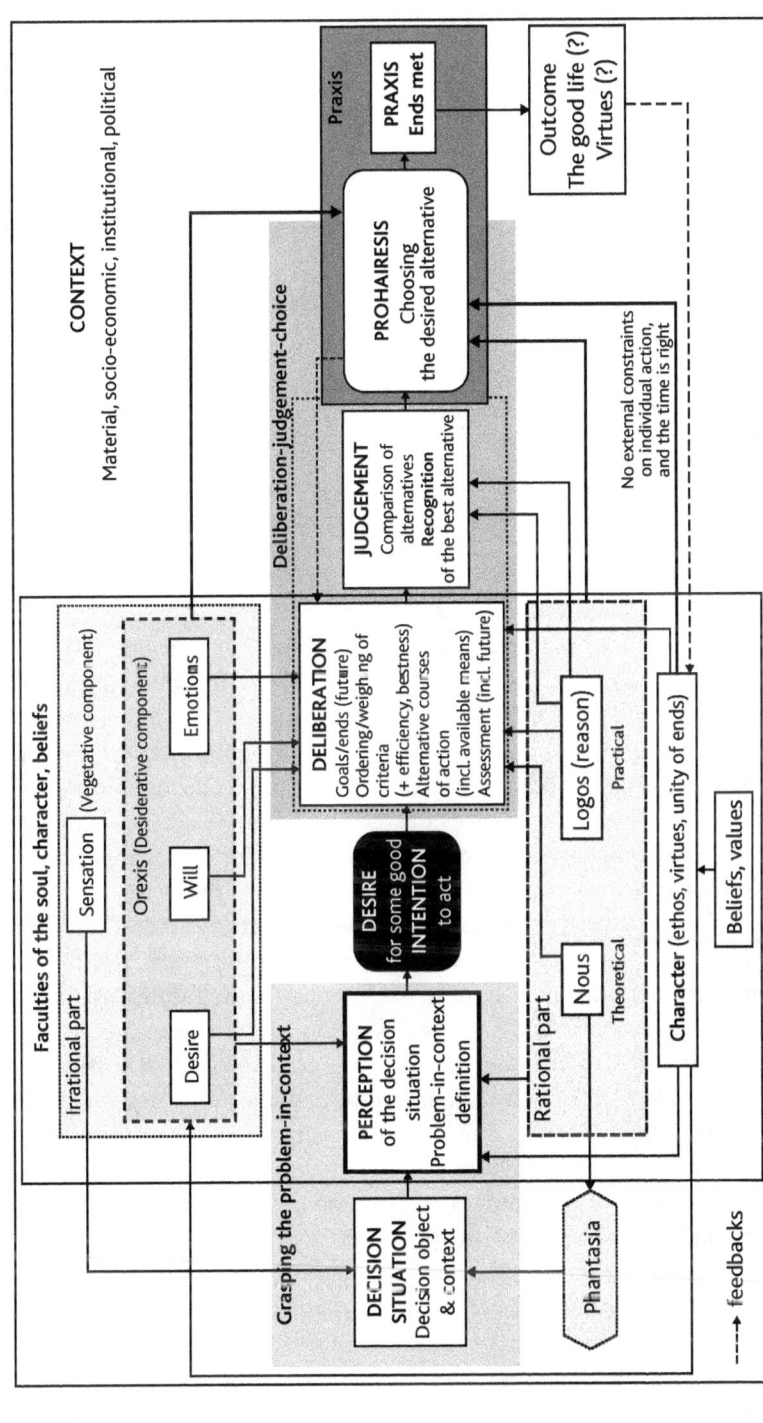

Source: Briassoulis, *Planning Theory*, 22:1, pp 58–84. Copyright © 2022 by Helen Briassoulis. Reprinted by Permission of SAGE Publications.

Table 3.5: Time in planning: some dimensions and factors in decisions

Time dimension (x4)	Factors (x5)				
1. Time as practised (field rhythm and doxa)	Importance	Resources	Knowledge*	Accountability	Solution/option
2. Time and speed (and time squeezing)	Importance	Resources	Knowledge*	Accountability	Solution/option
3. Time to think (reflexivity/ deliberation)	Importance	Resources	Knowledge*	Accountability	Solution/option
4. Measurement of time (and interventions)	Importance	Resources	Knowledge*	Accountability	Solution/option

Note: * Including the idea of *phronesis*.

Overall, the question of how and why time is used in application to a particular facet or task in planning is conditioned by the four considerations shown in the rows of Table 3.5, which concern practice culture, speed, reflexiveness and how time is measured or controlled, and the five practice 'factors' shown in the columns of Table 3.5, that is, importance, resources, knowledge, accountability and solution/options. The question of issue/task contingency involved or its deemed importance relates to the impact, criticality and repercussions of a planning decision set against a measure of time or restriction of time applied to it. Again, the issue of how much time/effort it is worthwhile expending is manifest. This conundrum is also shaped by any legal requirements, as well as by the prior investment that planners and politicians may have made in particular futures, and linked to questions of path dependency (see, for example, Fuchs and Scharmanski, 2009) that orient behaviour. Clearly, this could be linked to the level or attention paid in terms of deliberation. Such questions begin to open up for scrutiny how planners and others actually think about tasks, and how they operationalise their work.

The question of the resources, staffing and funding required to implement policy and ensure appropriate processes is open rather than fixed. This necessitates consideration of either how resource availability impacts on time taken or how further resources can be applied to meet agreed timeliness. This anticipates a rich vein of research to look at 'what planners *actually* do' (see, for example, Schoneboom et al, 2022), alongside our slightly more specific concern with 'what *time* is taken or is afforded to what they do'. In this, there is a connection to the question of what skills and knowledge are needed, and the issues of 'why', 'what' and 'how' regarding achieving a good planned outcome. Without such knowledge, a significant amount of time can be misdirected or wasted attempting to find appropriate courses of action.

Fourth is the issue of accountability and how time can be used inclusively, as well as performed to meet any legal or other expectations. This demonstrates why accountability of planners and others to public scrutiny may condition behaviour in and with time. The final of the five factors is solubility, which, along with any open-endedness of planning 'solutions' (that is, of policy fixes), reflects how policies and decisions are never closed or complete, particularly where there is controversy. A degree of policy looping, monitoring and revisiting is likely and desirable in such conditions.

Overall, this complex of considerations can aid planners and others in assessing what arrangements and process matters may need to be adjusted, or at least made more transparent. This must surely include making choices about time and speed in planning, as well as any resultant timescaping. Beyond these overt time dimensions and factors involved in decision making, Maslow's well-known hierarchy of needs is also a useful heuristic here. For those involved in planning, the implications of the hierarchy help begin to explain likely behaviours or responses to time management in planning. In combination with Figure 3.3, the hierarchy is applied in Table 3.6 and establishes levels of human need or preconditions for *phronimos*. Together, these schema help explain why particular behaviours may be observed or predicted. The levels expressed by Maslow are: (1) the physiological; rising through to (2) safety (including job security); (3) love and belonging needs (friendship); (4) esteem; and (5) self-actualisation.

Inspection of the relationship between the tiers of Maslow's hierarchy indicates how the absence or disturbance of a lower or base layer of the hierarchy destabilises another higher-level condition of being. What this means is that in order for effective engagement in practice, certain basic conditions are necessary. This overlay applies to all but perhaps particularly to professional planners, for whom planning forms their primary focus. This contrasts with a developer, for whom planning is a stage or obstacle to pass through or negotiate, or for a member of the public, who can dip into planning as an active participant, or a politician, who variously relies on others to advise them.

Time-based or temporal governance is as much about how pressure to act may foreclose deliberation or otherwise preference or disadvantage particular actors and aspects of 'good planning'. While the discussion of what constitutes good planning must necessarily be suspended here (we return to this in Chapter 5), it is important to acknowledge how that particular debate runs in parallel to our focus here on proper time. Given the theorisation of planning in and of time, we may attempt to recognise and maximise good planning by intimating that 'the multiple, material, situational, immanent

Table 3.6: Maslow's 'five needs' hierarchy and planning practice

Need	Descriptor	Relevance to planners and other interests in planning deliberation
1. Physiological needs	These most basic human survival needs include food and water, sufficient rest, clothing and shelter, overall health, and reproduction. These basic physiological needs must be addressed before humans move on to the next level of fulfilment.	As per all humans, a lack of some higher-level needs could impact on questions of health, for example. For communities, this need is a prerequisite for people to engage in planning process activity.
2. Safety needs	Next among the lower-level needs is safety. Safety needs include protection from violence and theft, emotional stability and well-being, health security, and financial security.	Pressure in workplace environments could impact on professional planners detrimentally. For communities, the way that the planning process is organised and delimited needs to be aware of questions of security in the process for all.
3. Love and belonging needs	These link to human interaction and include friendships and family bonds. Physical and emotional intimacy, ranging from sexual relationships to intimate emotional bonds, is important to achieving a feeling of elevated kinship. Additionally, membership in social groups contributes to meeting this need, from belonging to a team of co-workers to forging an identity in a club or group.	Time-based parameters of working practices may act to promote individualism or force group mobbing of work. For some community members, priorities to be attentive to such needs may marginalise wider civic engagement, such as participation. The approaches and opportunities in planning should be mindful of such time and psychological pressures.
4. Esteem needs	The primary elements here are self-respect (self-value and deserving of dignity) and self-esteem (confidence in potential for personal growth and accomplishments). This can be broken into two types: esteem that is based on respect and acknowledgement from others; and esteem that is based on self-assessment (self-confidence and independence stem from this latter type of self-esteem).	Inability to meet high standards in qualitative terms could impact negatively on confidence and esteem, both self and societal. Inputs to planning should be respected, and respectful discussion of inputs is needed to ensure that barriers are not created.
5. Self-actualisation needs	These aim towards the fulfilment of potential as a person. Self-fulfilment or self-actualisation needs include education, skill development, the refining of talents, caring for others and broader goals like learning skills and winning awards.	Focus on process and hitting targets and deadlines could facilitate awards of some type but could equally maintain narrower skills and talent. For participants in planning, recognition of legitimate goals and some degree of learning and progressive change is important.

and inherently moral character of planning analysis and practice' (Briassoulis, 2023: 76) needs to be routinely inspected, probed and defended.

The relationship between time and 'speed' or tempo and how it is asserted is critical to understandings of how time and its management are perceived and accepted in modern societies, as well as how timescaping can erode or promote the character and practices of planning. This brings into view the 'pace of planning' and a need to consider why particular speed/time assertions are constructed and justified as they are, and how they are enacted in practice. Such tempos may also be resisted or otherwise strategised (for example, 'deflected' or 'absorbed'), and conflicts over timings and measures to variously allow exceptions, avoid time constraints or the 'buying' of time are equally of interest here.

While some have critiqued time via assertions about speed, acceleration and velocity as ultimately destructive and against human nature (see, for example, McLuhan, 1980; Virilio, 1986; Habermas, 2009), we do not view speed as a challenge to planning a priori. The counterpoint is that proper time may be quite rapid, or more specifically variable, in some instances or 'stages' of planning. It is recognised that good use of time may involve alacrity; time can be valued in terms of speed or conversely in terms of the benefits of decisiveness, leadership, accretion or maturation. As Sorensen (2015) argues, recirculation of time can allow for positive feedback and aid improvement in planning, and, as we argue, help enable improved conditions for inclusivity, as well as trust and quality of outcome.

Process measures and imperatives are central to the organisation of time in and for planning, and these have been ripe for revision and critique. As we have already begun to expand upon here and in Chapter 2, the creation of deadlines and time allocations changes behaviours and influences outcomes. Time becomes a reason to justify particular approaches to planning. This observation is linked to a concern for just outcomes that are also procedurally sound (Hillier, 1998; Smith, 2003; Ottinger, 2013). This leads us to question whether we are sufficiently aware of how time and its use shape practice, impact on procedural justice and affect real-world outcomes. These questions are tied to interaction, communication and negotiating time to suit circumstances – that is the 'context' that Forester (2022) asserts. This understanding is key to setting up counter-arguments to challenge the assumptions about development speed, certainty and cost that dominate planning systems (as demonstrated in Chapter 4).

Planners operating in the public sector are heavily regulated and policed, resources are tight, and the range and variety of required considerations have increased. This context presents a combination of factors that weigh down systems unless resources are commensurate to the task. Since the 1960s at least, the evidence, voices, issues and interests that professional planners have had to account for have expanded. Such a plurality provides part of the backdrop to a widening realisation of the impact of particular uses and organisations of time, as well as the importance of planning in providing an arena for societal action (see Chapter 5).

Clifford (2016: 385), in his work examining the impacts of planning reforms on practitioners in England, mentions that 'the threat of intervention for poor performing authorities was strengthened, amidst rhetoric from government that the planning permission process created the sort of slow, expensive and uncertain process that reduces the appetite to build'; he also cites a local planner for whom time and regulation were linked: 'quite tight timeframes presented dilemmas about where to make trade-offs' (Clifford, 2018: 65). This was expressed at a time when the UK government was aiming to tighten the planning performance regime, so that planning decisions were 'made on time' (HM Treasury, 2015: 46). In reflecting on this situation, planners have acknowledged the need to make timely decisions yet question whether this should be prioritised above inclusion or quality considerations: "We should always just take the necessary time to balance off all of these competing interests and make sure nothing is missed. We don't rush decisions just to hit targets" (Local Authority Planner 'E').

Following our exploration of theory, the key factors that condition the temporalities of planning may be essentialised down to the rules and conventions that determine the (1) timing, (2) sequencing, (3) speed and (4) duration of actions. This view of planning is based on the assumption that planning has to be a reflective, deliberative practice and that such practice adheres to quality standards that are not only processual but also hinge on the analysis involved in the policy and decision elements of formal planning (and, as we propose later, the pillars of inclusivity, public interest and sustainable development are substantively present). In considering the various elements of the planning timescape, how the deployment or dispositional effects of time shape practice and key actors in planning becomes an important strand of research inquiry.

Some theorists have argued that we live in a 'timeless time', in the sense that everything is oriented to the present via acceleration, simultaneity and instantaneity, as such conditions of the present can marginalise the future(s) and underplay the past (Habermas, 2009). This has consequences for attempts to plan that are mindful of both past and future and take (proper) time to ensure adequate deliberation is exercised.

McGuirk (2001) notes that modern planning practice was constructed predominantly through a reliance on techno-scientific analysis and deductive logic. This approach enabled some forms of reasoning and, implicitly or effectively, tended to exclude a range of knowledge forms and value systems (that is, local, intuitive, tacit or group-based). In an era where a lack of trust in planning outcomes is apparent, it is notable that communicative and collaborative forms of planning theory were built, in part, on a case for renewing planning practice by critiquing both the epistemological foundations of modernist planning and the instrumental rationalities upon which its justification relied.

Clearly, different approaches taken towards the planning process and associated institutional arrangements privilege certain actors and knowledges within the system. This point raises the problem of the '*skhole*' of exclusion and restriction by elites (for a discussion, see Bourdieu, 2000). Acts of exclusion may occur due to limitations of resource or the simplification of planning challenges by design, or as a product of ignorance, and can be assumed to have persisted throughout institutionalised planning history. How we come to understand or reconcile competing 'times' becomes central to planning as a practice and, again, speaks to the idea that (good) planning is an inherently deliberative set of practices. Practitioners will need to source, assemble, digest and reflect on the information and ideas received.

Different parties and the temporalities that are maintained or promoted can potentially conflict given that the objectives of key actors are bound into a series of co-dependencies in time. Such divergences or alignments are choices and, in turn, shape the benefits and impact on the quality of planning, let alone raising questions of legitimacy. These questions are, in essence, ones of power and bring into view how planning decisions are taken, their basis and how outcomes are calibrated by speed. This perspective invites a more careful examination of the steps, stages and elements of planning practices. This will involve opening the black box of practice and examining the 'rules of the game', techniques, people and time involved or marginalised within each stage of planning. We cannot hope to detail all of this here, but we indicatively highlight this agenda through our particular interest in discussing time in and for planning.

Time effects/affects in planning

Time squeezes and other uses of time that prioritise speed or promote 'efficiency' deserve more regard because of the apparently tactical use of time achieved through the appropriation of process and the use of political time and timescaping. Forester (1980) argued persuasively that planning systems have the capacity to become self-serving or at least insular due to technical knowledge barriers and language hurdles. This perspective rings true and seems congruent with Bourdieu (2000) on time acting to structure opportunity and hopes, and the tendency for experts to wield power to shape such expectations. This is where the:

> experience of time is altered by relations of power which operate through an alignment of the subjective structure of hopes and expectations with the objective structure of probabilities. In other

words, there is a tendency for hope to increase proportionally with social power which enables an agent to manipulate the potentialities of the present in order to realize some future project. (McNay, 2001: 150)

This insight is a connector given that the assessment of questions of inclusion/exclusion in planning and by planners is extended by deploying theories of time.

Exclusion in and of planning: the classic participant view

In emphasising the exclusionary potentials of planning practice, Shin (2013: 269) points out that monolithic planning theory and its implementation can 'essentially exclude ordinary citizens from the planning process, and therefore produces plans that do not reflect citizens' values and cultures'. How time is organised to enable or otherwise constrain, or to include/exclude, is a critical question here. This is without, of course, ignoring other concerns relating to power, knowledge and institutional design that can otherwise include or exclude participation in an activity.

The cautionary note struck by Shin (2013) is not a new one; Davoudi and Atkinson (1999) highlight that planning may inadvertently sustain or exacerbate social exclusion, and point out the pernicious question of how under-represented groups fare in, and as a consequence of, planning processes. In Arnstein's path-breaking article produced in 1969, effective participation was recognised as producing a 'redistribution of power that enables the have-not citizens, presently excluded from the political and economic processes, to be deliberately included in the future' (Arnstein, 1969: 216). Beebeejaun (2012), for example, has explored the exclusion of minority groups in participatory planning, while Connelly and Richardson (2004) have argued that exclusion is inevitable in terms of decision making, regardless of how a system attempts to develop consensus.

Miller (2005) cites space–time activity theory as providing insights into social exclusion too. The space–time activity perspective highlights accessibility and extensibility in space and time as conditions for participating in activities, obtaining resources and acquiring information. On this view, 'accessibility' refers to a person's reach in space and time, while 'extensibility' refers to the ability to project presence beyond physical location in any given space and time. In this way, exclusion reflects constraints on people's abilities to access or extend themselves to activities, resources and information that are time-limited or available at few locations, or indeed where individuals find it problematic to fit into time frames that are imposed by others (see also Jensen et al, forthcoming).

Such contributions to the wider debate highlight that there are systemic aspects that conspire and combine to create a complex of potentially exclusionary intersectionalities. Moreover, time is clearly implicated in this, and each actor group has different 'proper times' shaped by an assemblage of money, networks, knowledge, capacity, markets or interest-based imperatives, which are also moulded by institutional frameworks and bureaucratic processes.

In terms of efforts to broker greater collaboration – to manage the assemblage of actors – time has been identified, unsurprisingly, as an issue to be reckoned with. This extends beyond the specific concerns of planning. Bain and Landau (2019: 405) argue that 'place-making [is] a policy exercise rooted in a politics of both space and time that can be studied through the temporal sequencing of discursive relations and governance networks'. While Thousand et al (2006: 245) highlight:

> time as a barrier, a strategy, and a precious and contested resource. Community members also talked about time – not having enough time, making time, serving time, or wasting time. Clearly, these different temporal ideas exerted influence. Time wound through collective meetings, cutting certain conversations short and impacting decisions about priorities. I watched participants' perceptions of time shape the trajectory of relationships and influence the scope and nature of their ambitions.

In this way, time as a resource affects the actual opportunity to participate; it is this that is squeezed. Considering time by each actor group demonstrates both a particularised power and an interest position. Schwanen and Kwan (2012: 2044) also recognise that space–times are multiple and 'rhythms, speeds, timings, and durations are lived and experienced differently in different situations and by different people'. Our highlighting of time in practice provides cause to think about how the different elements or episodes of planning are experienced and altered by actors – and what the implications of these are for 'good' planning.

As Graham and Healey (1999: 628) have noted: 'many different notions, experiences and representations of space-time continually collide and resonate within individual places'. Howlett and Goetz (2014: 486) see that 'through rules that determine when (timing), in what order (sequence), how quickly (speed) and for how long (duration) actions can be taken; and at the level of policy, which is concerned with allocation in time and over time', practice is shaped. Such views highlight how institutional time will work unequally because of the variety of dispositions held by participants. Moreover, for our purposes, a series of critical questions are raised: 'What time factors are accounted for to ensure actors are reasonably enabled?'; and 'How can planning meet tests of deliberative quality and associated questions of inclusivity?'

Practice is being almost continually challenged and moulded; however, clearly, there has never been an emphasis placed on 'proper time' or a sustained pursuit and implementation of inclusive planning. Given the preceding discussion, bringing questions of inclusion/exclusion together with time in planning presents the timescape as a factor that opens up and closes down possibilities for inputs and options, as well as for greater understanding, and that can erode or help develop trust in planning systems. The highlighting of planning temporalities is an inroad here towards a goal of renegotiating the very design and basis of planning.

Reflections on the planning process simply have not been attentive enough to how plans and planning impinge on different space–time capacities and produce uneven time–space access in practice. The concern to avoid exclusion and privileging brings into view a widened understanding of participation, which is core to legitimate planning activity. Indeed, the orthodox view of participation as something offered to one group by another is recentred, and we position planning as intrinsically participatory. Without 'participation', what is planning? This leads to the critical idea that the way time is marshalled shapes the form, basis and breadth of participation.

The exploration of practice examples (presented earlier in the second part of the chapter) is tied to both political motive and how time is itself understood and applied by policy actors. The instances described highlight the active role that time plays in performing actors and their interests in numerous stages and arenas of planning practice. Policy and decision making *in time* and *by time*, as well as instances of *times for deliberation*, were identified across the planning timescape in England.

What our examples have demonstrated is a parallel approach to the strict imposition of set clock times and the use of deadlines or the clepsydra, as well as channels for negotiated and bespoke time to operate. Across the instances shown, forms of proper time are made possible. We have a mixed economy of chrono-technologies and a timescape that is oriented to meet particular combinations of techno-rational and political and resource considerations. In this respect, the ideas of Bourdieu, Adam, Nowotny and Lazar become clearer in illustrating time–practice relationships, the use of time in service of particular goals and how this is politicised (as we examine in Chapter 4). Moreover, contributions from such authors as Strassheim, Hochschild and others provide useful insights that help position and explain the temporalities of planning policy and practice, as well as possible responses to this environment.

Attempts to both regulate and standardise timings may well form part of initiatives that involve change. This observation connects the instances of time and its deployment as part of the shifting timescape of planning to related ideas of speed, reform and various impacts of the timing, frequency and magnitude of change. This situation reflects a politicised environment that either suits or can be absorbed by the development industry, as well as aided by successively complicit administrations. As if to underline our points about the active temporal choreography and reframings in planning, the previously mentioned Planning Guarantee for non-major planning applications in England was changed from 26 to 16 weeks in November 2023. Similarly, the requirements for housing land supply measured in time were also adjusted in December 2023, as part of revised national planning policy. The ability for local authorities to make use of EoT agreements was also tightened during this period, calling their future into question. Therefore, the necessary caveat here is that the (seemingly continuous) changes to the policy environment governing planning in England, both small-scale tinkering and wholesale reform, serves to underscore the dynamic nature of the planning timescape in practice (and as presented here).

Our main issue to explore, as we turn towards Chapter 4, is how the dynamics of timescaping and chrono-synchronisation are oriented to reflect particular agendas, and how a dominant mode of neoliberal governmentality influences institutional orientation. Chapter 5 then considers the role of inclusion, deliberation and public interest as core attributes of proper time for planning, which go beyond the narrow neoliberal focus on speed and growth.

4

Time and neoliberalisation in planning

Neoliberalism and planning

We do not aim to chronicle the overall impacts of capitalism or neoliberalism on society or even upon planning systems here; indeed, such an enormous task has been attempted elsewhere within a burgeoning corpus of critical social science and planning literature. We can in general terms indicate sympathy for the view that neoliberalism has long featured core ideas and beliefs, with attempts to present those core beliefs as 'eternal truths' becoming routine; as have a variety of techniques to 'actively produce and impose conditions for the "free market" and the free-standing individual' as part of the project to assert the market as the model for social relations and exchange value as the 'only value' (Hall et al, 2013: 15).

This meta-contention links to our more focused question of time and places our view of how time is used to shape the practice of planning and how timescapes impact on often competing interests (particularly those marginalised by existing system arrangements). This focus is, however, inevitably drawn towards how dominant ideas influence timescapes in planning. It is beyond question that capitalist and neoliberal discourses form a dominant ideological orientation, shaping the political economy of most Western advanced liberal democracies and a large number of jurisdictions worldwide. As we will demonstrate, these discourses have had particular prominence and influence on political and economic thought and policy in the UK.

Engagement with the fashioning of the planning timescape does necessitate an understanding of the ongoing and multifaceted neoliberal orientation of politics and policy, as well as an assessment of neoliberal governance. This is primarily because the way that time has been organised and structured in political and economic institutions and policy agendas is bound up with attempts to orchestrate outcomes and actively produce behaviours (that is, practice). Thus, we cannot unpack project speed or existing arrangements and proposed reforms to planning without discussing the wider neoliberal context in which such discourses have been produced, promoted and routinised.

The neoliberal

The label 'neoliberal' and its application has become so widespread, if not ubiquitous, that, for some, the term has become meaningless (Buitelaar,

2020). While the sobriquet has become widely used and now rather stretched, it actually signals a multifaceted and changing set of ideas and practices that are applied variously. This may explain why the neoliberal has itself attracted numerous prefixes. Perhaps the significance lies in the variety of forms and formulations discussed in a vast literature, which indicates that neoliberalism may be better understood as a process rather than a state. Peck (2013: 146) argues that neoliberalisation may be regarded as 'a rolling and somewhat revolutionary program of macro-social and macro-institutional transformation, neoliberalization acts on and through these institutional landscapes; this is not a static neoliberalism'.

In attempting to pin down a definition and scope for such a complex, variegated and dynamic political and economic project as neoliberalism/neoliberalisation, we will inevitably miss some nuances. Yet, in its relation to planning, we relate the themes that are apparent across different conceptualisations and formulations. This is specifically with a view to explaining how these impact on time use in planning and in associated calls to reform planning systems and policies (which are discernible in the examples of the planning timescape depicted in Chapter 3).

Neoliberalism, in the more quotidian use of the term, refers to political approaches that commend market-based capitalism, minimise government spending and make use of deregulation. In the broadest of terms, the *Cambridge Dictionary* defines neoliberalism as 'the policy of supporting a large amount of freedom for markets, with little government control or spending, and low taxes'. The dictionary definition is simplistic, but in effect, the central claim of neoliberal proponents derives from neoclassical economics that the free market (not the state or civil society) is the most effective mechanism to organise, produce and distribute resources. From this perspective, any state intervention in markets is said to cause problems via 'distortions', and so, it follows, government deregulation and low tax and spending are claimed to be necessary to ensure efficiency and growth. On this view, the only legitimate role for governmental intervention is of a 'minimal state' acting as a 'night watchman' to protect the legal rights of individuals (Nozick, 1974).

Lord and O'Brien (2017) summarise the idea of the minimal state as a prevailing sentiment underpinning neoliberal discourses that concern planning, where such views similarly position planning regulation as a market distortion. However, neoliberalist views are being increasingly questioned as naive (see Biebricher and Johnson, 2012; Stiglitz, 2019) given the complex of interrelated issues that societies face across economic sectors, scales and time frames, as well as the challenges of tackling environmental and climate-related matters. Such concerns are further exacerbated given that neoliberalism and associated policy promotes a shift 'away from distributive policies, welfare considerations and direct service provision towards more market-oriented and market-dependent approaches aimed at pursuing economic promotion and competitive restructuring' (Swyngedouw et al, 2002: 547–8).

Despite widespread disdain for simplistic or naive neoliberalism, common themes can be seen as reducing the size and power of government, boosting competitive market forces, and encouraging private entrepreneurship (as well as public sector commercialisation). A divide between laissez-faire and state-led neoliberalism has featured in the literature, sometimes loosely categorised as a strategy of 'roll-back' and 'roll-out' neoliberalism, respectively. This binary categorisation has been further nuanced by arguments about its adaptability over time and in specific locations given that actors attempt to find combinations of tools and applications to suit the prevailing cultural or territorial circumstances, and the real politics that inevitably impact on ideologically infused approaches (what Keil [2009] terms the urban politics of 'roll with it' neoliberalisation). Thus, the literature paints a picture of a mix of conditions, tools and responses that present the apparent 'mongrel' characteristics of neoliberalism(s) (Roy, 2011; Peck, 2013) and of 'local neoliberalisms' (Peck and Theodore, 2019). As part of that multiplicity, we can add the temporal dimension to orient our attention here towards the *temporalities of neoliberal strategy* that attempt to reform the planning timescape.

This context is significant for our understanding of timescaping because the thinking behind neoliberal policy discourse places time firmly in view as something to be 'managed' in order for 'efficiency' to be assured, which manifests clearly in the NPM targeted at local government. This model stresses a consumer orientation, with 'delay' minimised and business and service imperatives promoted in governmental policy generally and through planning policy more specifically. We argue that such discourses, while distinct in their specific prescriptions, collectively form a key part of the environment for 'project speed' discussed in the following. This requires fast to immediate change and/or results that ostensibly service growth, which acts as an ultimate means and end of neoliberal government.

In parallel, reflecting on the rise of neoliberalism, Habermas (2001: 79) states that globalised markets 'drive out politics', meaning that the 'nation state increasingly loses its capacity to raise taxes and stimulate growth, and with them the ability to secure the essential foundations of its own legitimacy'. This undermines public sector activity and can jeopardise public interest decisions. The very logic of neoliberal thinking involves growth and resource allocation through markets, as encapsulated by the quote from Swyngedouw et al (2002) earlier, which itself provoked an academic debate over post-politicisation (see, for example, Legacy et al, 2019).

In linking the concept of the neoliberal with governmentality, Wargent (2021: 582, citing Lemke, 2001: 213) argues that a governmentality lens helps identify the neoliberal 'above all as a political project ... a political rationality that tries to render the social domain economic', and therefore not solely ideological rhetoric or a shaping of political-economic reality but also a set of conditions that alter behaviour. In terms of time, this means that neoliberalisation necessarily involves promoting particular time strategies and temporalities to service neoliberal (economic and related social) aims and to present these as both rational and normal (that is, as unquestioned doxa, in Bourdieu's terms), with practice consequences that impose on market and non-market actors alike.

One product of ongoing global and state neoliberalist policy formulations is that the so-called 'advanced liberal democracies' are seeing socio-economic inequality as a growing concern, with powerful factions in society pursuing their own agendas, while those marginalised in society are practically denied a genuine or facilitated voice in national or local political decisions. In the UK, this phenomenon was recently encapsulated in the 'left-behind places' agenda, which reflects socio-economic disparities and a social infrastructure deficit (Tomaney et al, 2023). Furthermore, the privatisation of public services, tax and (austerity) funding cuts, and the growing role of capital and finance are apparent in all spheres of society (Raco, 2016). These trends can serve to undermine civic solidarity and public debate over national and local political decisions, and can play out in exclusionary patterns in planning (Davoudi and Atkinson, 1999; Fainstein, 2017).

Unsurprisingly, the prefix of 'neoliberal' now appears regularly when discussing planning, prompting claims of its hegemony and for others to claim it has become tantamount to a swear word (Hartwich, 2009). The question of the impacts of neoliberal policy has been discussed at length in the planning literature, with Sager (2011, 2013) providing a review of the range of tools and mechanisms deployed with clear neoliberal credentials. The possible corrosive effect it can have on planning 'well' has also been cautioned against (Davoudi, 2017). In relation to planning in the UK, Lord and Tewdwr-Jones (2014: 346) point to key features as being a 'greater marketization of planning, a more prominent role for the private sector in determining policy, the replacement of local discretion in favour of an agenda created by a central government–business nexus and the deregulation of state planning with the removal of higher strategic levels of planning'.

The typical tropes found in neoliberal critiques of planning cite delay and hold this up as a key reason for the need to (further) deregulate or reform planning systems (see Evans, 2004; Ball, 2011; Cheshire, 2018). Yet, there is already a growing body of literature that counters the overly simplistic and narrow conceptualisations of regulation presented in mainstream economics (see Parker and Dobson, 2024), as well as the 'contemporary neoclassical economics framings of planning as merely imposing delays, risk, cost and uncertainty on developers' (Shepherd et al, 2022: 7).

While the relationship between modern capitalism and time has a much longer history than the last 40 years or so of neoliberalism (as set out in Chapter 2), we do see contemporary neoliberal policy approaches appealing to speed, efficiency and growth as a progression and intensification of this long-standing and complex relationship. As a consequence of ongoing efforts to harness time in service of capital accumulation, different ways of deconstructing capitalist forms are needed, with time already recognised as one element implicated in that project: 'Conceptual understandings of time and temporality can be employed to critique the political economy of global capitalism. Conversely, the insights of critical political economy reveal how dominant regimes of time and temporality are materially constructed' (Hope, 2009: 63). In other words, while the pursuit of growth through appealing to speed, efficiency and certainty tropes has long been legitimised by UK governments and urged by powerful land and development interests, 'project speed' has become increasingly fervent in the latest iterations of neoliberal governance 'waves' in England (what Allmendinger and Haughton [2013] term '"neoliberal" episodes in planning'). As such, there is a role for social theories of time to interrogate the assumptions and basis of those imperatives (that is, the temporalities of neoliberal strategy).

Neoliberal thinking is also a formulation that appears to abhor deliberation; an implicit concern is that it may slow down or impede market actors. While this ideological frame does not preclude some active role for communities, the evidence suggests that it is likely to be on terms preconditioned to serve neoliberal aims, with 'engagement' carefully orchestrated and compartmentalised in order to retain control. Inch (2018: 1090) also warns of a 'cultural battleground', where 'The hegemonic depth and weight of the discourse of efficiency therefore continues to function as a powerful problematisation of planning ideas and practices, not just disciplining prevailing practices but also generating pressure for further cycles of neoliberalising reform'. Planning temporalities form one such battleground between the competing logics and pressures placed on planners, oscillating between growth and speed, on the one hand, and participation, quality and public interest, on the other (Parker et al, 2022). The following section examines the political project of neoliberalising planning, with a focus on time and 'project speed', particularly since 2010, and the discourses that have been shaping ongoing planning reform agendas.

Project speed and planning reform

Planning systems are the primary form of state regulation exercised over land, property and development rights, and so are viewed by neoliberal proponents as a significant market barrier in the pursuit of economic growth. The critiques of planning stemming from neoclassical economics emphasise planning 'risk', conceptualised in relation to the speed and certainty of the land-use plan allocation and permission process for any given development. From this perspective, any activity counter to, or hindering of, such ends is routinely labelled as 'delay'.

Governments in the UK and other liberal democracies will, as a matter of course, need to justify planning and its reform in terms of procedural legitimacy and democratic accountability, but under neoliberalism, we see this as subordinate to the relationship of planning to servicing a political speed-growth agenda. The following government quote serves to illustrate the point:

> Our plans for a simpler and faster planning process need to be accompanied by a stronger emphasis on the faster delivery of development, especially for Growth areas where substantial development has been permitted. If local communities through the new Local Plan process have identified sites for substantial development over the next ten years and developers have secured planning consents, there should be a presumption that these sites will be built out quickly. (MHCLG, 2020: 36–7)

Yet, as we have seen through the examples in Chapter 3, some elements of time management or timescaping in planning over the past decade have ostensibly focused on speed but are actually about control. Developers are typically seen to want planning to be quicker and less burdensome. Time control becomes key, and the prompt for project speed seems to derive from the wish to have more control over planning processes, as this acts to manage risk as well as profitability. We presented some developer views on this in Chapter 3, added to which, the following developer promoted this view:

> 'Speed and planning aren't two words that you generally associate with one another ... the politics, local residents, consultees, resources, and then I would add into that the planning system, and all of those things together, at any given time, will slow the process down ... But it's not necessarily speed; it's certainty, I think that's what we really lack. I would take a more certain system for a quick system any day of the week.' (Housing Developer 'C')

It is primarily in the context of late capitalism and neoliberalism that we see discontent with 'slow planning' as a 'barrier' or 'delay' to economic growth expressed by successive UK government administrations. This problematisation forms the basis of many policy agendas that involve state (de)regulation internationally and accompanying narratives that prioritise speed and growth. Apparently, the wider costs and impacts of policies that orient planning to facilitate such priorities are not well understood or otherwise subordinated, or indeed both.

Solutions based on the speeding up of planning and the mobilisation of growth ignore or sideline questions of multiple objectives, long-termism or even place making. Tait et al (2020: 56) assert that simply in terms of who is involved, 'the development of the built and natural environment is characterised by very complex patterns of interaction by multiple actors dispersed across space and time (e.g. landowners, investors, developers, politicians, architects, traffic engineers, planners, citizens all play critical roles)'. Beyond the range of actors involved, the subject matters in scope are equally complex and multiple, and cannot reasonably be boiled down to simply the speed at which a decision is made.

Instead, time taken remains one of the critical elements in the negative imaginary of planning sustained through neoliberal tropes. Here, we have opted to label planning (reform) under conditions of neoliberal thinking 'project speed' in order to highlight our main focus in this chapter. The context for our use of the term 'project speed' is the hostile environment intermittently encouraged towards planning by the UK government over the past five decades. This corresponds with Adam's work (presented in Chapter 2), whereby the different elements of time control can be used in combination and directed at particular actors or interests. Adam (2004, 2008) broke down how control is exerted through the timescape, where the elements of time frame, tempo, time point, duration and succession have all become subject to forms of control.

Moreover, such attempts at control reflect political time for those acting in service of the 'right' goals. This prompts a succession of temporal preferencing tools, as well as exemptions and suspensions of time conditions. It also emphasises how political time appears to serve particular interests rather than society as a whole (which is discussed in more detail later).

In this way, the simultaneous attack on planning risk and delay has involved experimentation with deregulation, reregulation and 'flexible regulation'. This has been apparent in planning in England with the extension of such tools as enterprise zones (since the early 1980s in the UK) and freeports since the 2010s, and the extended use of 'permitted development' rights, most notably, since 2013, which are geared to not just speed up planning but also create new temporalities for development aimed at annihilating (regulatory/process) time.

This political-economic agenda of project speed carries across to numerous policy iterations, actions and amendments. This embraces a set of measures and exhortations that have been propelling planning activity to speed up. The use of clock time cannot be underestimated either in terms of its influence on the technologies underpinning project speed. Wider business discourses applied to planning critique are replete with temporal 'sledging'.

A statement by former UK Prime Minister David Cameron in 2011 is emblematic of the characterisation of planners as the 'enemies of enterprise', which has been reprised quite regularly. Cameron (2011) lamented the 'town hall officials who take forever with those planning decisions that can be make or break for a business – and the investment and jobs that go with it'. This sentiment was continued by the SoS in charge of planning in England in the same year:

> planning delays cost the economy £3bn a year. It is twice as expensive to get planning permission in London's West End as in Paris, and 10 times more than in Brussels. In a global economy, where skills and capital are more mobile than ever, our planning system is a deterrent to international investment, and a barrier to the expansion of home-grown enterprise. When planning acts as a brake on growth, and on the much needed new jobs and new businesses, reform is imperative. (Pickles, 2011)

We must stress that the 'project speed' label, as applied here, is much wider in its scope than the eponymous initiative commenced by the UK government in 2020, notably, by Robert Jenrick while SoS at the then MHCLG. Instead, the promotion of speed had been a priority for the past decade at least. While the label has become an informal sobriquet for a wider basket of measures, a specific project was also given this name, using the rather tortuous acronym SPEED, spelled out as 'swift, pragmatic, efficient, enhancement, delivery'. This served as a political policy hook for 'improved' delivery times for the development of infrastructure.

Indeed, the basis for much transport policy has rested on travel times and framed new infrastructure in terms of 'time saving' – as typified in the assessment set out by Bristow and Nellthorp (2000). The explicit SPEED initiative 'identified 10 key themes to lower costs and speed up the delivery of infrastructure schemes, such as rapidly increasing the use of innovative construction methods and removing complexity from planning processes' (DfT, 2021). While instructive, that particular initiative does not account for the range of measures that have or do feature in the English planning system and that characteristically involve time squeezing or related means that are clearly linked to the control of planning time to service growth goals, that is, our wider label of 'project speed'.

We use the 'project speed' label more liberally, and this embraces the wider list of planning examples and associated considerations discussed in Chapter 3. These are specifically directed at time saving and can be viewed as attempts to speed up planning authorities, reduce 'delay' for others and otherwise limit input time for other actors. They involve deadlines for the completion of planning decisions, organising timings for the preparation of a local plan, linking land supply to time (that is, five-year housing land supply), measures that indirectly involve time control (such as PPAs used to 'guarantee' time) and measures that anticipate expediting the future (such as 'permission in principle' [PiP]) (see Gallent et al, 2019).

The latter example of PiP was not discussed in Chapter 3 but is notable here. It was introduced through the Housing and Planning Act 2016 as a mechanism to identify brownfield sites ahead of any specific development proposal. PiP could be achieved in two ways: first, by local authorities designating PiP sites in their local development plan or brownfield register; or, second, by developers or landowners applying to a local authority to have sites designated for 'minor development'. The principle is to fast-track and help de-risk the development process given that:

> Would-be developers also need to account for the costs involved in securing planning permission in terms of expert advice, the costs of capital tied up and, crucially, time. Timing is important for two reasons: first, the longer the preliminary phases take, the more the developer incurs in holding costs – interest on loans, site security, etc. Second, delays in the preliminary phases have a knock-on effect on eventual revenues, especially given market cycles, decreasing their certainty and/or overall value. (Gallent et al, 2019: 675)

It is observable from the explicit aims, tenor and application of time/efficiency measures that the 'speed is good' mantra plays well politically and appears to satisfy business audiences. The language used, including the absorption of such terms as agility (in its narrower meaning of responsiveness), efficiency, innovation and competitiveness, is borrowed and applied to the complex set of challenges associated with spatial/land-use planning in order to justify alignment with the growth agenda.

Rather than attempt to understand the complexity of planning matters and apply the resources and time presumed, the preferred remedy is instead an attempt to reconcile time squeezes and control with a discourse of business flexibility. Hassan (2009: 73) asserts that 'business leaders, politicians and economists who were sympathetic to neoliberal ideology maintained that flexibility had to be inserted into every business entity, every process, and every economic relationship'. This highlights once again both how the idealised formulation of planning is critically about conflating time and its control, and why action words like 'competitive' and 'efficiency' are enrolled to legitimate particular technologies of timescaping.

Planning can be understood, in process terms at least, as the political and democratic context through which development activity happens. Involved are sets of activities designed to evidence, consider, enable and regulate land-use and property development, according to wider stakeholder interests and societal preferences. It is a process of decision making that accounts for a myriad of issues and considerations, and this is not without its challenges.

Given the complexity of planning and the often 'wicked' problems that are addressed (Rittel and Weber, 1973), there is a tendency, in line with the Dunning–Kruger effect (Dunning, 2011), to underestimate the difficulties involved in good planning and the knowledge and abilities needed to analyse the problem(s) or render appropriate solutions. This is notwithstanding imperatives to address 'whole problems' rather than seeking to simply carve off parts that suit us (Wright et al, 2019) or to redefine systems or problems to mirror a particular interest-based agenda. Misconceptions about the role and scope of planning (as a state regulatory mechanism) and its importance are sustained by more or less sophisticated arguments that challenge or seek to reform it and which become useful in promoting timescaping measures.

The RTPI (2020) *Invest and Prosper* report made the case that strategic planning provides a range of benefits to communities and businesses by ensuring that access is provided to essential services and infrastructure, and that negative externalities from development are accounted for and minimised, particularly where they have a negative impact on human health or the environment. It identifies the problem that while:

> [p]lanning plays a key role in delivering these benefits ... they are poorly understood and seldom attributed to the planning system. Without effective planning systems, many of these benefits would not be captured, affecting the quality of life for residents and imposing costs on both the public and private sectors. (RTPI, 2020: 4)

These issues of attribution and measurement make it hard to defend the planning system in economic terms and leave it open to simplistic critiques of inefficiency and delay. Instead of further deregulation, the report asserts that the main cause of delay in processing planning applications is a lack of funding and resources, and hence inadequate numbers and quality of staff to undertake the work.

Planning time, discretion and certainty

Given the argument about the complexities involved in planning issues and challenges, it is germane to highlight how UK planning systems are characterised by a combined or hybrid approach to decisions. These are ultimately made on a discretionary case-by-case basis, underpinned by national and local policy; such policy, in the form of not only quantifiable measures and targets but also thresholds and more open, interpretive criteria, organise planning decisions. Local planning officers and locally elected politicians take the decisions, and communities provide input into the process to determine which developments receive planning permission. This process has required a host of technical and democratic inputs from a range of stakeholders to shape policy and make development decisions appropriate, or sustainable, in their specific spatial and temporal context.

Critics of the discretionary aspects of UK planning systems (particularly those that advocate for a shift to a more rule-based/codified approach more typical of zoning planning systems found internationally) often argue that 'political' inputs (either via civil society or elected politicians locally) introduce too much uncertainty and should be limited in order to provide greater speed and ameliorate risk for market actors. On this view, inputs should be minimised or 'front-loaded' where possible. This can be seen in serial attempts to deregulate, or 'cut red tape', which often equate to time squeezing.

As we detail in the following, the deregulatory strand of policy is a favoured approach of the wider political ideology associated with neoliberalism. We can see such rhetoric in the following quote from then Prime Minister Boris Johnson in advance of formally launching English planning system reform proposals in 2020:

> Time is money and the newt-counting delays in our system are a massive drag on the prosperity of this country. And so we will build better, build greener and we will also build faster. That is why the chancellor and I have set up Project Speed to scythe through red tape and get things done. (Johnson, 2020)

This ongoing and seemingly dominant political narrative of speed being good has become a useful device, used to justify a wide range of measures. It is useful to consider the typical tropes or logics of neoliberal thinking when evaluating the claims that are made to justify reforms or sustain particular timescaping measures.

Neoliberalism and project speed can be viewed not as a coherent master strategy enacted by successive UK government administrations but, rather, as a series of loosely congruent, related initiatives, statements, funding arrangements and proposals that rather uncritically discount the value of other arguments, actors and goals outside of the mainstream economic and business discourses, all of which tend to valorise speed/efficiency as being good for growth. Such appeals can be attractive for politicians looking to reassure business interests that the government understands their needs and is responsive to them.

Others have been highly critical of policy and reform of planning in England, not least because of their narrow basis. In response to the UK government's 2020 planning white paper *Planning for the Future* (MHCLG, 2020), the Town and Country Planning Association (TCPA, 2020a) produced a report entitled *The Wrong Answers to the Wrong Questions*, which critiqued those reform proposals. In the foreword to this report, TCPA Director of Policy Hugh Ellis

(2020: 2) made the case that any changes to the planning system needed to be based on 'authoritative evidence' and not founded on uncritically accepted business claims, and he explicitly cited the 'project speed' tag:

> Future change must be founded on authoritative evidence as to the problems facing the system and on building shared values as to its long term purpose. That purpose must be to achieve the health and well being of people inside the wider goal of sustainable development. The government's current commitment to 'project speed' must urgently be replaced by 'project people'.

The project speed programme, as characterised in the debates concerning the 2020 planning reform agenda, is not particularly novel in form and content. In reality, it is a supplement or, as we have presented it, part of a combination of iterations proposed and implemented by successive governments (and informed by sympathetic think tanks [see Haughton and Allmendinger, 2016; Dinan and Miller, 2022; Foye, 2022]). In this way, Foye (2022) argues that the framing strategies deployed by think tanks have been drawing on a 'causal narrative' of planning as a constraint, one that sets up a logical solution pathway that leads to planning as being in need of deregulation, or speeding up.

The longer history that pre-dates the 'project speed' label is reflected in the following statement from one such think tank, Policy Exchange, referring to the operation of the UK planning system in 2007:

> delay means that investment takes place later than it should (if it has not been abandoned), with a consequent loss of efficiency. Associated with the delays built into the system is the level of detail which the British planning system tries to control, a factor which, of itself, builds in delays. We then look at the relationship between land use planning, economic growth and competitiveness. The planning system was one of the main features of the UK economy which inhibited economic growth. (Evans and Hartwich, 2007: 10)

Indeed, these arguments resurfaced again in 2020 to set off the renewed round of debate on planning reform (prompted incidentally via the same sympathetic think tank that had made the same argument some 13 years earlier). The Policy Exchange report *Rethinking the Planning System for the 21st Century* (Airey and Doughty, 2020: 15) provided a strong catalyst for the 2020 government white paper in arguing that:

> The planning system in its current form increases the cost of living and the cost of doing business in this country, unnecessarily and often

by obscene amounts. Without reform, the Government's efforts to increase access to property wealth, improve economic competitiveness, build beautiful homes at a rate that meets housing demand; and, reach net zero emissions will be frustrated ... the costs of our current system of planning far outweigh the benefits and many of these costs are simply not taken into account in mainstream political and policy debate ... Reforming the planning system will ... unleash growth in the economy, housing supply and innovation more than any other supply-side structural reform.

Similar arguments attributing blame to the planning system were also made in the *Planning for the Future* report by the Centre for Cities (Breach, 2020: 3) around the same time:

The problem at the heart of the housing crisis is the discretionary element in the planning system, which rations the supply of land for development and new homes. It is wasteful and inefficient and must be reformed. England and the devolved nations need to shift from this discretionary approach to a flexible zoning system to reconnect the supply of housing to demand and end the housing crisis.

Shortly after publication, the think-tank reports just cited were effectively endorsed by then Prime Minister Boris Johnson (2020: 6) in the foreword to the 2020 *Planning for the Future* white paper, where he wrote:

Thanks to our planning system, we have nowhere near enough homes in the right places. People cannot afford to move to where their talents can be matched with opportunity. Businesses cannot afford to grow and create jobs. The whole thing is beginning to crumble and the time has come to do what too many have for too long lacked the courage to do – tear it down and start again ... Radical reform unlike anything we have seen since the Second World War. Not more fiddling around the edges, not simply painting over the damp patches, but levelling the foundations and building, from the ground up, a whole new planning system for England.

The 2020 reform proposals centred around moving away from the case-by-case discretionary planning system substantially created under the Town and Country Planning Act 1947, with time and speed a clear feature of the proposals as highlighted in this chapter: 'Our plans for a simpler and faster planning process need to be accompanied by a stronger emphasis on the faster delivery of development, especially for Growth areas' (MHCLG, 2020: 36). Following Lazar (2019), such rhetorical-temporal political strategies were presented as a means of 'Modernising the planning system to get Britain

Building'. It is also clear that in his foreword to the white paper, Johnson was using time to do political work in order to cast the old system as antiquated and no longer fit for purpose. This set up the government's proposed solution of a new 'faster' zonal system in the reform proposals.

Similarly, in the briefly infamous 'growth plan' speech to the UK Parliament in 2022, former UK Chancellor Kwasi Kwarteng (2022) drew on the now-familiar tropes of planning being 'too slow' and involving 'complex' regulation, which holds back growth:

> Today, our planning system for major infrastructure is too slow and fragmented. The time it takes to get consent for nationally significant projects is getting slower, not quicker, while our international competitors forge ahead ... We will bring forward a new Bill to unpick the complex patchwork of planning restrictions and EU [European Union]-derived laws that constrain our growth ... we are getting out of the way to get Britain building ... We will liberalise planning rules in specified agreed sites, releasing land and accelerating development.

While these soundbites often make the news and reach a wider public audience, it is worth noting that an alternative vision for the future of the planning system was presented a few years earlier. The 2018 *Planning 2020* report (TCPA, 2018: 118), which concluded the Raynsford Review of Planning in England, was not taken forward by the government, but it did present an alternative political and temporal narrative for planning, and, crucially, one that specifically did not prioritise speed, efficiency and growth:

> [The] planning system ... has been subject to a bewildering scale of change. There is currently no sign of an end point to these changes, which are not always well understood by the wider public. From the conversion of buildings on industrial estates to low-quality homes, to the lack of national co-ordination for infrastructure and housing delivery, England is now increasingly 'un-planned'. And that matters for our collective future, given the scale of the challenges in matters such as housing and climate change that lie ahead ... Such a choice should be the subject of national debate, because the future of our communities depends on effective and fair organisation. It is no overstatement to say that the simple choice between planning and non-planning ... is a defining test of our democracy.

The Raynsford Review summarised the two main views on planning in response to the question: 'What is the justification for a spatial planning system in a market economy?' The first view accords with the neoliberal perspective, that is, that the purpose of planning is to 'facilitate the private market through a residual form of land licensing to support "growth"'; the second, more encompassing, perspective is that planning is designed 'to regulate the market to achieve long-term public interest objectives in relation to sustainable development' (TCPA, 2018: 74). The review sided with the latter position, arguing that reliance on markets and property rights cannot substitute for the need to deliver on public interest and democratic engagement through the system:

- A free market in land and development leads to a range of complex sub-optimal outcomes which have serious impacts on wider society ... The state has, therefore, a legitimate role to play in the regulation of land and the built environment to secure important public interest outcomes ...
- There is no evidence that the market alone can deal with these challenges in a way that balances the interests of the environment and economy while securing people's safety, health and wellbeing ...
- People have a right to a voice in the decisions that affect them – which goes beyond the expression of property rights. This is a primary distinction between democratic planning and a system of residual land licensing. As a result, the planning system must work within the grain of our existing democracy and civil rights. (TCPA, 2018: 75)

The TCPA drew on similar arguments in the 2020 debate, citing reforms being pursued without evidence and standing against proposals that would bypass public interest and democratic controls:

The UK government has announced 'radical reforms' to the planning system in England which it frames as an outdated blockage to the development we need to 'build back better' from the economic impacts of COVID-19 ... [but] we are deeply concerned that this agenda has been driven by ideologically-motivated free-market think tanks and self-interested property lobbies rather than sound evidence ... the proposals are incoherent, will undermine democratic controls, reduce the quality of new development, and waste an important opportunity to build safer, healthier, more equal, and more environmentally sustainable places. (TCPA, 2020a: 3)

The 2022 *Levelling Up the United Kingdom* white paper (DLUHC, 2022c) appeared to change tack in some significant ways from the planning reforms proposed in the 2020 *Planning for the Future* document (MHCLG, 2020). This offered an apparent acknowledgement of the value of the planning system and a concern to spread opportunity more equally across the country in support of 'left-behind places'. How such laudable but complex aims are achieved, as set out in the following excerpt, is fuzzy at best, and they may be viewed more as a 'wish list' than a coherent plan; yet, planning is somewhat recast here by the UK Government:

> A strong planning system is vital to level up communities across the country and give them a say in how their land is used and where beautiful, sustainable houses are built … wider changes to the planning system will secure enhanced social and economic outcomes by fostering beautiful places that people can be proud of; improving democracy and engagement in planning decisions; supporting environmental protection, including support for the transition to Net Zero; and securing clear benefits for neighbourhoods and local people. (DLUHC, 2022c: 227–8)

While this refocus on the role of planning and its reform by government was broadly welcomed, the approach still attracted criticism from the TCPA that planning was still absent in this agenda:

> [T]hrowing pots of money at localities, or at big infrastructure projects … is an extremely wasteful use of public money, if not combined with strategic thinking, whether in plans or in some shared public conversations about regional disparities. Spatial and locational fairness and efficiency must go hand in hand. Levelling Up has to be planned, if it is not to fall flat on its face. When Governments in the past have set out to address regional inequalities and the 'North/South Divide', they have taken a serious approach using indices of deprivation across the country to target investment. No such seriousness or evidence-based policy is yet forthcoming from the 'Levelling Up' agenda pursued by this Government. Levelling Up is a slogan not a policy – with careful planning nowhere to be seen. (TCPA, 2021: 5)

Here, we can see the familiar neoliberal distrust of government and planning being highlighted, even when it comes to an explicit policy of spatial redistribution and infrastructure/transport projects. Instead, 'levelling up' is regarded as an approach that relies on leverage funding and deregulation to stimulate market-led growth in deprived areas. This demonstrates how the neoliberal 'offer' undergoes regular review, revision, repositioning and extension. It remains to be seen the extent to which the subsequent 2023 Levelling Up and Regeneration Act delivers on the government's stated aims to speed up planning, build more homes and 'level up' the country.

The temporal politics of planning and growth

Nowhere was the neoliberal ideal of 'growth at all costs' more apparent than in the speech made by, briefly, Prime Minister Liz Truss in presenting her 'growth plan' in 2022. Useful now as an insight into neoliberal thinking, if nothing else, the wording is certainly instructive. In this speech, Truss conjured up a folk devil image – the 'anti-growth coalition' – to act as an enemy that needed to be overcome, or an opposition to be faced down, in order to deliver growth for the country:

> I have three priorities for our economy: growth, growth and growth ... Previously, we faced barriers to growth like militant unions, nationalised industries and outdated City regulation. Now, we must break down the barriers to growth built up in our system over decades ... Instead, we will ensure regulation is pro-business and pro-growth ... I will not allow the anti-growth coalition to hold us back. Labour, the Lib Dems and the SNP, the militant unions, the vested interests dressed up as think-tanks, the talking heads, the Brexit deniers and Extinction Rebellion ... they peddle the same old answers. It's always more taxes, more regulation and more meddling. Wrong, wrong, wrong ... We see the anti-growth coalition at work across the country. (Truss, 2022)

These reflect greater frustrations, but they also concern planning and how it is conceptualised. The counterpoint we present is that rather than being a barrier to growth, planning involves and reflects the acceptance of material and temporal limits to growth. As Jackson (2021: 3) highlights:

> Every culture, every society, clings to a myth by which it lives. Ours is the myth of growth. For as long as the economy continues to expand, we feel assured that life is getting better. We believe that we are progressing – not just as individuals but as a society. We convince ourselves that the world tomorrow will be a brighter, shinier place for our children and for their children.

The vision of economic growth that can continue indefinitely has been increasingly called into question, not least given the carrying capacity of a finite planet. There are thus clear issues here because planning becomes a key tool whereby agendas that appear to be 'anti-growth' coalesce. The concern for sustainable development and the myriad considerations that are also deemed important beyond economic growth are regarded as barriers rather than checks and balances. Kate Raworth (2017) argues that a healthy economy should be one that promotes 'thriving' as the outcome rather than one that pursues endless growth as its main goal. She presents the need for a 'doughnut economics' approach that recognises the need for balance between meeting the basic social needs of humanity and not compromising the natural environment:

> Below the Doughnut's social foundation lie shortfalls in human well-being, faced by those who lack life's essentials such as food, education and housing. Beyond the ecological ceiling lies an overshoot of pressure on Earth's life-giving systems, such as through climate change, ocean acidification and chemical pollution. But between these two sets of boundaries lies a sweet spot – shaped unmistakably like a doughnut – that is both an ecologically safe and socially just space for humanity. The twenty-first century task is an unprecedented one: to bring all of humanity into that safe and just space. (Raworth, 2017: 44)

Economic growth was a powerful force during the Industrial Revolution and post-war reconstruction of countries across the 19th and 20th centuries, yet the 21st century poses different challenges. The world population is increasing at an unprecedented rate (UN, 2022), and with it, so is the potential for anthropogenic climate change, biodiversity loss and mass viral outbreaks (such as COVID-19), among other global challenges. These are not issues that can prudently or morally be ignored or pushed into the future (MacAskill, 2022), and they lead to questions about whose present and future are being secured under these conditions:

> On 15 November 2022, the world's population is projected to reach 8 billion people, having grown by 1 billion since 2010. This is a remarkable milestone given that the human population numbered under 1 billion for millennia until around 1800, and that it took more than 100 years to grow from 1 to 2 billion. By comparison, the increase of the world's population over the last century has been quite rapid. Despite a gradual slowing in the pace of growth, the global population is projected to surpass 9 billion around 2037 and 10 billion around 2058. (UN, 2022: 1)

If planetary-scale population growth and attendant environmental and social considerations were not enough to force careful reconsideration of the value of planning, then the simplistic premise that having higher gross domestic product (GDP) will mean a better quality of life for all should be seen for what it is rather than held up as a panacea for all (particularly for those exploited, left behind or excluded from the market and its benefits). Increasingly, such assumptions sit uneasily with the evidence that wealth becomes concentrated at the top and social inequality grows.

Stiglitz (2019: 1) asserts that neoliberal ideas are on 'life support' and that while:

> elites claimed that their promises were based on scientific economic models and 'evidence-based research' ... after 40 years, the numbers

are in: growth has slowed, and the fruits of that growth went overwhelmingly to a very few at the top. As wages stagnated and the stock market soared, income and wealth flowed up, rather than trickling down.

To sustain the myth of growth, various forms of denial or 'cognitive dissonance' have helped to avoid engaging with contrary evidence. This situation has led commenters to claim that 'neoliberalism is dead but dominant' (Smith, 2008) and to accusations of 'zombie' neoliberalism (Peck, 2010).

Bringing the discussion back to deliberation and time, John Friedman (2011: 232), when discussing future approaches to growth and resources, argues we need to live within a 'world of limits'. This, he argues, will involve properly accounting for different values and means of valuation. He links this to enabling better, wiser decisions, arguing the case that the underpinning of democratic virtue is to be partly achieved through deliberative practices, and that decision making and institutional design must be based on a mix of knowledge, aspiration and moral orientation. This counterpoint highlights how project speed becomes associated with the denial of limits, with planning temporalities organised as part of a quest for 'unlimited everything' – a perfect time for capital akin to Nowotny's (1994) *uchronia*.

As Carney (2021) points out, the current mainstream economic approach to determine market price and valuation is poorly equipped to deal with (different forms of) value(s) outside of the economic sphere of business. Denial of the material limits of a finite planet is itself a denial of time – most significantly, a political denial of the future. In the neoliberal, we can see Adam's recognition of the attempted colonisation of the future, as rehearsed in Chapter 2, promoted to sustain the present, where the interests of capital are placed over future generations:

> Capitalism is distinct in its relationship to the future whether this be in its systems of credit and interest, insurance or financial trading ... The economy therefore operates in the sphere between present and future with a view to using the future to secure the present. To achieve that task, it borrows from the future to finance the present. The radical present orientation is demonstrated at its fiercest in the discounting of the future ... [where] the value of the future is calculated with reference to the use and extractive value it holds for the present ... be this in economics, science or politics, makes parasitic use of the future – our own and that of successor generations. (Adam, 2004: 141–2)

Reports by the RTPI (Adams and Watkins, 2014; Adams et al, 2016) have demonstrated the (more than economic) value of planning, but neoclassical economics struggles to price the social and environmental benefits resulting from planning activity. Such challenges are most visible in calculating national GDP, where anything that cannot be standardised and rendered calculable for markets is either made to conform, under-represented or even ignored:

> The genius of GDP is that it somehow manages to squeeze all human activity into a single number ... To create a single number requires measuring everything in the same unit, which in economics means converting everything into dollars and cents. When it comes to something hard to price – say volunteer work, life expectancy, clean air or a sense of community – you must either figure out a way of attaching a dollar amount to it or just forget all about it ... But prices cannot be a proxy for everything. That means much of what we care about as human beings is either left out of our economic calculations or converted, using some jiggery-pokery, into a dollar amount that can be included. (Pilling, 2019: 285–6)

This can be seen clearly with planning, as Tait et al (2020: 57) explain, when 'faced with the difficulty of measuring the performance of planning, governments have tended to fall back on simplistic indicators of procedural efficiency – such as the speed of decision making – rather than attempting any substantive evaluation of outcomes'. It is much more difficult to measure 'quality' than duration and much easier to rely on market price than to value public goods.

Following mainstream economic interests, particularly under neoliberal influence, project speed places market value as the priority and then seeks to secure certainty for this over others. To effect this, a discourse has needed to be sustained that anything that is not primarily supporting market growth is causing delay and is a barrier that is a candidate for removal. Shepherd et al (2022: 2–3) highlight that, in this way, 'framing of the planning system, as limiting housing land supply and imposing uncertainties and risks on developer interests, has influenced successive rounds of planning reform in England', where much of the government's reform agenda has positioned planning as 'being somehow in opposition to the market due to the risks it imposes, with the implication being that developers are uniformly of the view that the English planning system needs to be simpler, more predictable, less risky for landowners and developers'. In this context, Lord and O'Brien (2017: 218) explain that 'the inaccurate impression that planning is an activity that principally bears only costs has become close to an accepted wisdom amongst the political élite in nations such as Britain'.

Other evidence countering claims of planning delay has been forthcoming, with the LGA (2020) pointing out that 'the number of planning permissions granted for new homes has almost doubled since 2012/13 with councils approving 9 in 10 applications' and that more than a million homes granted planning permission in England over the preceding decade had not yet been built. Such alternative narratives point towards the responsibility of other actors, while some seek to reposition planning to align with the idea that:

> Planning should not be seen as a drag anchor on growth, but as an engine for the creation of visionary new ideas to tackle burning social issues over a long term time-scale. It offers a way of rethinking places to produce the types of change that we all urgently need. A thoughtless 'Build, build, build' agenda will achieve the opposite of this: short-term thinking, poor-quality spaces, unecological and unsustainable building, and the pursuit of profit over health and wellbeing. (Tait et al, 2020: 62)

This is not a lone or isolated call; the Campaign for Better Planning in the UK boasts a membership of 34 organisations, and in its 'Six tests for planning' (CBP, 2021: 2), they expressed concern over governmental proposals for a 'reduced time-scale for plan preparation' and argued that the planning system in England should 'allow for significant and early local engagement in the shaping of master plans and design codes/briefs'.

Such views not only evince questions about good planning being a matter of requiring more time, or 'slow planning' in a simplistic sense, but also embrace the value of good planning and consider the role of time in reflecting the nature of the challenges faced and the development of appropriate responses. This requires reflecting more widely and deeply on the multiple interests, uses and values of time in and for planning beyond the neoliberal paradigm and project speed that set the dominant temporal politics of growth in the UK and elsewhere.

In particular, attention should be paid to how political time is used to promote agendas that either discount or colonise the future in favour of the present. This includes allowing alternatives to be considered, such as the possibilities for post-growth trajectories (Savini et al, 2022) or managed degrowth (Jackson, 2009). We can perhaps best view the impacts of adopting a short-term and present-oriented temporal politics in claims made for 'sustainable development'.

The guiding principle (or meta-narrative) of sustainable development has been established in planning for some time now. We have witnessed over time, however, that the interpretation and application in practice of what can be justified in the name of 'sustainable development' evidences its subversion. The indicative power of sustainable development as a concept can clearly be undermined or discredited (see Russel and Kirsop-Taylor, 2022), and, in planning terms, manipulated to support a great variety of development schemes.

In the 2023 version of the NPPF for England, the purpose of the planning system in England is again purportedly geared to achieving 'sustainable development', and this also includes explicit reference to the 17 United Nations Sustainable Development Goals (SDGs): 'The purpose of the planning system is to contribute to the achievement of sustainable development ... These address social progress, economic well-being and environmental protection. Achieving sustainable development means that the planning system has three overarching objectives, which are interdependent and need to be pursued in mutually supportive ways' (National Planning Policy Framework, 2023: 5). Despite the implied balance or reconciliation required for achieving sustainable development between these three overarching objectives in national policy, the economic dimension has been preferenced in English planning while operating within a neoliberalised policy context. An instructive example of this lies in how economic viability arguments in planning have been enabled and deployed (notably, in the same national policy document [see also Henneberry, 2016]). We can also see economic preferencing being cast as a temporal 'crisis' narrative, such as the UK housing crisis, which positions the immediate increase in the supply of new homes in England as a priority of 'sustainable development', one that can trump other linked concerns for quality, design, infrastructure and so on. This type of political use of time can also be seen in legitimating permitted development rights for housing that effectively bypass plans and planning scrutiny (that is, 'delay'). In such cases, a growth-first approach is adopted.

Political time and neoliberal planning timescapes

Thus far, this chapter has demonstrated how governments who are influenced by neoliberal ideas have embraced time as a political resource to justify pursuing a speed-growth policy agenda and associated reforms. We now turn our attention to the wider insights that political time can provide for understanding practice and the (real and imagined) planning timescape.

Recalling Chapter 2, political time refers to the rules, norms, conventions and understandings that serve as a resource and constraint for political institutions and actors. The idea of political time has a policy dimension concerned with rules relating to timing, sequencing, speed and duration in decision making. This typically involves temporal policy features, such as the distribution of the costs and benefits of major policies across time. Thus, the political use of time brings into relief (re)consideration of how time is conceived and deployed.

Lazar (2019) stresses the political construction of time in highlighting how political strategies are enacted through 'temporal-rhetorical framings' and 'time talk', constructed to produce or maintain political legitimacy and facilitate particular political projects. Within such temporal framings, opposing or apparently incongruent temporalities structure how a political problem is understood and then, it follows, what will count as an ideologically, practically and/or politically acceptable solution. The quotes drawn from a succession of UK politicians in this chapter underscore the use and manifestation of time talk and the framing of planning and delay. In particular, we can see (project) speed as an energising device to which all other planning logics must align: quicker growth, greater (time) efficiency, operating at the pace that business requires and tolerating participation that does not 'hold things up'.

Nowotny (1994) argues that time is a central dimension of power, where 'chrono-technologies' are deployed in attempts to shape what and how activities are to be performed. Similarly, Zielonka (2023: 29–30) asserts that '[i]n the world of politics, the crucial question is: who makes time, and how? ... Time is a powerful political instrument because our life is dependent on it and the ways in which it is regulated by governments.' The examination of political time and how neoliberal theory and policy has approached time is instructive for understanding their influence on the orientation of systems, policies and procedures associated with land-use planning. Taken together, these serve to form the planning timescape.

In the context of political time in service of neoliberal goals, we can see that the near-incessant political rhetoric for planning reform to make the system faster and more efficient aligns with Adam's (2004) view that the control of time is largely about realising economic gain and social advantage. Furthermore, this illuminates that the link between time and growth is that of practice, that is, efforts to enable growth require practices to align accordingly, and time is a key resource applied to the solution. This is where Bourdieu's (2000) assertion that 'time makes practice' can be extended to 'political time makes practice' – that is, tailored to neoliberal ends.

The neoliberal problematisation of planning has featured the extensive use of political-rhetorical framing and time-related metaphors, as well as explicit challenges about time and delay. These motifs abound; for example, the *Daily Telegraph* promoted the idea that 'The glacial pace of Britain's clogged-up planning system will trigger a slump in housebuilding, experts have warned' (Rees, 2022). A prominent UK planning consultancy hired by the Home Builders Federation (HBF) have also been attempting to cost 'delay', saying: 'The costs of delay are real. The continuing malaise in plan making locks up growth' (Lichfields, 2023).

It is clear that time has been a consistent resource for governments and others to deploy in an attempt to control planning speed and practice more widely. This has been a means to orient planning actors to a more market-oriented and business-friendly practice culture. In this context, the English planning system has been subject to myriad forms of 'neoliberal spatial governance' (Allmendinger, 2016). Whilst much has been written about the spatial and scalar dimensions of planning reform, much less focus has been directed towards the temporal dimensions of reform. As part of that, we have been concerned with formulations of *neoliberal temporal governance* and its importance where the timescapes of planning have been shaped and reshaped to better fit prevailing neoliberal goals. The impacts of neoliberal thinking and policy prescription on planning practice are likely to be varied across space and time. The array of technologies has altered as waves of reform have been initiated and small iterations, tweaks, nudges and elaborations, or 'micro-reform' elements, have mounted up as successive UK governments have sought to make changes to the planning timescape.

One of the most insightful ways that power operates through time in politics and policy making is by implying an unrealisable temporal future. The end state is the idea of *uchronia*, or perfect time(scape). By creating a vision for a utopian temporal future (the '*uchronia*'), the problems of the present, it is assumed, can be solved by realigning time. This legitimises actions taken towards reforming governance arrangements that 'are not just about time but about the socially and politically situated experiences of time embedded in specific power relations' (Raco et al, 2018: 1190–1). This is how power uses policy making and its temporal organisation; however, as Nowotny (1994: 139) puts it, 'the uchronia which only demands more time does not escape the quantitative logic of money and its accumulation'.

Despite the *uchronia* of a planning system organised around the neoliberal goals presented in mainstream political and economic discourses, we see that while business interests play off conflations of time and efficiency, speed alone is not the main aim. Instead, predictability and control of time is what is actually desired by the development industry. To achieve this, deregulation is not the only requirement, nor indeed the main issue; rather, it is certainty, not the cutting of 'red tape' that binds development to specific obligations. Contrary to suggesting a cruder outright deregulation, we contend that it is the organisation of regulation and timings that suit neoliberal ends that are the desired outcome. We have termed this a 'blue tape' exercise that adapts and evolves, as per the mongrel pedigree expressed in Peck's (2013) assessment of neoliberalist durability. In effect, what is being pursued is a *uchronic* re-regulation that is flexible for some and rigid or observably exclusionary for others. This involves a 're-regulation of subjectivities' (Raco, 2005: 341) to support a set of arrangements that normalise an acceptance of the rational merit of 'project speed', regardless of its actual content or effect. The underlying aims of power and control remain implicit beneath appeals to reform.

The stakes of political time and neoliberal aims being used to shape planning are high because they impinge on the core tenets of the profession around inclusion, deliberation and public interest:

> the most sensitive political questions are raised by time-related regulations dealing with citizenship, judiciary and democratic representation ... If time is used in an unjust manner, why do citizens not rebel? Why are time-related regulations hardly ever an object of political bargaining, if not conflict? ... Time, like any other democratic good, should be made 'by' citizens, and not merely 'for' citizens by their respective governments. (Zielonka, 2023: 41–5)

A main concern in planning is that a narrow political construction oriented to speed can impact on attitudes taken towards affording time for participation, with Wilson et al (2020: 44) arguing: 'the emphasis on speed in planning decisions for the past four decades, and the increasing and now overwhelming power of landowners through that time, have made planners sceptical about citizen engagement in planning'. This leads to concerns that speed, efficiency and delay narratives marginalise wider groups and interests. In this context, Brownill (2020: 44) urges us to 'recognise that consultation takes time and costs money and that the quality of planning outcomes that results is as important as the speed of planning decisions'.

Similarly, as Rosling et al (2018) argue, a focus on speed can have a number of negative consequences, such that it can act to undermine diligence, evidence and experience, promote a prioritisation of the short term (for example, particular development consents), encourage containerisation (that is, a focus on isolated topics, such as housing or 'design'), and routinise compromised outcomes, including a willingness to trade off public goods (for example, poorer design, affordable housing and environmental standards). As such, the true corrosion of planning as public service is measured not in *how* or *when* something is delivered but in terms of *what* is delivered. This brings into stark view the warning presented earlier in the book by Rosling et al (2018: 228) that many matters are 'almost never that urgent, and it's almost never an either/or (scenario)'.

The investigation of time and its deployment in planning discourse and practice shows how powerful narratives of project speed can belie the nature of the problems faced and the ability to generate appropriate solutions. Such concerns need to account for the definitional framing of planning and its accepted role in developing solutions. How this is organised and managed reflects the legitimacy of both scope and process. A slow, or in our terms 'proper', planning is one that features not only considered deceleration but also improved resources, tools, institutional structures and clear organising principles. Together, these can allow time resources for the proper democratic and technical oversight of development, as well as the introduction of new forms of regulation (Weber, 2015). Such a task can draw on such ideas as promoting 'co-evolved times' (Johnson and Johnson, 2021), where more emphasis is placed on understanding the capacities and needs of the different parties in planning, and a focus on when and how to undertake planning as a deliberative, co-productive effort becomes more significant.

Thus far, we have set out the ways in which time has been explicitly used as a means to shape planning practice and the dominant reasons why, using the English system as a case in point. We now move on to consider an alternative to neoliberalised planning timescapes, specifically, one that allows for deliberation and proper time in planning, and that is centred around normative principles of inclusion and public interest.

5

Time and deliberation in planning

Rational and collaborative time: modernist and postmodernist planning

We have been keen to orient the focus towards the importance of time for shaping planning practice. In doing so, we have presented a review of key ideas drawn from social theory and a framework that highlights questions of power, politics and practice. We coalesced these key concepts around the view of an overarching planning 'timescape' and a range of examples drawn from the main stages and tools that together make up the existing planning timescape in England. These provide an illustrative case in point. Shaping these are the neoliberal objectives of speed, efficiency and growth, which have been highlighted as the key drivers in the production, maintenance and reform of the planning timescape.

Throughout the previous chapters, we have alluded to the need for an alternative to the political construction of time in service of a neoliberal speed-growth paradigm, one that allows proper time for inclusion and participation. We now consider the wider 'public interest' justification for planning to meet a range of present and future needs, as well as the role of democratic processes and deliberation as a means to enable 'good' planning.

We begin this task by considering the perspectives of modernist and postmodernist planning and the collaborative approaches conceived in an attempt to overcome tensions over planning legitimacy. We have explained that the control and the colonisation of time are expressions of power that have inclusionary and exclusionary potentials for different actors and their interests. Despite inherent and uneven power relations, no one actor has full control over time and no arrangements are likely to produce some perfect or *uchronic* timescape. This means that addressing planning via time parameters on its own does not necessarily fix the challenges or problems that are apparent in any given planning system.

The numerous factors that shape development and decision making are complex, contingent and affected by deep structural and institutional legacies. Indeed, wider cross-cutting literatures on this exist discussing the temporalities of institutional change (Innes and Booher, 2010; Moulaert et al, 2016; Lauermann and Temenos, 2022), and recent engagement with planning over time or through 'diachronic' planning (Hutter and Weichman,

2022), as well as planning for time (Lennon and Tubridy, 2022) and rethinking time for deliberation (Jensen et al, forthcoming), has appeared.

Attempts to simplify and regulate using the elements of the planning timescape depicted in previous chapters have shown that resultant temporalities have been more likely to exclude rather than offer deliberation that can, in turn, foster knowledge sharing and greater inclusion. As our review of the existing timescape in England showed, many exceptions, suspensions and other responses have also been made possible, indicating the difficulties of both applying standardised approaches and servicing growth-oriented actors.

We now consider how collaborative and deliberative forms of planning may begin to bridge the multiple temporalities of participants and better reflect the complexities of planning issues. We also note that deliberative forms will need to be recognised as themselves enmeshed with power and the possibility of subversion. Such a perspective is set within the context of democratic systems and institutions with established differences in approach, derived from a system based on an aggregative model and one moving towards a more deliberative system.

In the aggregative approach, politics establishes a compromise between rational individuals, whose interests are combined or 'aggregated'. The deliberative perspective considers politics not as a set of trade-offs or compromises but as a result of a convergence of preferences geared towards socially optimal decisions. The premise of the latter is that these can be shaped through public debate and knowledge building. There are apparent differences too in terms of how time is viewed and deployed. This reduces down to either time being a resource to be conserved, rationed or squeezed for efficiency reasons or, in the deliberative paradigm, time(s) becoming a resource to be invested and applied in order to enable inclusive planning.

The context in which planning operates and the critiques levelled at forms of democratic engagement confront how time in planning is and may be deployed deliberatively and in order to further progressive ends. Collaborative and deliberative forms of planning have suffered from the criticisms and challenges also posed to wider democratic practices presented in the political theory and philosophy literature, namely, that they are naive in the face of power and underestimate the plurality of interests and values in contemporary fragmented societies.

In outlining collaborative planning theory (see Healey, 1997), we start from an initial standpoint that questions how planning processes can pass tests of public confidence, let alone reflect multiple issues and societal aims. As Allmendinger (2017: 241) puts it:

> How can we 'make sense' of what is happening and plan for the future within a dynamic and increasingly complex society? When there is

wholesale distrust of the political process, a fragmentation into single-issue politics and a plurality of positions, how can we come to agree on matters of concern?

We can begin to see that this is where the intersection between time and democratic values becomes complex. Even if 'proper time' was made available for stakeholders to engage in planning, 'consensus' is unlikely. Any given deliberative planning process may, for example, acknowledge the multiple temporalities of participants and, consequentially, entail opened-up processes. This does not, however, guarantee that any 'right' decision can be achieved, or one that could be persuasively or legitimately posed as a unified expression of 'public interest'. A more mature assessment recognises both the power enacted through the control of time and the impact of other factors that shape participatory expression and inclusive responses. In such circumstances, the prospect of more pragmatic endeavours seems inevitable, yet the dangers of such a position should be obvious: what elisions and imperfections are acceptable?

This is where ethics plays its part in seeking to pursue just or equitable planning forms, arrangements that are not only 'situated' (Campbell, 2006) but also contingent and care based (Hendler, 2017), as well as crafted to the context (Forester, 2022). Proper timing can allow for a more just planning practice, but this is far from 'perfect fix' territory (Allmendinger and Haughton, 2013). As with the idea of *uchronia* (an idealised perfect time), a search for a 'perfect' set of time arrangements in planning appears quixotic. Recognising the limits of reaching any final position on planning (as reform agendas imply), a system geared to facilitating ongoing deliberation is instead needed in order to respond to (ever-)changing values and goals as part of a more open culture where multiple times are fully recognised and accommodated.

We characterise the past ebb and flow of planning epistemology as a miscellany of efforts to grapple with postmodernity and pluralism, with profound implications for policy aims and processes. However, before moving on to these debates, it is important to state that the roots of such theories and critiques are found in the assertions made by modernists, subsequently challenged by postmodernist thinkers, regarding claims to knowledge/expertise and public interest assumed by planners in the past. This is particularly relevant in regard to opposing epistemological and ontological positions.

Briefly, in the most general sense, we allow that epistemology, as well as an epistemological position or approach, involves a particularised recognition of the theory of knowledge, especially with regard to appropriate methods, considerations of validity and scope. When we consider the ontological as a meta-question of world view and existentialism, that is, of how and why the world works, it is clear that how we frame and evaluate the production and application of 'knowledge' itself conditions practice. This gives shape to the factors contributing to an overall 'world view' and the tacit boundaries of acceptable epistemologies that shape the *techne* and *logos* of practice.

The ideas popularised during the 'Enlightenment' period of universal reason and science as the driving forces of human progress are typically associated with modernism. This perspective places instrumental rationality as its highest form of reasoning. The use and role of speed and time taken are often implicated in this paradigm. Stuart Hall (1996: 17) gives one perspective on this: 'Essential to the idea of modernity is the belief that everything is destined to be speeded-up, dissolved, displaced, transformed and/or reshaped ... Its essential traits are of restlessness, innovation and constant progress.'

For our purposes, the UK planning system was created under such conditions in the mid-20th century, and among prevailing attitudes, much planning practice and theory is still shaped by the legacy of modernism and an associated instrumental rationality. The modernist perspective is also closely aligned with positivist thinking and empiricism. On this view, time was regarded as a resource to be made objective and quantifiable. Furthermore, time was to become universal and measurable (for an explanation, see Adam, 2004; see also Chapter 2).

When such a view is combined with conditions of limited resources and politicisation, the mix attracts significant scrutiny from postmodern planning theorists, as Sandercock (1998: 4) argues:

> Modernist architects, planners, engineers ... saw themselves as experts who could utilize the laws of development to provide societal guidance. The hubris of the city-building professions was their faith in the liberating potential of their technical knowledge and their corresponding belief in their ability to transcend the interests of capital, labour and the state, and to arrive at an objective assessment of the 'public interest'.

Instead of 'objective' governance led by techno-rational experts and policy makers, what we have witnessed is that 'the processes of reification, quantification and commodification have paved the way for an instrumental treatment of temporality, turning it increasingly into the subject of market pressures for speed, productivity and profit maximisation' (Madanipour, 2017: 6). That is to say, rather than being enrolled in a neutral technocratic process, time has been used and deployed to suit powerful economic and political agendas (as reflected in policy approaches like 'project speed'), which can be masked by drawing on useful narratives and open-ended ideas, such as the 'public interest', and through appeals to national competitiveness and economic growth as being 'good for all' (as discussed in Chapter 4).

Arguments drawn from a range of critical social theorists have rejected modernist assumptions that normalise and accept time as neutral, objective and involving a natural ordering of the world. This leads to a set of uncomfortable questions for planning professionals when the basis of their legitimacy is challenged and has prompted an unresolved debate about how society makes tenable decisions about the future of places if: (1) professional planners cannot determine an objective public interest; (2) planning cannot be based (solely) on scientific techno-rational techniques; and (3) planning will not be considered impartial given competing interests?

The answer from a postmodern perspective is that the 'systems' and 'rational' and 'procedural' planning paradigms served by the aggregative model must accept the inherent limitations of that world view and associated epistemologies. In response, a clear option that seeks to recognise and address such critiques is to reorient and engage in more collaborative and deliberative forms of co-produced planning. While these have been promoted for many years, the question remains as to how such approaches can be sustained.

The postmodern perspective reconceptualises time as a resource that is socially constructed, subjective and relative, as well as bound up with power relations and (economic, political and social) practices extant between groups in society. As Nowotny (1994: 143) reminds us: 'Time is made by human beings and has to do with power which they exercise over one another with the aid of strategies of time.'

We can see attempts to claim a 'scientific', and therefore objective, status persisting in other disciplines, such as economics. Therein, modernist approaches, most often rooted in neoclassical economic theory, seeks to remove 'social' elements, such as politics and human behaviour. This is necessary for those models to represent market exchange in a 'rational' world and promote the idea that 'economies' can only be measured and controlled through techno-rational supply and demand:

> In the intellectual world, economists wanted to make their discipline seem 'scientific' – more like physics and less like sociology – with the result that they dispensed with its earlier political and social connotations ... while economics students used to get a rich and varied education in the idea of value, learning what different schools of economic thought had to say about it, today they are taught only that value is determined by the dynamics of price, due to scarcity and preference. (Mazzucato, 2018: 8)

If we accept the postmodern view in general terms, then there can be no universally knowable or rational 'right' course of action or values, nor, as per our focus, an indisputably correct time frame or ideal timescape (*uchronia*) when planning for land and development. This is where understanding values and embracing deliberation become important for the future of democratic institutions and just practices.

It is these thorny challenges that the following sections contend with, before the chapter closes by reflecting on what these considerations mean for deliberation and collaboration in planning practice, and for the role of time and timescapes. We now consider time and the question of public interest given its claimed central role in legitimising the planning system and its prominence in providing legitimisation for planned action.

Public interest, democracy and time in planning

Bound up with questions of process and time taken are more substantial questions of the aims of planning (for more on this, see Klosterman, 1985; Allmendinger, 2017). Widely aired and often poorly explained, public interest is used as a broad justification for modern town planning; therefore, while we set out the wider literature on time and planning, we also draw on debates about deliberative democracy and public interest in order to consider what could be involved in conceptualising a 'proper time' for planning that goes beyond labels of 'fast' or 'slow'.

The idea of public interest as a guiding principle has attracted a great deal of attention over the decades. The basic assumption of communicative theory is that public interest could be co-produced and used as a guiding, if opaque, principle for evaluating alternatives. Commentators like Alexander (1992), Howe (1992), Campbell and Marshall (2002), Moroni (2014), Maidment (2016), Lennon (2017) and Schoneboom et al (2022) have all added to consideration of the public interest criterion and how it may be understood and observed by planners. This attention has been sustained because this rather nebulous concept is still seen as critical in order to legitimate both planning activity and the profession (Hendler, 1995, 2017).

The difficulties of defining public interest in a specific context have prompted some to say that it is a 'phantom' idea (Moroni, 2014), but many recognise that it still serves as a means of orienting discussions over the aims of planning (that is, as a counterpoint to planning not necessarily servicing or being in harness to any particular private interest, or neglecting other interests). In similar fashion, Campbell and Marshall (2002: 181), while being critical of its loose application, view public interest as 'the pivot around which debates about the nature of planning and its purposes turn'.

Alexander (1992) argued that public interest was taken for granted during the heyday of modernist comprehensive planning. Professional planners were assumed to possess the skills and knowledge to be able to identify public interest and enact it accordingly. The issue that has persisted is how to arrive at a point where a decision is made 'in the public interest' legitimately and meaningfully, and, moreover, what role time plays in that process.

Accordingly, part of the dynamics of public interest planning involves knowledge exchange and sharing of perspectives, and this ineluctably requires the greater representation and involvement of wider publics. Diversity is not only celebrated as a strength but also acknowledged as a significant challenge when considering how to accommodate divergent attitudes, priorities and ideas within the same political system. This has led to significant debates, not least over determining public 'values', 'consensus' and 'common good' for diverse social groupings.

Understanding this and seeking ways to minimise exclusion or justify detrimental impacts are critical to good (public interest) planning. A closer inspection of this concept and debate highlights difficulties rooted in practical issues of actualisation. Rather than simply accept a basis for such a formulation rooted in collaborative planning theory, where discursive interaction establishes 'public interest' (Healey, 1997: 297), we recognise that a version of public interest could prevail that is quite apart from a public interest that is superficially consensual, objective or fixed.

Indeed, Howe (1992) argued that the public interest could be approached in four ways, which indicates a variety of criteria and start points: first, as a pluralist aggregation, where the overall net benefit for a population provides justification; second, through an economic approach that relies on a suite of assumptions about utility, cost–benefit and rationality to arrive at an optimal public interest; third, by assessing the 'common interest', where the common good is a supra-individual or extra-individual value (this is where communitarian conceptions of the public interest focus on the 'community' as the first ethical priority, that is, what is good for the community as a whole); and, fourth, as a 'good reasons' or care-based formulation that allows for special interests or minority needs to be considered carefully, so that public interest embraces both difference and flexibility. It should be clear that any approaches or associated mechanisms influenced by these conceptions may not produce consensus or deliver a no-cost outcome. This tells us that unlimited time is unlikely to be the solution but that 'more' time or time better used can assist across any of the four public interest formulations outlined and as applied to planning.

We may also examine how processes of planning and its governance actively seek wider evidence and inputs in order to legitimise and underpin a public interest claim. Collaborative planning theorists argue that in a pluralist society, more deliberative processes can help determine public interest and develop greater understanding of the aims and trade-offs involved in policy orientation and other planning decisions. Notably, differences appear between theorists who favour Habermasian ideas and see the development of a universalised interest as a possible product of deliberation (that is, a communicative rationality) and others who argue that such approaches do 'not seem to provide an adequate normative model if we wish to see [an] increase in people's motivation to enter into discourses or comply with norms' (Mattila, 2016: 361).

Maidment (2016: 367) makes a clear association between shaping the decisions that serve the 'public interest' with participation in planning and 'the need for the greater use of deliberative, or participatory, forms of democracy'. Together, these raise questions about how and where publics can make effective and helpful deliberative inputs, and how public interest decisions, as more than simply aggregative or majoritarian calculations, can be reached. Both this concern to serve and evidence public interest, on the one side, and an apparent failure to satisfy public demand for active roles and inputs, on the other, are part of a powerful social critique. This furthers our problematisation of exclusion in planning through the identified manipulation of time and the application of chrono-technologies and timescaping that, overall, limit, ration and squeeze time for deliberation in favour of speed and efficiency performance metrics, and, as such, undermine claims to public interest.

The argument presented here is that time for deliberation can at least help achieve greater rationality in decision making or recognise differences between subjects and groups in contemporary societies. Time, as part of the institutional fabric (that is, the timescape), needs to be actively facilitated even if practice arrangements are flawed in philosophical terms or are imperfect in implementation.

To complicate our main concern here, there is evidence which indicates that the *quantum* of time taken over matters like public consultation is less important than the *quality* of the process and the effort applied to that end. This is particularly so when interaction or deliberation promote feelings of fairness in planning processes (Firestone et al, 2018). The role of time is most relevant to public interest planning if the aim is to foster particular conceptions of public interest, with time as a component necessary to enable deliberation that has public interest in view.

(Post-)Democratic theory and planning

We explicitly link time and its institutional use to planning and democratic renewal, noting that democratic engagement in planning has long been criticised. We take a high-level view of the state of engagement and participation within contemporary democracies. Even with the claimed safeguard of democratic institutions, any claims to 'right speech and deep listening' are largely missing in institutionally mandated engagement practices.

This speaks to wider criticisms of traditional 'citizenship as membership' being passive and points towards debates over deep citizenship and the active roles expected of individuals and groups in society (Clarke, 1996; Young, 2002; Dobson, 2003). Such questions of active citizenship, when linked to ideas of time, depth of process and extent of knowledge or experience (as well as questions of power relations), act to challenge the extent of such action and the basis upon which individuals are politically and socially responsibilised (see Flinders and Moon, 2011; Sager, 2013). Felt (2016) also sees these conditions as part of the attempted 'temporal choreographies' that influence responsibility, citizenship and democracy. Similarly, Cohen (2018) shows how time use and deadlines in legal and political processes can either confer or deny citizenship rights, arguing that the devaluation of some (marginalised) groups' political time constitutes an unnoticed form of 'temporal injustice' within democratic justice systems.

Enhanced democratic engagement and reflective practice is not some sort of antidote to project speed (as discussed in Chapter 4), and time use by private citizens should not be assumed, but 'proper time' for different planning activity should be secured and reflected on consciously. This does not propose time as the sole factor in resolving or challenging problems of engagement, deliberation and power. Yet, time squeezes threaten the ability of planners and citizens to plan well, particularly if commensurate or partnering resources are lacking.

Public trust in democracy and democratic institutions across Western liberal societies has been increasingly called into question. Rather than absorbing new approaches and institutional arrangements that foster participation, many have been circumvented or invoked but not actually or widely practised. This is despite claims being made about social innovation and co-production (see Moulaert and MacCullum, 2019). Instances of overtly deliberative activity are promoted, yet mainstream practice lags. Planned outcomes and the perceived lack of time and resources put into planning has not helped address theory–practice gaps either, despite persistent appeals based on sustained attention in the academic literature.

Parallel calls to govern through mechanisms that deliver community 'empowerment' and via forms of 'localism' tend to conjoin with calls to adopt specific practices that are more inclusive and deliberative. Yet, actually existing forms of mandated localism, such as the Localism Act 2011 in England, often become captured by power and service political agendas, such as neoliberalism. In this case, the flagship policy of neighbourhood planning was couched in terms of empowering local communities to have more say and control over development in their local area but, covertly, was actually a political project to make housing and growth more palatable to such communities (for example, such plans could only allow for more and not less growth).

Such issues have been raised and assessed through an assortment of 'post-democracy' critiques, and sustain an ongoing debate over how to shift to more deliberative practices as part of a project to legitimise planning activity:

> planning processes, as well as possessing value in mediating between social actors, serve as vehicles for establishing new avenues of more

deliberative and participatory modes of democratic governance in addition to liberal representative institutions ... [Yet] among scholars and in the community of planning practitioners, there seems to be substantial uncertainty about how to assess the democratic effects of collaborative planning processes. (Agger and Löfgren, 2008: 146)

In attempting to appraise the broader situation, Miller (2020) argues that the vast majority of ordinary citizens living in democratic countries are not, in fact, democratic citizens at all, at least not according to any tenable interpretation of the concept. Miller (2020) invites us to consider instead what it means to be a post-democratic citizen given the rather paradoxical situation or perception that one both is and is not a democratic citizen when assessed in the light of apparent political powerlessness persisting within modern liberal democracies:

The central problem of post-democratic theory, then, is reconciling the failure of democratic institutions and subsequent loss of democratic citizenship with an enduring democratic cultural horizon: in other words, how to move beyond the ideological fantasy of democratic citizenship to a more honest engagement with the broader implications of post-democratic sovereignty. (Miller, 2020: 33)

Part of the incongruity involved in this is the political use of time that structures time to serve ideological ends. Rights of citizenship have expanded and include rights to participate, protest and have voice. Beyond rights to vote, efforts to deepen citizenship have realised many other social, economic and political rights (Turner, 1990; Barnett and Low, 2004). Rights to participate in planning are limited by quality, extent and, of course, the use of time and timescaping. As we have contended, the use of timescaping in various ways needs to be explored more thoroughly in recognition of the important structuring and depoliticising effects of planning cultures, capacity and mandated requirements (Brody et al, 2003; Taylor, 2013).

Statements of community involvement (SCIs) in England provide an indication of how local authorities have carefully guaranteed only the statutory minimum participatory rights in planning while, at the same time, acknowledging, without committing to, a whole range of participatory tools and options (OECD, 2020; Dobson and Parker, 2023a). Only a very few LPAs have deployed practices that could be termed 'innovative approaches to engagement'. Many have instead relied on standard consultation approaches: 'SCIs have served to structure and maintain pre-existing relations, and the participation offered by LPAs is made contingent and moreover offered on their terms' (Dobson and Parker, 2023a: 3). This situation serves as a vignette; our concern over time is made stronger based on arguments about local planning not having 'time' or resources to sustain deliberative approaches, let alone a willingness to do so.

The use of public reason between free and equal individuals may seem a viable basis for liberal democracies, but there is still the challenge raised by the political theorist Isaiah Berlin of 'value pluralism' (see Gray, 2013). Pluralists argue that values are incommensurable and therefore cannot be meaningfully compared, measured or combined with others. This means that trade-offs have to be made in the choices selected and none can claim their value(s) as having greater merit. Rawls (1997) accepts that people will agree or disagree on reasonable political matters but argues that a reasonable pluralism requires us not insisting on the truth of our own values and beliefs when deliberating over them. Some democratic theorists writing from the agonistic pluralism perspective assert that disagreement is a permanent feature of political life and conflict is therefore ineradicable. Agonistic democrats argue that any claimed consensus masks (unequal) power relations (Mouffe, 2005). This presents a powerful challenge to claims of achieving a unified and discursively established public interest, and instead warns of a post-politicisation of public life, where policy, regulation and the timescape are organised to avoid or suppress conflict, which is an orchestrated or choreographed form of democratic engagement.

Promises to devolve greater power and control away from central government to citizens is a policy trajectory that has been sustained rhetorically for at least 30 years. Disparities between claimed aspirations and outcomes raise questions over the legitimacy of existing forms of democratic governance and highlight the paradoxical position of the post-democratic citizen in an increasingly interconnected and fragmented society.

Despite the increasing 'hyper-pluralism' within societies, post-democratic theories hold that public reason can still be used as the basis for free and equal deliberation over the types of values that a particular society holds up as important and how they are then constructed in practice through social institutions, policies and so on:

> public reason does not compete with citizens' comprehensive doctrines, but instead seeks to show how citizens who possess different and conflicting comprehensive doctrines might live together peaceably and on equal terms within a common democratic framework ... When they do conflict, we must seek to deliberate from common ground or risk one group imposing its way of life on others' way of life. (O'Flynn, 2022: 104–5)

What we demonstrated in Chapter 3 is that the timescape elements arranged in England can be exploited more readily by those who can profit from growth. The preceding discussion indicates that it may also be convenient for others seeking to ignore or marginalise debate. Such a situation highlights the ongoing process of asserting, adjusting and re-regulating actors in planning. Time figures here as a resource and a barrier to processes that would support deliberation. In this context, Inch (2015: 411) argues:

> The hegemonic position of pro-growth planning means that development is effectively synonymous with the public interest, the primary good that the planning system should seek to promote. This suggests that participation is subordinate to the goal of pursuing light touch planning and ensuring that any perceived 'costs of delay' in decision-making are minimised in the interests of development and growth.

Given the preceding discussion, it would be naive not to acknowledge the broader critiques of democratic engagement and the role of power that structure such institutions and arrangements. Rethinking time in, and deliberation over, planning can be an important part of a potential antidote both to 'project speed' and to wider, often simplistic, cost arguments used to deflect calls for intensive forms of engagement or otherwise deny timely deliberation.

Planning time for deliberative democracy

When reflecting on public interest earlier, we flirted with the close association that deliberative practices and collaborative planning forms have with claims to establishing public interest. What we can say is that planning practices, or 'events', take time; that much is obvious. But how much time? How should this be organised? And what inputs and renderings are needed to produce good planning? We do not propose to pursue such questions fully here but, instead, rest on the idea that widely accountable and open processes should help fulfil tests of public interest and good planning. Our argument for proper time helps in brokering context-specific and time-sensitive solutions, and if nothing else, we have opened up for scrutiny the current timescape and squeezing of good planning.

In terms of the credentials of deliberation, critical commentators like Michael Walzer (1999: 66) argue that genuine deliberation is out of kilter with 'political reality', where 'victory is rarely won by making good arguments'. Instead, deliberation as practised can be tainted by partisanship, prejudice, hyperbole and ulterior motives that undermine the open exchange of ideas and the reaching of a shared view. Others argue that it is unrealistic not to expect people to impose their views on others (O'Flynn, 2022) – perhaps most evident in the 'culture wars'.

In terms of deliberative democracy and forms of democracy, Curato et al (2019: 4–5) argue that the three aspirational standards for deliberative democracy should be inclusiveness, authenticity and consequentiality. The first standard for inclusivity is the 'all-affected principle', whereby all those affected by a collective decision must have (a realistic) opportunity to provide input. The second standard for authenticity requires that deliberation is governed by norms of openness and reciprocity. The final standard for consequentiality refers to the outcomes of deliberation, which provide its legitimacy.

Furthermore, theorists have specifically attended to questions of time in policy making and point to appropriate 'times of policymaking' to explain where progressive rehearsal and reimagining are sustained by discursive and deliberative means (Nowotny, 1994; Strassheim, 2016). As O'Flynn (2022: 1) argues:

> The notion of a deliberative democracy is rooted in the intuitive ideal of a democratic association in which the justification of the terms and conditions of association proceeds through public argument and reasoning among equal citizens. Citizens in such an order share a commitment to the resolution of problems of collective choice through public reasoning, and regard their basic institutions as legitimate in so far as they establish the framework for free public deliberation.

This sets a high bar for the legitimacy attached to institutional processes and decision making generally, let alone planning. Furthermore, '[m]ost especially, deliberative democrats have been concerned with the prospect for reforming democratic institutions so that minority and disadvantaged groups can have a genuinely equal say' (O'Flynn, 2022: 97).

We concur with Mansbridge (1994: 53) that, 'In democracies we must use power to get things done', and this includes recognising the political work enacted through space(s) and time(s) for engagement. While progress has been made in liberal democracies, rights and freedoms still require defence, and 'Democracies always entail some form of coercion to realise their objectives, whether it is equal treatment of citizens' interests, or rendering some form of substantive justice. The challenge is to nurture spaces where citizens can constantly fight the very power that underpins their democratic polities' (Curato et al, 2019: 176).

Moreover, beyond concerns over psychological biasing (such as confirmation bias, echo chambers and cognitive dissonance) in deliberative processes, there are further issues concerning motivation and capacity to become informed and involved in shared public discussion. This widened focus moves somewhat beyond our scope, but clearly, if inclusion is to be taken seriously, then reliance on self-motivated informed citizens is not enough. Without active support and mobilisation (and paying heed to other rational-choice considerations), such approaches to participation are likely to fail (see Mace and Tewdwr-Jones, 2019).

Another related set of issues are difficulties in measuring 'effect' or outcomes, which are presented by instigators, on the one side, as discrete, measurable and linear rather than diverse and open (Chilvers and Kearnes, 2020), or, on the other, as simply unclear and uncertain. Some practices of public participation are commonly measured 'against theoretically defined and pre-given procedural standards, for example of inclusiveness, representativeness, social learning, and so on' (Chilvers and Kearnes, 2020: 6). Chilvers and Kearnes (2016, 2020) have identified in both affirmative and critical discourses a 'residual realist' imaginary of participation, the key dimensions of which are summarised in their tabulation of participation and contrasted with a relational conceptualisation shown in Table 5.1.

This comparison highlights how expectations and conceptualisations of who are involved, what practices are to be considered and to what ends all are affected a priori by resource considerations and, critically, by time(scape). Our viewpoint is to seek to merge and combine these creatively, using time as our lens to assess how to construct proper times in planning. What

Table 5.1: Narrower and wider conceptualisations of participation: realist versus relational and co-produced

Key features	Residual realist participation	Relational co-productivist participation
Ontology of publics	External and naturally occurring	Mediated and constructed through the performance of participatory practices
Publics are ...	(Aggregations of) Autonomous individuals	Multiple socio-material collectives
Models and normativities of participation are ...	Fixed, pre-given and ready made	Experimental, co-produced and in the making
Participatory practices are ...	Specific prescribed formats, techniques, tools and procedures	Co-produced, socio-material and highly diverse
Participation happens in ...	Discrete, isolated and ephemeral events	Systems and ecologies of multiple interrelating participatory collectives
Virtues and qualities of good participation are ...	Inclusion, representativeness, participant learning and decision impact	Reflexivity, humility, diversity, responsibility, responsiveness and experimental
Relationship between participation and change	Linear cause–effect understanding of participation impact	Participation as non-linear and multiply productive
Relation to science and democracy	Participation as separate from science and democracy	Participation as constitutive of science and democracy

Source: Chilvers and Kearnes (2020: 353)

Chilvers and Kearnes draw attention to is how certain conceptions will suit particular conditions. Therefore, how participation is conceptualised will sustain quite different tools. Indeed, Felt (2016: 183) argues:

> what is regarded as an adequate duration and temporal structure of participatory events obviously impacts the ways in which matters of concern take form and are debated. This perception shapes what types of scenarios are elaborated and tested and whether and how the right to take time for deliberation can be exercised.

In turn, those tools or techniques employ time, or specifically allow time, reflecting the fourfold elements discussed in Chapter 3 – the timing, sequencing, speed and duration of actions – along with the generation of *phronimos*, that is, the assembly of knowledges and understandings needed to develop 'good planning' outcomes. Furthermore, it is acknowledged how:

> specific temporal structures [impact] on both how we see the world and how we imagine its development. It is this perception of time that enables us to imagine that we can – also through performing participatory exercises – 'colonise the future' and to conceptualise it as open to exploration and exploitation, calculation and control. (Felt, 2016: 187)

Part of the implied co-productivist approach that would stem from the preceding discussion may well have to bear similarity to the 'residual realist' episodes and virtues outlined in Table 5.1. To operationalise a planning system without deliberation and to rest on instrumental means of pursuing planning easily fall foul of legitimacy tests. Therefore, some of the potential challenges to democracy in unequal and pluralist liberal societies, as well as the opportunities for developing deliberative democracy, are linked to our concern for time and its uses in planning.

Given that much of the literature and empirical evidence presented about deliberation in public life is derived from beyond the specifics of planning, the purpose or focus of the deliberative activity being queried clearly varies, and complexities are present. As Sager (2013: xxi) warns: 'Even more than before, public planners must expect opposition from strong market actors who challenge any notion of public interest by pursuing private goals using power strategies that disrupt open and fair deliberation.' When discussing deliberative planning, an active involvement in planning is implied. Co-production has been identified as the basis where combinations of deliberation, collaboration and use of proper time in planning can assist in such an agenda.

Albrechts (2013) highlights how co-production was initially a service-delivery strategy, while Watson (2014: 71) sees co-production as aiming to transform state–society engagement through both planning and delivery stages but that some co-production initiatives are 'more concerned with skilling and empowering marginalized communities to manage their own living environments, to deal effectively with state structures, to structurally advance citizen control over state resources and political power, and to pass on tactics for achieving this to other communities'. Moreover, Galuszka (2019: 144) argues that the term 'co-production' is used interchangeably with other concepts, such as co-creation, and that 'the concept is more and more often discussed as a form of engagement by different stakeholders at a policy and planning level, in particular as embedded via various bodies established within the sphere of formal governance'. This positions flexibility and shared ownership of the process as commonly identified prerequisites for co-production, but it is notable how time is rarely mentioned when considering such approaches.

Arguments in favour of (some forms of) co-production view it as a means of deepening democracy and realising social justice (Turnhout et al, 2020; Fishkin, 2009. Co-production aims to move beyond deliberation to challenge existing norms, whereas wider arguments for deliberative democracy highlight a concern for joint problem solving based on collective reasoning. This requires time and effort to understand the different issues/points of view and develop an objective judgement. Yet, it seems unlikely that, in practical terms, more than a small number of the (national or local) populous can be directly involved in this type of process.

In contending with this situation, deliberative tools can take on many different formulations, and the most common forms of 'mini-publics' are aimed at addressing such difficulties through citizen juries, citizen assemblies and deliberative polls, as well as forms of sortition that hold promise (see, for example, Landwehr, 2014; Bouricius, 2017; Miller and Lawson, 2021). While they appear attractive, the representativeness and diversity of those included helps minimise cognitive biasing and boosts inclusivity. If mini-publics can be useful tools to garner informed public opinion on issues, they are unlikely to be sufficient in themselves and need to be embedded within a wider set of democratic procedures to form a deliberative system.

This highlights the role of systems theory thinking in deliberative democracy given that 'no single forum, however ideally constituted, could possess deliberative capacity sufficient to legitimate most of the decisions and policies that democracies adopt'; rather, 'the system should be judged as a whole in addition to the parts being judged independently. We need to ask not only what good deliberation would be both in general and in particular settings, but also what a good deliberative system would entail' (Mansbridge et al, 2012: 1, 5). This, for us, needs to account for the sensibility that our emphasis on participatory planning implies.

This must be allied to clearer 'principle-based' planning systems that set out aims and rules for planning to underpin any specific methods of deliberative engagement. The work of the Raynsford Review (Raynsford, 2018), sponsored by the TCPA, did include a recommendation for a more considered and principled approach in the UK context, asserting that 'it is not beyond our country's means to introduce new and improved guiding principles, structures, relationships and processes to the planning system with the potential to deliver real economic, social and environmental advances', and that 'any review of planning in England must explore the founding principles of the system and test whether they have relevance for the problems we face today' (TCPA, 2018: 3, 7). Without being explicit, such a call must surely feature proper time as part of a new and improved approach to the principles, structures, relationships and processes in planning.

Examples of deliberation in planning

Despite some swingeing critique based on a combination of past failure, a lack of transformative outcomes, depoliticisation effects and the inability to challenge power relations, we have argued that a component in the rehabilitation of good planning is progressive deliberation. This is part of what some have termed 'empowered participatory governance' in planning (Fung and Wright, 2003). There exist a range of techniques and tools to aid deliberation, and there is a need to recognise that:

> the politics of co-production both in practices and in research will require a rethinking and a repoliticization of these processes that goes beyond simplistic checklists of do's and don'ts. We suggest that it is important to understand co-production as both a knowledge-making and a political practice which is inevitably imbued with unequal power relations that need to be acknowledged but cannot be managed away. Instead, it will be vital to allow for pluralism, create scope to highlight differences and, enable the contestation of interests, views, and knowledge claims. (Turnhout et al, 2020: 20)

Given our concern to fashion proper time for planning, and reflecting on the examples of timescaping explored in Chapter 3, elements of the timescape indicate where temporal adjustment or chrono-synchronisation may be applied. The dynamics of time frames, duration, timings, tempo and sequencing, as well as the distilled elements of the (1) timing, (2) sequencing, (3) speed and (4) duration of actions considered earlier, are relevant and come together as ingredients, though with Turnhout et al's (2020) warning about the political import of such measures as a necessary rider.

The explicit recognition of time as a critical factor in participatory planning sits alongside the dialogical, social and causal dimensions of engagement (De Liddo and Buckingham-Shum, 2010). Consideration of the timing of participation and deliberation, along with more mundane issues, such as scheduling of when and how time is to be applied, are all relevant. Some positive, albeit limited, examples of deliberative democracy do exist in England and include the Uttlesford community forums, designed to enhance local plan inputs:

> the Community Stakeholder Forum has been established to complement and enhance the consultation process by providing a platform for discussion among a wide range of local stakeholders, helping to inform and inspire contributions from the wider community. All meetings are live-streamed on Zoom and YouTube, with recordings remaining on the Council's YouTube channel afterwards. (Uttlesford District Council, 2021)

Similarly, Rugeley in the West Midlands has convened community planning weekends, initially held in 2018, where intensive public discussions were held to consider a large development proposal. This may be counterposed with ongoing engagement and open-systems approaches that may avoid 'delay' in the terms discussed in Chapter 4. These could allow greater inclusion and awareness raising by moving time and concentrating time for deliberation at key stages and in defined circumstances.

The idea of 'revisability' features in the deliberative democracy literature, which emphasises the provisional status of decisions made by a majority that can (and should) always be revisited at some point in the future. We argue that the key principles for community participation and the methods used to achieve and monitor engagement should be open to such revisability over time (and built into the timescape to ensure this) rather than becoming fixed over long periods. A more flexible and robustly defined community engagement strategy, with questions of proper time in sight, could be one element to help bring a greater range and number of people into planning.

The idea and technologies to 'move time' and 'save time' overall, as well as how these aid either good planning or perhaps a specific interest, or both, is clearly relevant. A good example is where a developer decides to engage with a local community over a development proposal far before they have finalised their scheme or submitted a planning application. This highlights the use of time in a sequence that suits them and their development's time-cost projection. Another example, on the policy side of planning practice, is exemplified by investing in 'front-loading', where a wider range of inputs are facilitated early in a process of policy formulation or decision making. This concept has been endorsed by UK administrations for some time in relation to planning participation, and prominently so within a set of six involvement 'principles' endorsed in 2004. These were set out in national planning policy at the time:

- community involvement that is appropriate to the level of planning – arrangements need to be built on a clear understanding of the needs of the community and to be fit for purpose;
- front loading of involvement – there should be opportunities for early community involvement and a sense of ownership of local policy decisions;
- using methods of involvement which are relevant to the communities concerned;
- clearly articulated opportunities for continuing involvement as part of a continuous programme, not a one-off event;
- transparency and accessibility; and
- planning for involvement – community involvement should be planned into the process for the preparation and revision of local development documents. (ODPM, 2004: 8)

The recognition of front-loading as a technique and possible 'timesaver' was more recently endorsed in the 2020 English planning white paper outlining planning reforms. Concerns were raised about the potential for reduced public input overall in a front-loaded system, leading the government to make the subsequent assurances:

> Government believes that engagement with communities and neighbourhoods is a central pillar of an effective planning system. The Government agrees with the Committee's recommendation on the importance of understanding the extent of public involvement in the planning system ... and how changes to the system could be approached with frontloading and deliberation in mind. (DLUHC, 2022a: 10)

Deliberation and delay

The speed and sequencing of participation episodes indicate measurement that is relative, and provoke the question: relative to what? How can speed be adjudged unless by recourse to reifications or valorisations? It is unclear how deadlines and time limits have been arrived at, but, as we discussed in Chapter 3 when presenting the planning timescape, they have helped form a time-based 'performance' basis to criticise the planning system.

Such criticism cites delay without explanation of the wider factors complicating 'speed'. This is a typical trope in neoliberal critiques of planning, and this demonisation is held up as a reason to deregulate or reform, as outlined in Chapter 4. In this vein, Ball (2011: 349–50) argues: 'Developers' desires to build can be severely dented when faced with slow, expensive and uncertain processes involved in a planning authority deciding whether a proposed development meets prescribed rules.' Such criticisms of time taken in planning introduce the idea of 'delay' but without providing any reference point. In presenting delay as a generalised abstraction, there is no consideration of why time may be needed and what issues are being faced. Indeed the 1975 Dobry report cites planning delay in the first paragraph as the main problem to be addressed. Yet in his interim report to the UK government a year earlier, Dobry acknowledged that 'not all delay is unacceptable: it is the price we must pay for the democratic planning of the environment' (Dobry 1974, p 3). Notably these government-comissioned reports on 'delay' pre-date the advent of neoliberalism in the UK ushered in by the Thatcher administration from 1979. This underscores that the calibration of what is acceptable time taken and when and how time should be expended reflects particular power dynamics, resource decisions and priorities more widely than *only* the neoliberal concerns outlined in Chapter 4.

Moreover, issues of 'delay' have since been interrogated by the RTPI in their work looking at the value of planning, which highlights that: 'The framing of delay as a cost arises from an economic position that factors time as a major component of market decisions. This has been particularly influenced through theories based on transaction costs, often in direct contradiction to theories of welfare economics that tend to focus on outcomes' (Adams et al, 2016: 18). In terms of the multiple factors that combine to add clock time to planning outcomes, the same study pointed out that 'a key criticism of many studies of delay ... is the narrow focus on timescales of decision-making with little appreciation of how other aspects of the market can contribute to slow performance (such as the supply of credit, developer behaviour and structure, and broader land market operations)' (Adams et al, 2016: 18).

This underscores deeper issues with market values influencing social ones, prompting Carney (2021: 11) to argue that 'markets are social constructs, whose effectiveness is determined partly by the rules of the state and partly by the values of society. If left unattended they will corrode those values.' In the UK, certainly England, planning has been substantially captured by economic and political narratives, predominantly adopting values aligned to neoliberalism over the past four decades. Reclaiming time goes some way to rebalancing what is valued, reflecting the view that 'Value in the market is increasingly determining the values of society'; instead, we need to 'channel the value of the market back into the service of the values of humanity' (Carney, 2021: 12).

Creatively organising time and other resources could produce multiple deliberative events that take place side by side, overlap and embrace co-production. This can aid the channelling of more resource into planning at key moments or episodes. Such 'time stacking' builds from its established use in considering how actors prioritise and use different technologies to work through complex or multi-layered processes (Klein et al, 2003).

Table 5.2 lists five key considerations, which, in short, cover questions of engagement forms, principles and rules, visioning, culture and leadership, and knowledge and rational choice concerns, such as 'What is at stake here?' All hold implications for time and its application in planning, when embracing participatory, deliberative systems.

As we see in Table 5.2, the literatures on deliberation tend to assume enough time to undertake adequate activity and instead place stress on knowledge, leadership, vision or aims, the stakes involved, and, lastly, being the closest or most relevant here, the rules involved. From our perspective, these should address questions of time explicitly.

It is also worth highlighting the relevance of the education and training of professional planners as an ongoing consideration in respect of time *in* and *for* planning. There seems to be a gap around time awareness and understanding the use of political time, along with how particular skills and knowledges for deliberation are needed. Overall, there appears a clear research agenda here to help better understand how linear, 'stacked' or intensive planning processes can be used and sustained. As stated earlier, question marks that are raised about perfect fixes cannot be sufficient reasons to impede improvement that reflects the aforementioned points. If inclusivity, deliberation, public interest and principles of revisability are explicit at the outset, what approach to plan making might be created and, indeed, improved iteratively?

Normative principles and deliberative planning

This chapter has presented an alternative deliberative planning timescape centred on the normative principles of inclusion and public interest. We view these as central for underpinning the democratic legitimacy and quality of planning practice. We have also considered the challenges to fostering such an approach, not least power and claims of post-democracy.

The focus we have directed on time brings into view how time is not evenly distributed but consolidated and strategically deployed, much like other resources (including knowledge), to suit objectives that are shaped by the dynamics of power relations. As Raco et al (2018: 1190–1) point out: 'The temporalities of planning lie at the heart of broader debates over contemporary forms of urban governance, democratic engagement and policy outcomes ... temporalities are not just about time but about the socially and politically situated experiences of time embedded in specific

Table 5.2: Five key factors for deliberation

Deliberation factors	Implications for community engagement and time applied
1. Rules (and principles)	Deliberative exchange takes place in planning over uncomfortable topics. This requires formal or informal rules of engagement – explicit rules must prop up deliberative initiatives. Infuse a context with the right procedures and organise it to conform to the right norms, then deliberation can take place. Rules of equality, civility and inclusivity may prompt deliberation and may institutionalise deliberation as a routine process. These link to the importance of clear principles (or at least parameters) for engagement that can be used to hold all stakeholders honest and accountable to their role in the process.
2. Stories (and visions)	If individuals do not understand the issues or feel connected to the problem and/or accountable for outcomes then their participation is unlikely. Successful deliberation seems to require a form of talk that combines the act of making sense (cognition) with the act of making meaning (culture). Storytelling/stories can anchor reality by organising experience and function as a medium for framing discussions (that is, these link to political / policy narratives as well as strands of planning theory around visioning and persuasive storytelling). These might make it easier for laypeople to become involved by telling the story of their area.
3. Leadership (and culture)	Leadership can initiate or maintain a shift towards a deliberative track. Public opinion is largely a product of elite cues, so leaders who engage in more thoughtful rhetoric may prime citizens to adopt a more deliberative posture. Leaders can steer towards non-deliberative conversations by insisting on the salience of particular cues. However, leaders often manipulate cues/processes to achieve personal political goals.
4. Stakes (and benefits)	This relates to questions of 'Why do it?' and what the consequences are of participating or not. Individuals are more likely to sustain deliberative reasoning when outcomes matter to them. Forester (1999) argues the same principle: individuals who are included in a policy-making process from the beginning become more invested in the process than individuals brought in at the end to choose among a range of predetermined options. Put simply, deliberation works best when individuals are invested in the outcome.
5. Prior knowledge	People tend to prefer non-deliberative forms of reasoning, and laypeople have little experience with deliberation (and presumably little skill). This prompts calls for renewed civic education. Basic knowledge is necessary, but it is not a sufficient spur to deliberation; rather, deliberation is a way of doing politics and deliberation is shaped by culture and society. One might imagine education as a form of 'apprenticeship learning', that is, guided activity of deliberating in real contexts and by establishing deliberative mechanisms, providing effective leaders, and guiding ordinary people through the process. This links to the facilitation of skills and capacity.

power relations and conjunctions'. Proper time for deliberation in planning should be welcomed, but this does not guarantee any improved outcomes. Time is not sufficient alone, and without consideration of the broader power relations and politics that structure the system, the institutional arrangements and practices required to assure and enact proper time in planning will remain underdeveloped, circumvented or absent. Indeed, political time can use the guise of democracy to suit power.

Time taken in planning is clearly a concern for business and some governments, who not only fear time as wasteful and 'inefficient' but also worry about the potential loss of control of planning (as we detailed at length in Chapter 4). It is in the context of the neoliberal and project speed where this view overtly portrays planning as a cause for delay and has had significant traction. As a threat to powerful interests, the dangers of 'wasting time' can be offered up as a justification for time squeezing, deadlines and limits – thus circumventing wider participation.

In addressing these issues, we have argued that the insights from democratic theory, particularly deliberative democracy, can help shine a light on the challenges and potential for improved forms of citizen engagement and participatory planning. We align with O'Flynn (2022: 134–5), in that 'deliberative democracy is our best hope. It is fundamental to the reform of representative institutions and practices – and much more besides.' This is not to downplay the significance of post-democratic or post-political citizenship, or the plurality of views and issues that are there to contend with; however, to accept or yield to forces that undermine democracy, rather than deepen it, represents a fatalism that will negate efforts to improve systems and institutions for the future.

If it is accepted that efforts to foster democratic engagement and inclusivity are legitimate and positive endeavours, then we must also guard against an uncritical deployment of clock time as an appropriate means of managing and judging planning performance. By placing the idea of public interest alongside questions of planning timescapes, an important (repoliticisation) function can be served in highlighting that time allocation is not some sort of panacea to resolve or accommodate plurality, or avoid the political nature of planning.

Public interest is dynamic and fluid, and despite other reservations, the aim of addressing timescapes in aid of greater attention to public interest is useful for several reasons. First, time has not been confronted in this way, and questions of public interest can be addressed episodically and at scale. Second, we should discount the idea that any one solution or one decision alone can stand up to a high bar of public interest, as suggested in some of the theoretical treatments of the concept. This means, third, we should allow professional judgement that is informed by plurality and the appropriate marshalling of guiding principles (that is, public interest and inclusivity), appropriate methods and processes (that is, deliberative techniques), and the informed use of timescaping (that is, aiming at 'proper' time). In essence, we are calling for thoughtful timescaping to generate and help provide a basis for better planning practice overall.

This chapter has brought together our main focus on time in planning with questions of democracy through considering what we view as central normative principles of public interest, deliberation and inclusion. We have argued that the timescaping of planning needs to have purpose; however, the type of purposes highlighted in Chapters 3 and 4 show up an emaciated view of time in planning. Underpinned by the different ways in which time has been conceptualised, as set out in Chapter 2, the opportunity for deliberation and proper time is revealed as an important component of enhanced and rejuvenated approaches to planning.

Following Zielonka (2023: 161), we see that 'a solution for embracing the future is not less but more democracy'. Despite the criticisms presented here, democratic innovation is still the best hope in allowing for wider debates that go beyond short-term political and economic 'business as usual' approaches that fetishise speed and growth as the primary goals of the 21st century.

6

Time, planning and timescapes for the future

Problematising planning time: neoliberal and normative principles

While some of the social theory of time presented here can be considered 'high-level' esoteric theorisations on such grand topics as practice, capitalism, power and politics, we have attempted to demonstrate their relevance to planning in revealing how they draw attention to questions of time and its control, the political use of time, and the role of time in shaping practice and vice versa. Together, these assist in problematising our existing approach(es) to planning.

This final chapter serves as a distillation of the key arguments made throughout the book and presents our reflection on the significance of time and its uses in planning. We started this process in Chapter 1 in seeking to highlight the relationship between planning and time, and its import as an area for critical inquiry. We then presented a review of the social theory of time in Chapter 2, drawing attention to the work of key thinkers, such as Bourdieu, Adam, Nowotny and Lazar, among others. Chapter 3 sketched out some of the key features of the planning timescape in England by presenting 13 examples from practice, as well as examining how such temporal arrangements have exclusionary as well as privileging potentials for those participating in the system. The neoliberal critique of planning as causing 'delay' and stunting development, founding the impetus behind proposed planning reforms and orienting the latest 'project speed' agenda, was outlined in Chapter 4, along with key counter-arguments. In attempting to break with a narrow view of time and planning, Chapter 5 considered the challenges and opportunities for a 'proper time' in planning for public interest based on pluralistic inclusion and democratic deliberation.

At the heart of this book, we have presented two competing ideological views on the role of time in planning: (1) the neoliberal and (2) what we term 'normative' or 'substantive principles'. In doing so, we have used the intelligible carrying labels of 'project speed' and 'proper time' (or 'slow planning') to evince the core features of these perspectives and implications for planning.

We have seen that governments that adopt a neoliberal-informed perspective, such as in the UK, typically mobilise political time in support of policies and reforms that prioritise a dominant speed-growth agenda, which acts as both the means and end of the state. While we have been mindful not to fall into the trap of criticising speed or growth in all cases, we have been critical of applying a 'fast growth' or 'growth at all costs' approach to planning. This neoliberal perspective views planning as a barrier and seeks to transform it into an economic tool, particularly through control over time. Yet, planning systems developed out of a concern for preventing or mitigating the impacts of (unregulated) development to protect public health and safety and the environment, and time taken in plan and decision making should be directed to this end, notwithstanding any widening of public participation and concern to mediate proposals in the public interest.

Time and tensions between neoliberalised planning and normative principles

We see a tension between the planning timescape oriented towards neoliberal objectives and one that allows time for inclusion and deliberation over public interest and alternative goals. It is not that neoliberal governments are against greater participation and deliberation (and the time afforded to these activities) per se but, rather, that these remove certainty over the process and therefore a degree of control over achieving outcomes. Indeed, neoliberal governments will often attempt to marry citizen 'empowerment' and public participation (especially where these bypass the state) with achieving development, that is, to align liberalism and growth.

In England, this can be seen in the case of neighbourhood planning, which was introduced as part of a 'localism agenda' that ostensibly claimed to put communities 'back in control' of their local area but was designed and operationalised to incentivise neighbourhoods to accept and plan for greater housing development. Despite the empirical evidence of communities undertaking neighbourhood planning being resistant to housing, the government was at pains to evidence that the policy was empowering citizens that were planning positively for additional housing (Salter et al, 2023). In other words, the neoliberal perspective seeks to free individuals from the state to pursue their 'natural' desire for growth (*homo economicus*), and when this does not happen, they attempt to distort reality instead to preserve their world view (What happens when free citizens do not want growth?). This has led us to conceptualise neighbourhood planning as a *simulacrum* orchestrated to validate the neoliberal world view (Dobson and Parker, 2023b). Indeed, one consequence of the 'freedom' to engage in neighbourhood planning has been some communities opening up the policy issues being considered in their local area to include more progressive agendas (see Brownill and Bradley, 2017).

It should be clear that whether one accepts either the neoliberal or the normative principles view of planning, there will be a significant impact on the planning timescape – both for how it is arranged and for what it is in service of. In the UK, what we observe under a neoliberal policy approach is a concerted effort to narrowly define planning in terms of its scope and to mobilise efforts to organise planning under tightened aims (that is, growth and housing). This has required a legitimising (temporal) discourse / narrative that requires planning to be accepted as a source of delay and in which speed is presented as a positive good, thus justifying reforms to the timescape.

Our exegesis of how time has been manipulated for the purposes of project speed could be discounted if growth were actually the main consideration for the enterprise of spatial planning. Without wishing to attempt to define planning, what we can surely say is that good planning engages with multiple issues and challenges simultaneously. Planners will think about spatial relationships and take a long-term view of likely impacts. In contrast, orienting planning in service of 'growth' seems both a stunted and short-term simplification that has been roundly criticised elsewhere. Rydin (2013) demonstrates how a growth-dependent model for planning is only appropriate for some places that have strong market demand and that are in a position to negotiate for some of the accrued wider benefits of economic development in the area – an approach that leaves many 'left behind'. As such, there is a need to look beyond singular growth models applied in all places (and at all times).

Allmendinger (2016) has made the case that neoliberal reforms targeting different spatial boundaries and scales of planning have formed a 'neoliberal spatial governance' strategy that has experimented with finding the 'silver bullet' for the operationalisation of neoliberal planning. This is most evident in the dismantling of strategic spatial planning, the removal of regional government in England and a rescaling towards localism, including the activation of the neighbourhood level for planning activity. We have sought to add to this spatial dimension of neoliberal strategy in drawing attention to *neoliberal temporal governance*, which has experimented with the timings of planning activity through successive reform agendas to find the best temporalities suited to the realisation of growth (what we view as a rather quixotic search for an ideal or *uchronic* arrangement). In both cases, we see the effect as subordinating the normative aims of planning.

The politics of time and planning, and the resources applied to the task, seem somewhat out of kilter with need given the number of 'crises' identified across contemporary societies that present significant environmental, social and economic problems (for example, the climate crisis, nature crisis, housing crisis, ageing/overpopulation crisis, cost-of-living crisis and so on). These prompt thinking more deeply about time and the role of spatial planning (and 'planners') in helping to address them given that almost anything that impacts or relies on land use requires good planning.

The main arguments presented in this book have sought to counter and recalibrate the planning system away from neoliberal discourse. We also add to the growing calls for greater consideration of the participatory nature of planning and the key poles of inclusivity, deliberation and a rehabilitation of public interest planning. In doing so, we have challenged the orthodox view of participation as something offered to one group by another and only on set issues and time frames. Instead, we have sought to recentre this dynamically as critical to the act of planning itself (that is, that planning is participatory). We see such a reorientation, both in cultural and in institutional mindset terms, as the first step towards fostering greater levels of inclusion and deliberation in planning.

Recasting the term 'participation' (where other terms have been used, such as 'visioning', 'analysis' or 'deliberation') is pertinent here, as a widened view of who and what is constituting planning practice has become more accepted. Yet, while that perspective is broadly accepted, we see that participation of professional planners has become 'planning' and involvement in planning from others has been distanced as 'participation'. We argue that such a separation needs to be broken down. As Felt (2016) notes, how people engage in planning and their behaviours are shaped by the understanding of inputs and the time allocated. Redefining the purpose and timing(s) of participation can be a progressively iterative process, creating a positive feedback loop rather than one that attempts to reduce and standardise planning practice and the time afforded.

This underscores that, on its own, simply allowing more time for participation is not enough. Therefore, while we contend that a new timescape is a prerequisite for improving planning, we also need to foster better engagement processes and the time to deliberate and reflect within that more accommodating timescape. This brings us to a crucial point set up in the introduction, which can now be aired in light of the preceding chapters: there is more at stake than simply planning fast or slow; rather, much more emphasis is required about what we are planning *for* and *why*.

Planning fast and slow reprised

As Zielonka (2023: 94) highlights: 'the objective is not necessarily to slow down capitalism and reduce its territorial reach. We first need to have a democratic discourse about the implications of speed and a few simple measures to protect us from pathological manifestations of turbo-capitalism.' We would agree that the answer is not necessarily to slow down economic development, but we would certainly advocate making it more democratic and sustainable. Indeed, simply speeding up or slowing down a process a priori make little sense in the abstract given that 'notions of slowness and speed are relative and context dependent' (Zielonka, 2023: 100). It is the intention and goal that is important, as power can operate with different temporalities, fast or slow, depending on which best suits the agenda in any given circumstance.

Fast-paced decision making can undermine democracy, but so can slowing the process down, each can be effective tools to 'modulate' wider inputs and interests (see Parker and Street, 2015):

> The present day acceleration and time compression perverts democratic procedures and leads to the ruling by decree of a small group of ruling-party politicians in charge of the executive branch of government. Incessant time pressure leaves little room for research, negotiation and compromise ... since we instantly move from one crisis to another with no 'slow' periods for reflection and the correction of mistakes, the policy process leads to outcomes that are not only irrational, but also utterly ineffective in most cases ... [Conversely] Advocates of slow-paced legislative deliberation often have vested interests in maintaining the status quo and resisting any meaningful changes. In short, *speeding up and slowing down have unequal implications for different groups of people and regions*. (Zielonka, 2023: 97–9, emphasis added)

We can see that the picture is much more complex when power can adapt to make use of different temporal strategies and where a 'fast/slow dichotomy cannot hope to capture the simultaneous coexistence of multiple temporalities that characterises the experience of modernity' (Wajcman, 2015: 176). That is to say, power can shape time to suit its different needs.

We can see examples where 'slow development' is in the interest of power in maximising capital returns. In the UK, for example, despite the government rhetoric of a housing crisis and the need to build 300,000 homes a year, volume house builders will drip-feed new housing supply onto the market over time rather than build a site out as quickly as possible (Archer and Cole, 2016). This is in order to maintain product scarcity and therefore value in the local housing market (that is, to control the supply and demand over time in the interest of profit) (Archer and Cole, 2021). Similarly, large developers can store land for future development, that is, 'land-bank', as a means to maintain a steady-state supply pipeline (a form of time bank). Such a business model is predicated on managing/supressing the temporalities of housing delivery yet is not viewed as 'delay' because it is driven by the private sector. That is, as Colenutt (2020) puts it, because these actions are in the interest of the 'property lobby'. Furthermore, the land purchase, construction and marketing phases sit adjacent to, but outside of, the planning system and are assumed to be aligned with growth and not regarded as a 'barrier'.

In such examples, we can see that time is not the main issue; rather, it is the level of certainty and control over the development process, as best supported by faster or slower temporalities. As Raco et al (2018: 1180–1) show, the picture is more nuanced:

> Too often debates over development times simplify this fluidity and present the development sector as a unified interest with a clear subjectivity that want 'fast' returns from investment decisions … Calls for the 'speeding up' of planning deliberations may benefit some types of investors but not others, who may value-engineer slower planning timeframes in the pursuit of greater longer-term profits.

As such, we can see similar problems with 'project slow' or slow neoliberalism if the outcomes are still exclusionary, devoid of meaningful deliberation and undertaken without consideration of wider public interest or long-term sustainability. We come back to Adam (2004: 123–4) in asserting that 'the quest for control is to a large extent about obtaining dominion over time for economic gain and social advantage'. Therefore, the question remains not how much time is taken but for what and for whom time is being used. Which interests are gaining and losing from any formulation of timescape?

Planning timescapes for the future

We have used the concept of timescape throughout the book to highlight the power enacted through time and within specific spaces of planning. Planning involves a variety of temporal influences beyond simple ideas of clock time taken to write a plan or to make a decision. The often-cited element of the verb 'to plan' talks of the future and of directing and managing actions for the future; therefore, in that sense, planning is bound up *with time*, but it also *takes time*. We have attempted to highlight the multiple temporalities of planning and how they fit within the different elements that make up the planning timescape. In doing so, we have highlighted that different actors and interests will each have their own conception of 'proper time' in relation to planning, and that these can and do conflict in practice. We have also shown how power and politics can shape time to preference certain interests over others. In the neoliberal canon, this is often oriented towards facilitating speed and growth aims; as such, neoliberal timescaping can crowd out other considerations.

This focus on timescaping leads us to the contention that *the colonisation of planning time is tantamount to the colonisation of planning itself* given that temporal conditions and (re)deployments have the ability to shape practice and enable or undermine good planning. Following Adam (2004) in understanding that control of the present is control over the future, we now consider alternatives that could prompt a reconceptualisation of planning timescapes for the future.

Multiple temporalities and timescapes

The (recognition of the) existence of multiple forms of temporality can be viewed as a positive in a liberal democracy and pluralist society, where time has different roles and functions for individuals, professions and institutions. Indeed, timescapes and timescaping involve multiple institutional arrangements, including legal arrangements, both general and specific to planning law, and rules applied though regulations. Yet, multiple temporalities are not treated equally, and powerful interests can seek to control planning time to suit their own agendas.

In considering political time and policies that impact on time distribution and use, we can see significant influence on the temporalities of planning systems. Time is clearly important in the disciplining of behaviour and is a dimension in which the use of power to govern conduct in planning practice has been exercised. Indeed, the very term 'time' obscures a complex set of power relations, resource allocations, structural imbalances and political ideology, and this focus brings to light whose time is being promoted or discounted.

It is moot, therefore, whether we can say that there is one planning timescape at all or, instead, different actors' perspectives, responses and experiences of planning. We see that any given planning timescape(s), as applied or relaxed, favour particular actors and their interests over others, and such changes will result in variable contours of temporal equity as the (re)formed timescapes are variously received, applied, negotiated or contested. The actual practice and experience of timescape(s) is therefore different from what can be drawn from any abstract reading of regulation and policy. To consolidate these points, there are five key features or dynamics involved here:

- how planning itself is conceptualised ('*why*');
- the different actor groups (*who* is involved);
- frequent timescape changes (*what* is involved);
- different local responses (*how* the timescape is absorbed); and
- how the timescape is received (the *effect* on outcomes).

Attempts to control through time and the variable ability to utilise timescape impositions are complex. One imperfect but rather nice way of conjuring up an image of the 'moving parts' of planning and its timescape is by recourse to the orrery. It is a metaphor here, of course, but its creation was an attempt to depict the operation of the solar system. Figure 6.1 depicts an orrery designed to show the relative movement of the planets around the sun, each with their own orbits, trajectories and speeds. This calls to mind the

Figure 6.1: The orrery

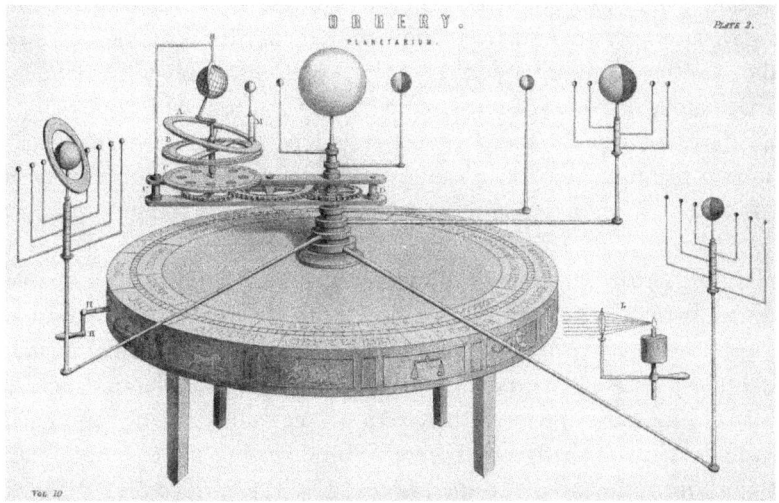

Source: D87NYB – Contributor: Chronicle/Alamy Stock Photo

interdependencies and multiple moving parts involved in planning across active interested parties, and how the juxtapositions present themselves to different actors.

Notably, of course, the operation of an orrery sees these different parts come into alignment at certain times, possibly one might say there are '*uchronic* moments'. What this helps with is the idea that attempts to both impose and then fashion a *uchronic* arrangement is rather quixotic; instead, greater attention can be beneficial, and even fleeting alignment may help serve public interest. The timescape will suit some interests at some times in some places, and we might characterise this as presenting the possibility of either 'localised' or 'episodic' proper times.

Thus, we see a more nuanced project in place in English planning, where the range of policy initiatives exhibit time-bound outputs and expectations that, as Datta (2019) portrays, are actually flexible; the key is that control of time is still retained to some degree by the state institutions and actors that enact planning. This is where time is seen as integral to a reorientation of institutional arrangements in planning. By way of illustration, we now summarise the two alternative planning timescapes that we have discussed throughout the book: the project speed timescape and the slow planning timescape.

Project speed as timescape

Neoliberalist orientations of the planning timescape, which we have characterised here as 'project speed', involve a series of time squeezes, time limits and other measures to secure planning 'performance' (see Chapter 3). Accompanying this set of measures have been a series of rhetorical framings that have attempted to equate planning with delay (that is, this is tantamount to the idea that planning *is* delay). This sits uncomfortably with planning as a participatory activity, and tensions are clearly apparent when one compares proponents of project speed to other voices that have warned against designing planning to service the growth agenda. The latter have posited planning as a far more expansive and important undertaking:

> planning's real purpose: to allow local, democratic say over spatial decision-making; to ensure that development is targeted where it is most needed, not where it is most profitable; to improve people's quality of life and health outcomes; to provide the amenities and infrastructure that communities need to thrive; to protect valuable environments, mitigate climate change, and preserve biodiversity; and to redistribute wealth from the richest to the poorest. (TCPA, 2020b: 2)

While influenced by business and development interests, the timescape of project speed has been oriented towards those deemed delivery agents, which have included not only the development industry but also those members of the public who have been willing to operate within such conditions and pivot in support of the growth agenda. In the case of neighbourhood planning in England, the timescape involved has been shaped to accommodate such involvement rather than squeeze it, and other constraints faced by participants have instead ensured that a growth orientation is sustained (Dobson and Parker, 2023b).

Indeed, Moore-Cherry and Bonnin (2022) highlight that temporal politics plays a crucial role in framing urban experience under capitalism, to the extent that urban redevelopment is considered as a 'success' or 'failure' depending on the temporal framing that is being privileged. This leads them to argue that cities are shaped by multiple, fluid and contingent framings and temporalities that complicate the ability to analyse policy outcomes conclusively.

If we consider the policy 'success' of the planning timescape in terms of facilitating a neoliberal speed and growth agenda, suited to a narrow development and finance interest perspective, then the outcomes sought from planning are seen from the starting point of meeting these ends, thus framing calls for further reforms. The neoliberal approach is, by now, the 'business as usual' approach in the UK, but the challenges being faced in the early 21st century are mounting, and there are calls for a different approach to protect the future:

> High-speed capitalism and culture only reinforce this resistance to change, because in a high-speed society changes are more prominent

than ever. As a result, the future is being ignored or suppressed. The danger of things going badly wrong in the future is being underplayed. Our capacity to handle eventual catastrophes is being declared with pathetic, and unmerited, confidence ... Actions to avert the collapse of the pension system, climate change or traffic congestion are being mimicked, with no real intention to deliver any meaningful adjustments. (Zielonka, 2023: 154)

While these issues will require a form of rapid action, time is needed to openly deliberate what the implications of our current approaches are and seriously consider potential alternatives.

Slow planning as timescape

If neoliberalist timescaping is supported by the characterisation of planning as a cause of delay and change is made in order to orient planning systems and policy to support the pursuit of growth, then we may contrast this with the deliberately contrary idea of 'slow planning'. As we have explained, this book is not set up to advocate for 'slow planning' if slow planning means something that is unnecessarily prolonged. Instead, we are arguing that project speed does not align planning with inputs or resources sufficient to secure proper time and attendant deliberative practices that accommodate the 'event' and those involved. This does not mean that planning requires more linear or clock time, but it does need greater recognition of planning as participatory and requires applying temporal innovation that challenges the status quo:

> Part of the problem is that the short-term horizons of profit-driven, neoliberal economics have made it difficult for democratic institutions to implement any ambitious, long-term projects – in effect confining them to quick, futile fixes ... With little time for democratic deliberation, it is hard to come to any satisfying decisions ... Rushed negotiations between parties representing diverse interests generate few durable compromises. (Zielonka, 2023: 95)

Proper timing of planning is not just about time allocations or time taken per se but involves the enabling of a complex of different people with varied perspectives, appropriate skills and knowledges, and evidence. Accountabilities are also needed to accompany such arrangements. Some of the theoretical content, examples shown and alternative times outlined in previous chapters clearly provide plenty to consider in refashioning time *in* and *for* planning. We argue in the following that the timescapes of planning can relate or can sit uneasily with the contemporary challenges and issues facing society, with time playing an important role. In essence, we see proper time(s) in planning as part of the answer to the question: 'how can we make time in collaborative processes for temporalities to be explored, and for critical temporalities to be developed' (Matthews, 2014: 52). As Nowotny (1994, 144–5) explains:

> proper time is made possible only through the time of others. Only when a common time is created as a frame of reference, which neither belongs completely to the one or completely to the other ... can the constraint of time at least be loosened, even if it cannot be totally removed ... this presupposes a process of constant development, of negotiation and argument by means of their continued temporal strategies ... the interval of time is the basic element for structuring interhuman relations.

Timescapes for the future

In highlighting how planning and time have been manipulated to service a particular agenda, the critical points raised alert us to how control of time acts to control planning activity. Where planning has been subject to project speed, we argue that it has been set on an unsustainable trajectory and that an exclusionary timescape has been fashioned. We contend that the existing arrangements are therefore unsatisfactory. This timescape is both problematic now and for the future, critically, because a narrow and short-term view of planning has been asserted and that cannot be justified processually.

There seems little point in calling for a simplistic 'slow it all down' system, but individuals can urge for time and its organisation in planning to be better understood and to enable proper deliberation of complex issues. Equally, where better planning relations and outcomes are likely, the politics of planning should also become less febrile. In Bourdieuian terms, this rethink can provide the tools for developing a 'new social gaze' on time and practice while understanding the means by which time has been controlled in the past. For planning practitioners, any advocacy for 'slow planning' can be justified as one that urges for quality processes and outcomes of planning. It is the deployment and utilisation of the governance of time that are key here rather than simply a focus on the duration of any given activities.

This view highlights that different actors recognise distinct pressures and foster their own *uchronic* assumptions and strategies as part of their proper time. The imaginary of actors in planning is driven by a number of different factors, and there is not a set speed or assemblage of processes that is ideal for each. Indeed, in this mode, Toffler (1970: 21) wrote that 'the future ... invades the present at differing speeds. Thus it becomes possible to compare the speed of different processes as they unfold ... time is the currency of exchange that makes it possible to compare the rates at which very different processes play themselves out.'

This observation of visions of (competing) future(s) invading the present is deeply embedded in planning practice as a future-facing activity, as well as a complex process with multiple timescales that evolve at different speeds, from conception through to implementation. This serves as a reminder that the organisation of time and timescape acts to influence control of the future through the present. Going beyond this differential, we have also asserted that actors are battling over control of planning *through* time. Greater consideration of the ways that time is apportioned, regulated and managed in planning is therefore appropriate not only in terms of the principles discussed but also due to the intensely practical implications found in the consideration and reconciliation of the complex of planning issues. Arbitrary time allocations for specific actions, stages or processes attempt to simplify planning rather than refashion it in a way that can address wider complexities – the imposition of time limits affect choices about what to do, how to do it and with whom, that is, time parameters perform planning behaviours, which supports the central nostrum in this book that time makes practice.

The 'What we are planning for?' dimension is also affected, that is, how practice makes time. This suggests a need for a more effective and explicit defence of allowing 'proper time' for planning activity, where necessary, providing a challenge to instances where the four main time tactics of neoliberal temporal governance – speeding up, slowing down, the 'suspension' of time and setting actions 'off the clock' – are (mis)applied to suit the interests of power and capital. This must contend with the multiple temporalities of planning and the recognition that no set, standardised time can be fashioned that suits all actors in the planning process, or can service the multifaceted planning agenda perfectly. There is, in reality, no planning '*uchronia*'.

Few would argue against the need for timely decision making, yet planning is a complex profession and an endeavour with multiple participants and high-stakes outcomes. The essence of good planning requires that time is taken: to reflect on, and absorb the implications of, a variety of inputs; to think about past and future; to explain options and choices; and to recognise a need for processes that are inclusive or sufficiently deliberative. We align with Felt (2016: 183) in arguing:

> what is regarded as an adequate duration and temporal structure of participatory events obviously impacts the ways in which matters of concern take form and are debated. This perception shapes what types of scenarios are elaborated and tested and whether and how the right to take time for deliberation can be exercised.

Collectively, we need much wider and deeper democratic discussions and guiding principles about what future we want to create and whether this is being served by the existing approaches (and limits) that have become dominant across the planet. If we align with the neoliberal timescape, then the speed of decision-making processes and planning approvals may be enough, as the 'market' will determine the shape of the future built and natural environment. However, if we want something more, then part of that is allowing proper time to plan, to include, to deliberate, to mediate and to reflect on the multiple users, interests and aims of the planning system. For us, such attempts would form a worthy planning timescape *for* the future.

In overview, the logic path of the book has served to navigate the following stages of the argument:

1. Time is not neutral but constitutive of power relations and therefore practice.
2. Planning is participatory, and this is shaped by the timescape and vice versa, impacting the (claimed) normative aims of the system, which are ostensibly to serve public interest and deliver sustainable development.
3. Each actor has their own proper time when participating in planning, and prioritising one set of time interests has a (knock-on) effect/affect on all others in the timescape.
4. Given the foregoing, control of time in planning is tantamount to control *over* planning.
5. More reflection and research are needed on the role of time in shaping planning and how timescapes are experienced by different actors, as well as what imaginaries are at work in constructing plans and policies in and through time.

It is to this final stage that we now turn in setting out some ideas for further developing time and timescapes as a mainstream research agenda and which could bring about a 'temporal turn' in planning theory and practice.

Time as a research agenda

This treatise on time in planning should help to extend the debate over the temporalities of planning and perhaps act as a nudge towards a 'reset' of the planning field. Reflection about the full ramifications of attempts to control time are needed, and 'proper time' for planning activity is seen as necessary to help realise positive systemic change and future-proofing. While questions of time have largely been neglected or given limited attention in the planning literature to date, this is beginning to change as the role and importance of time in shaping power relations and practices has begun to be applied to the field and be critically questioned (see Raco et al, 2018; Laurian and Inch, 2019; Hutter and Weichman, 2022; Lennon and Tubridy, 2022; Jensen et al, forthcoming). The effects/affects of time on planning have thus far been highlighted by the advent of 'performance management' measures and the concomitant imperatives of 'delivery' accompanying broader reforms to public services, local government and planning.

The thinking behind neoliberal policy discourses, including forms of NPM, places time firmly in view as something to be 'managed' in order for 'efficiency' to be assured and 'delay' minimised. Such business and service imperatives are promoted in governmental policy generally and planning policy specifically. We have argued that such political and business discourses, while distinct in their specific prescriptions, collectively form the bulwarks of 'project speed': an endeavour that requires fast to immediate change and/ or results in order to service growth as the primary goal to be pursued via planning systems and a planning imaginary.

Writing in the context of late capitalism and neoliberalism, we can see the regular pejorative use of 'slow planning' in mainstream political and business discourses. The depiction of planning as a 'barrier' to economic growth makes use of delay and speed frequently and forms the basis of (reform) agendas in planning. Contrasting this with wider critiques, we can see a disjuncture: there is a growing concern that such narratives prioritise speed and growth regardless of the wider costs and impacts to people and the planet. Clearly, there are a number of environmental challenges in the 21st century that cannot be ignored, with climate change and biodiversity protection being critical issues to address globally, notwithstanding social questions over inequality, development quality, well-being or accountability to lived communities (Raworth, 2017). A reasserted public interest agenda must surely help secure these aims, with greater knowledge and understanding of time being a critical servant to that goal.

Our work has delved into how the English planning system has been timescaped to suit particular agendas, and we have drawn in both secondary and primary data to set out our exploration of political time and practice. This work has revealed multiple avenues for research to understand the temporalities of planning. This agenda implies a challenge to the dominant singular perspective of project speed and, instead, points to the highlighting of multiple temporalities involved in planning and the impacts the timescape has on actors. This activity can also begin to sketch out alternative times given that, as Abram (2014: 129) notes, since planning 'is concerned with transformation through time ... close attention to planning practices indicates that such temporalities are doubted, contested, and mediated'.

The roles of power and control are central features in this agenda. As Raco et al (2018: 1190) highlight: 'time is a resource within the development process' and, like other resources, it represents 'a source of both power and control'. Similarly, Laurian and Inch (2019: 269) emphasise that time 'is a scarce resource and an unescapable constraint' and 'knowledge of time is power', which can be used to shape agendas or to promote interests. It is such insights that have led us to consider the importance of timescapes and processes of chrono-synchronisation or the 'timescaping' of practice. Together, these prompt a call for greater examination of the impacts and possibilities of time and proper time in planning.

The relationship of planning to modern reifications of time is both formative and influential upon system design, scope and anticipations of the future. How we conceptualise and organise time substantially creates the conditions of possibility for planning as a means of applying complex reasoning to decisions that shape the future. That is to say, the creation of dominant understandings of time conditions how we behave as individuals and societies, and how we broker solutions. For planners, it affects how they practise (that is, the very act of planning).

Much greater understanding of time and time squeezes on planners and others is needed too, and an analytical focus on time can provide a fruitful research agenda for planning theory and practice. There is rich potential for deep qualitative empirical research into how 'delay' emerges in planning by tracking planning activity in detail (such as the production dynamics of a local plan), including how it unfolds over time, how time is used and how the actors involved respond. How time is regulated also impacts on different actors in more or less intended and unintended ways, and such matters are critical. Research in this area can help foster an approach that engages effectively with the far-reaching issues of concern to spatial planning.

The political use of time in neoliberal accounts invariably presents planning delay as synonymous with it being 'unnecessary' or avoidable. There appear to be myriad reasons for taking time in planning that is necessary for due process and democratic engagement, but this can all too easily be badged up as a delay and used as an excuse to ignore the complexities and trade-offs that need to be aired and considered when making important decisions.

Rarely, if ever, have studies looked at what causes 'delay' and then examined planning processes in terms of the complexity of the task in the 21st century. Delay may be legitimate if, for example, a government is updating national planning policy or progressing new legislation. As a result, continuing to pursue plan making in the context of such uncertainty would be fruitless. Similarly, if a local authority does not have enough planners or other resources to process the volume, type and timeliness of work expected, then empirical evidence is also needed to understand this better. We need to know more about why an (arbitrary) clock-time target was missed and examine whether this was explainable in terms of the specific context, issues and strategies employed to meet such pressures before condemning it as a product of lassitude.

We therefore see merit in looking at the claims, causes and justifications for delay as part of this research agenda, and to consider the barriers to good planning that is not only 'efficient' but also inclusive and deliberative. As such, a wide research agenda based on the study of time in planning might do well to embrace questions of:

- From where do temporal discourses/narratives of planning delay emerge and how are they evidenced?
- How do individual planners experience speed imperatives, that is, what strategies are adopted and to what consequence?
- How do communities and the diversity of local populations experience existing planning timescapes?
- Where and why is 'delay', or more specifically interruption, in the plan-making process encountered, and what impact does this have, and on whom?
- When and why are time restrictions or squeezes lifted or negotiated?
- How and to what extent can 'proper timing' and deliberative forums assist in inclusion and build trust in planning?

The list is not exhaustive, and indeed closer examination of the development industry appears necessary, but we conclude by reflecting that planning activity is an inherently temporal as much as a spatial activity. It seeks to shape and manage not only the existing built and natural environment but also vision those of the future. We are planning in time and for time, and so the stakes are indeed high. Consideration of the temporalities of planning are not merely a technical or philosophical exercise but a practical and political one infused with attempts to exert power, provide legitimation and exercise control. How time is conceptualised, challenged, managed and practised by different actors with a stake in planning, as well as its outcomes, appear critical to just, sustainable futures.

References

Abram, S. (2014) 'The time it takes': temporalities of planning. *Journal of the Royal Anthropological Institute*, 20: 129–47.
Abram, S. and Weszkalnys, G. (2011) Introduction: anthropologies of planning. Temporality, imagination, and ethnography. *Focal*, 61: 3–18.
Adam, B. (1990) *Time and Social Theory*. Cambridge: Polity Press.
Adam, B. (1995) *Timewatch: A Social Analysis of Time*. Cambridge: Polity Press.
Adam, B. (2004) *Time*. Cambridge: Polity Press.
Adam, B. (2008) Of timespaces, futurescapes and timeprints. Lecture presented at Lüneburg University, 17 June.
Adams, D. and Watkins, C. (2014) *Value of Planning*, RTPI Research Report No. 5, June. London: RTPI.
Adams, D., O'Sullivan, M., Inch, A., Tait, M., Watkins, C. and Harris, M. (2016) *Delivering the Value of Planning*, RTPI Research Report No. 16, August. London: RTPI.
Adkins, L. (2004) Reflexivity: freedom or habit of gender? In L. Adkins and B. Skeggs (eds) *Feminism after Bourdieu*. Oxford: Blackwell, pp 191–210.
Adkins, L. (2009) Sociological futures: from clock time to event time. *Sociological Research Online*, 14(4): 88–92.
Agger, A. and Löfgren, K. (2008) Democratic assessment of collaborative planning processes. *Planning Theory*, 7(2): 145–64.
Airey, J. and Doughty, C. (2020) *Rethinking the Planning System for the 21st Century*. London: Policy Exchange.
Albrechts, L. (2013) Reframing strategic spatial planning by using a coproduction perspective. *Planning Theory*, 12(1): 46–63.
Alexander, E. (1992) *Approaches to Planning*. Philadelphia, PA: Gordon and Breach.
Allmendinger, P. (2016) *Neoliberal Spatial Governance*. London: Routledge.
Allmendinger, P. (2017) *Planning Theory*, 3rd edn. London: Bloomsbury Publishing.
Allmendinger, P. and Haughton, G. (2013) The evolution and trajectories of English spatial governance: 'neoliberal' episodes in planning. *Planning Practice & Research*, 28(1): 6–26.
Archer, T. and Cole, I. (2016) *Profits before Volume? Major Housebuilders and the Crisis of Housing Supply*. Sheffield: Centre for Regional Economic and Social Research, Sheffield Hallum University.
Archer, T. and Cole, I. (2021) The financialisation of housing production: exploring capital flows and value extraction among major housebuilders in the UK. *Journal of Housing and the Built Environment*: 1–21.
Arnstein, S.R. (1969) A ladder of citizen participation. *Journal of the American Institute of Planners*, 35(4): 216–24.

References

Atkinson, W. (2019) Time for Bourdieu: insights and oversights. *Time & Society*, 28(3): 951–70.

Austin, I. (2011) *A Guide to Planning Performance Agreements*. London: British Property Federation and Department of Communities and Local Government.

Bain, A. and Landau, F. (2019) Artists, temporality, and the governance of collaborative place-making. *Urban Affairs Review*, 55(2): 405–27.

Ball, M. (2011) Planning delay and the responsiveness of English housing supply. *Urban Studies*, 48(2): 349–62.

Barnet Council (2023) Pre-application and fast track guidance notes and fees schedule. Available at: www.barnet.gov.uk/sites/default/files/2022-12/planning-pricing-brochure-pre-app-and-fast-track-fees-2023.pdf (accessed 28 March 2023).

Barnett, C. and Low, M. (eds) (2004) *Spaces of Democracy: Geographical Perspectives on Citizenship, Participation and Representation*. London: Sage.

Bastian, M. (2014) Time and community: a scoping study. *Time & Society*, 23(2): 137–166.

Beebeejaun, Y. (2012) Including the excluded? Changing the understandings of ethnicity in contemporary English planning. *Planning Theory & Practice*, 13(4): 529–48.

Biebricher, T. and Johnson, E. (2012) What's wrong with neoliberalism? *New Political Science*, 34(2): 202–11.

Booth, P. (2003) *Planning by Consent: The Origins and Nature of British Development Control*. London: Routledge.

Booth, P. (2020) Will zoning offer more flexibility, speed and efficiency than the discretionary system? In TCPA (ed) *The Wrong Answers to the Wrong Questions?* London: TCPA, pp 29–32.

Bourdieu, P. (1977) *Outline of a Theory of Practice*. Cambridge: Cambridge University Press.

Bourdieu, P. (1984) *Distinction. A Social Critique of the Judgement of Taste*. London: Routledge.

Bourdieu, P. (1992) *The Logic of Practice*. New York, NJ: Wiley & Sons.

Bourdieu, P. (1998) *Practical Reason. On the Theory of Action*. Stanford, CA: Stanford University Press.

Bourdieu, P. (2000) *Pascalian Meditations*. Cambridge: Polity Press.

Bourdieu, P. and Passeron, J.-P. (1977) *Reproduction in Education, Society and Culture*. London: Sage.

Bourdieu, P. and Wacquant, L. (1992) *An Invitation to Reflexive Sociology*. Chicago, IL: University of Chicago Press.

Bouricius, T. (2017) Sortition: envisaging a new form of democracy that enables decision-making for long-term sustainability. In J. Hartz-Karp and D. Marinova (eds) *Methods for Sustainability Research*. Cheltenham: Edward Elgar, pp 129–41.

Breach, A. (2020) *Planning for the Future: How Flexible Zoning Will End the Housing Crisis*. London: Centre for Cities.

Briassoulis, H. (2023) The making of good public plans. Phronesis, phronetic planning research and assemblage thinking. *Planning Theory*, 22(1): 58–84.

Bristow, A. and Nellthorp, J. (2000) Transport project appraisal in the European Union. *Transport Policy*, 7(1): 51–60.

Bristow, T. (2008) Evaluating the effectiveness of planning performance agreements in involving communities in the orchestration of complex development proposals. MSc Dissertation, University College London, UK.

Brody, S., Godschalk, D. and Burby, R. (2003) Mandating citizen participation in plan making: six strategic planning choices. *Journal of the American Planning Association*, 69(3): 245–64.

Brownill, S. (2020) How can we make planning more democratic? In TCPA (ed) *The Right Answers to the Right Questions*. London: Town and Country Planning Association.

Brownill, S. and Bradley, Q. (2017) *Localism and Neighbourhood Planning. Power to the People?* Bristol: Policy Press.

Buitelaar, E. (2020) If neoliberalism is everything, maybe it is nothing. *Planning Theory*, 19(4): 485–8.

Cameron, D. (2011) Speech to the Conservative Party Spring Forum. 6 March, Cardiff, UK.

Campbell, H. (2002) Planning: an idea of value. *Town Planning Review*, 73(3): 271–88.

Campbell, H. (2006) Just planning: the art of situated ethical judgment. *Journal of Planning Education and Research*, 26(1): 92–106.

Campbell, H. and Marshall, R. (2002) Utilitarianism's bad breath? A re-evaluation of the public interest justification for planning. *Planning Theory*, 1(2): 163–87.

Carney, M. (2021) *Values: An Economist's Guide to Everything That Matters*. London: William Collins.

CBP (Campaign for Better Planning) (2021) Six tests for planning. July. Available at: www.cpre.org.uk/resources/six-tests-for-planning/ (accessed 17 February 2023).

Chancellor, E. (2022) *The Price of Time: The Real Story of Interest*. London: Allen Lane.

Charbgoo, N. and Mareggi, M. (2020) A framework for time studies in urban planning: assessment of comprehensive planning in the case of Tehran. *Environment and Planning B: Urban Analytics and City Science*, 47(6): 1098–114.

Cheshire, P. (2018) Broken market or broken policy? The unintended consequences of restrictive planning. *National Institute Economic Review*, 245(1): 9–19.

References

Chilvers, J. and Kearnes, M. (eds) (2016) *Remaking Participation: Science, Environment and Emergent Publics*. Abingdon: Routledge.

Chilvers, J. and Kearnes, M. (2020) Remaking participation in science and democracy. *Science, Technology, & Human Values*, 45(3): 347–80.

Clarke, P. (1996) *Deep Citizenship*. London: Pluto Press.

Clegg, S. (1989) *Frameworks of Power*. London: Sage.

Clifford, B. (2016) 'Clock-watching and box-ticking': British local authority planners, professionalism and performance targets. *Planning Practice & Research*, 31(4): 383–401.

Clifford, B. (2018) Contemporary challenges in development management. In J. Tomaney and J. Ferm (eds) *Planning Practice. Critical Perspectives from the UK*. London: Routledge, pp 55–69.

Cohen, E.F. (2018) *The Political Value of Time: Citizenship, Duration, and Democratic Justice*. Cambridge: Cambridge University Press.

Colenutt, B. (2020) *The Property Lobby: The Hidden Reality behind the Housing Crisis*. Bristol: Policy Press.

Connelly, S. and Richardson, T. (2004) Exclusion: the necessary difference between ideal and practical consensus. *Journal of Environmental Planning and Management*, 47(1): 3–17.

Curato, N., Hammond, M. and Min, J. (2019) *Power in Deliberative Democracy: Norms, Forums, Systems*. Basingstoke: Palgrave Macmillan.

Czarniawska, B. (2004) On time, space, and action nets. *Organization*, 11(6): 773–91.

Datta, A. (2019) Postcolonial urban futures: imagining and governing India's smart urban age. *Environment and Planning D: Society and Space*, 37(3): 393–410.

Davoudi, S. (2017) Spatial planning: the promised land or rolled-out neoliberalism? In M. Gunder, A. Madanipour and V. Watson (eds) *The Routledge Handbook of Planning Theory*. London: Routledge, pp 15–27.

Davoudi, S. and Atkinson, R. (1999) Social exclusion and the British planning system. *Planning Practice and Research*, 14(2): 225–36.

DCLG (Department for Communities and Local Government) (2009) *Development Management: Proactive Planning from Pre-application to Delivery*. London: DCLG.

DCLG (2013) *Planning Performance and the Planning Guarantee: Government Response to Consultation*. London: DCLG.

DCLG (2014) Determining a planning application. National Planning Guidance Para 002 Reference ID: 21b-002-20140306, updated 6 March. Available at: www.gov.uk/guidance/determining-a-planning-application (accessed 13 November 2022).

De Liddo, A. and Buckingham-Shum, S. (2010) Capturing and representing deliberation in participatory planning practices. Paper presented at the Fourth International Conference on Online Deliberation (OD2010), 30 June–2 July, Leeds, UK.

De Magalhães, C., Sonia Freire-Trigo, S., Gallent, N., Scanlon, K. and Christine Whitehead, C. (2018) *Planning Risk and Development*, RTPI Research Paper, April. London: RTPI.

Dean, M. (1994) *Critical and Effective Histories: Foucault's Methods and Historical Sociology*. London: Routledge.

Deer, C. (2012) Doxa, In M. Grenfell (ed) *Pierre Bourdieu: Key Concepts*. London: Routledge, pp 118–24.

DfT (Department for Transport) (2021) Launch of Project SPEED challenges rail industry to cut time and costs of rail upgrades. Available at: https://www.gov.uk/government/news/launch-of-project-speed-challenges-rail-industry-to-cut-time-and-costs-of-rail-upgrades (last accessed 9 February 2023).

Dinan, W. and Miller, D. (2022) Managing the climate apocalypse: think tanks, policy planning groups, and the corporate capture of sustainable development. In A. Hansen and R. Cox (eds) *The Routledge Handbook of Environment and Communication*. London: Routledge, pp 86–99.

DLUHC (Department of Levelling Up, Housing and Communities) (2019) Determining a planning application. National Planning Guidance Para. 024 Reference ID: 21b-024-20190315, updated 15 March. Available at: www.gov.uk/guidance/determining-a-planning-application (accessed 17 July 2023).

DLUHC (2022a) *Government Response to the Levelling Up, Housing and Communities Select Committee Report on the Future of the Planning System in England*, Policy Paper CP673. London: DLUHC.

DLUHC (2022b) Housing delivery test: 2021 measurement. Available at: www.gov.uk/government/publications/housing-delivery-test-2021-measurement (accessed 8 November 2022).

DLUHC (2022c) Levelling up: levelling up the United Kingdom. White Paper. UK Government. Available at: https://www.gov.uk/government/publications/levelling-up-the-united-kingdom

DLUHC (2023) *Increasing Planning Fees and Performance: Technical Consultation*. London: DLUHC. Available at: www.gov.uk/government/consultations/increasing-planning-fees-and-performance-technical-consultation (accessed 3 March 2023).

Dobry, G. (1974) *Review of the Development Control System: Interim Report*. London: HMSO.

Dobry, G. (1975) *Review of the Development Control System: Final Report*. February. London: HMSO.

References

Dobson, A. (2003) *Citizenship and the Environment*. Oxford: Oxford University Press.

Dobson, M. and Parker, G. (2023a) Words (in)action: the orchestration of participation in planning through statements of community involvement in England. *Town Planning Review*, 94(5): 491–512.

Dobson, M. and Parker, G. (2023b) The moral economy of localism in England: neighbourhood planning as neoliberal 'apprentice piece'. *Territory, Politics and Governance*, DOI: 10.1080/21622671.2023.2184856

Dunning, D. (2011) The Dunning–Kruger effect: on being ignorant of one's own ignorance. In Zanna, M.P. and Olson, J.M. (eds) *Advances in Experimental Social Psychology*, Vol 44. Amsterdam: Academic Press, pp 247–96.

Dunt, I. (2023) *How Westminster Works … and Why It Doesn't*. London: Weidenfeld and Nicolson.

Eastleigh Borough Council (2017) Local plan 2016–2036: local development scheme. Available at: https://www.eastleigh.gov.uk/planning-and-building/planning-policy-and-implementation/local-plan (accessed 6 November 2022).

Elias, N. (1992) *Time: An Essay*. Oxford: Blackwell.

Ellis, H. (2020) Foreword. In Town and Country Planning Association (ed) *The Wrong Answers to the Wrong Questions: Countering the Misconceptions Driving the Government's Planning Reform Agenda*. London: TCPA, pp 1–2.

Evans, A. (2004) *Economics and Land Use Planning*. Oxford: Blackwell Publishing.

Evans, A. and Hartwich, O. (2007) *The Best Laid Plans: How Planning Prevents Economic Growth*. London: Policy Exchange. Available at: https://policyexchange.org.uk/wp-content/uploads/2016/09/the-best-laid-plans-jan-07.pdf (accessed 21 February 2023).

Ewing, D. (1972) The time dimension. In D. Ewing (ed) *Long Range Planning for Management*. New York: Harper & Row, pp 439–50.

Fainstein, S. (2017) Urban planning and social justice. In M. Gunder, A. Madanipour and V. Watson (eds) *Routledge Handbook of Planning Theory*. London: Routledge, pp 130–42.

Felt, U. (2016) The temporal geographies of participation. In J. Chilvers and M. Kearnes (eds) *Remaking Participation: Science, Environment and Emergent Publics*. Abingdon: Routledge, pp 178–98.

Ferm, J., Clifford, B., Canelas, P. and Livingstone, N. (2021) Emerging problematics of deregulating the urban: the case of permitted development in England. *Urban Studies*, 58(10): 2040–58.

Firestone, J., Hoen, B., Rand, J., Elliott, D., Hübner, G. and Pohl, J. (2018) Reconsidering barriers to wind power projects: community engagement, developer transparency and place. *Journal of Environmental Policy & Planning*, 20(3): 370–86.

Fishkin, J. (2009) *When the People Speak: Deliberative Democracy and Public Consultation*. Oxford: Oxford University Press.

Fletcher, N. (2023) Request for a debate on 15 minute cities and 20 minute neighbourhoods. Hansard, 9 February, Business of the House, Vol 727, Col 1042. Available at: https://hansard.parliament.uk/Commons/2023-02-09/debates/306A686A-9B53-42BE-9367-C12AB4771504/BusinesOfTheHouse#contribution-94431A3F-FEB8-4A2C-B979-1EE81B5F1FFF (accessed 16 February 2023).

Flinders, M. and Moon, D. (2011) The problem of letting go: the 'Big Society', accountable governance and 'the curse of the decentralizing minister'. *Local Economy*, 26(8): 652–62.

Flyvbjerg, B. (2001) *Making Social Science Matter*. Cambridge: Cambridge University Press.

Flyvbjerg, B. (2004) Phronetic planning research: theoretical and methodological reflections. *Planning Theory and Practice*, 5(3): 283–306.

Forester, J. (1980) Critical theory and planning practice. *Journal of the American Planning Association*, 46(3): 275–86.

Forester, J. (1999) *The Deliberative Practitioner: Encouraging Participatory Planning Processes*. Cambridge, MA: MIT Press.

Forester, J. (2022) Options analysis as context-responsiveness in practice: integrating diagnosis, expertise, and negotiation (refining communicative planning and critical pragmatism). *Planning Theory & Practice*, 23(5): 663–80.

Foye, C. (2022) Framing the housing crisis: how think-tanks frame politics and science to advance policy agendas. *Geoforum*, 134: 71–81.

Friedman, J. (2011) *Insurgencies: Essays in Planning Theory*. London: Routledge.

Friedman, W. (1990) *About Time: Inventing the Fourth Dimension*. Cambridge, MA: MIT Press.

Fuchs, M. and Scharmanski, A. (2009) Counteracting path dependencies: 'rational' investment decisions in the globalising commercial property market. *Environment and Planning A*, 41(11): 2724–40.

Fung, A. and Wright, E. (2003) *Deepening Democracy. Institutional Innovations in Empowered Participatory Governance*. London: Verso.

Gallent, N., De Magalhaes, C., Freire-Trigo, S., Scanlon, K. and Whitehead, C. (2019) Can 'permission in principle' for new housing in England increase certainty, reduce 'planning risk', and accelerate housing supply? *Planning Theory & Practice*, 20(5): 673–88.

Galuszka, J. (2019) What makes urban governance co-productive? Contradictions in the current debate on co-production. *Planning Theory*, 18(1): 143–60.

GLA (Greater London Authority) (2018) Affordable housing and viability supplementary planning guidance. Available at: www.london.gov.uk/programmes-strategies/planning/implementing-london-plan/london-plan-guidance-and-spgs/affordable-housing-and-viability-supplementary-planning-guidance-spg (accessed 28 March 2023).

Goetz, K. and Mayer-Sahling, J.-H. (2009) Political time in the EU: dimensions, perspectives, theories. *Journal of European Public Policy*, 16(2): 180–201.

Graham, S. and Healey, P. (1999) Relational concepts of space and place: issues for planning theory and practice. *European Planning Studies*, 7(5): 623–46.

Gray, J. (2013) *Isaiah Berlin: An Interpretation of His Thought*. Princeton, NJ: Princeton University Press.

Grenfell, M. (ed) (2012) *Pierre Bourdieu: Key Concepts*. Second Edition. London: Routledge.

Grube, D. (2022) *Why Governments Get It Wrong. And How They Can Get It Right*. London: Pan Books.

Guildford Borough Council (2019) Guildford Borough local plan strategy and sites (2015–2034). Available at: https://www.guildford.gov.uk/guildfordlocalplan (accessed 19 October 2022).

Gunder, M. (2010) Making planning theory matter: a Lacanian encounter with phronesis. *International Planning Studies*, 15(1): 37–51.

Gunder, M. and Hillier, J. (2016) *Planning in Ten Words or Less: A Lacanian Entanglement with Spatial Planning*. London: Routledge.

Habermas, J. (2001) *The Postnational Constellation: Political Essays*. Cambridge: MIT Press.

Habermas, J. (2009) *Europe: The Faltering Project*. Cambridge: Polity Press.

Hall, S. (1996) Introduction. In S. Hall, D. Held, D. Hubert and K. Thompson (eds) *Modernity: An Introduction to Modern Societies*. Cambridge: Blackwell, pp 3–18.

Hall, S., Massey, D. and Rustin, M. (2013) After neoliberalism: analysing the present. *Soundings*, 53: 8–22.

Hardy, C. (2012) Hysteresis. In M. Grenfell (ed) *Pierre Bourdieu: Key Concepts*. London: Routledge, pp 131–48.

Hartmann, T. (2012) Wicked problems and clumsy solutions: planning as expectation management. *Planning Theory*, 11(3): 242–56.

Hartwich, O. (2009) *Neoliberalism: The Genesis of a Political Swearword*, CIS Occasional Paper No. 114. Sydney: Centre for Independent Studies.

Hassan, R. (2009) *Empires of Speed: Time and the Acceleration of Politics and Society*. Leiden: Brill.

Haughton, G. and Allmendinger, P. (2016) Think tanks and the pressures for planning reform in England. *Environment and Planning C: Government and Policy*, 34(8): 1676–92.

Hayward, C. (2004) Doxa and deliberation. *Critical Review of International Social and Political Philosophy*, 7(1): 1–24.

Head, B. and Alford, J. (2015) Wicked problems: implications for public policy and management. *Administration & Society*, 47(6): 711–39.

Healey, P. (1997) *Collaborative Planning: Shaping Places in Fragmented Societies*. Basingstoke: Macmillan.

Hendler, S. (ed) (1995) *Planning Ethics. A Reader in Planning Theory, Practice and Education*. New Brunswick, NJ: CUPR.

Hendler, S. (2017) Planning ethics. In S. Mandelbaum, L. Mazza and M. Burchell (eds) *Explorations in Planning Theory*, 3rd edn. New Jersey, NJ: CUPR.

Henneberry, J. (2016) Development viability. In J. Henneberry, C. Whitehead and A. Crook (eds) *Planning Gain: Providing Infrastructure and Affordable Housing*. Chichester: John Wiley, pp 115–39.

Hillier, J. (1998) Beyond confused noise: ideas toward communicative procedural justice. *Journal of Planning Education and Research*, 18(1): 14–24.

Hillier, J. and Rooksby, E. (eds) (2005) *Habitus: A Sense of Place*. Aldershot: Ashgate.

HM Treasury (2015) *Fixing the Foundations: Creating a More Prosperous Nation*. UK Government. https://assets.publishing.service.gov.uk/media/5a7f7fb9e5274a2e8ab4c8b4/Productivity_Plan_print.pdf

Hochschild, A. (2005) *On the Edge of the Time Bind*. New York: Henry Holt.

Honoré, C. (2005) *In Praise of Slow: How a Worldwide Movement Is Challenging the Cult of Speed*. London: Orion Press.

Hope, W. (2009) Conflicting temporalities: state, nation, economy and democracy under global capitalism. *Time & Society*, 18(1): 62–85.

House of Commons Housing, Communities and Local Government Committee (2021). *The Future of the Planning System in England*. https://committees.parliament.uk/publications/6180/documents/80920/default/

Howard, C. (2005) The policy cycle: a model of post-Machiavellian policy making. *Australian Journal of Public Administration*, 64(3): 3–13.

Howe, E. (1992) Professional roles and the public interest in planning. *Journal of Planning Literature*, 6(3): 230–48.

Howe, J. and Langdon, C. (2002) Towards a reflexive planning theory. *Planning Theory*, 1(3): 209–25.

Howlett, M. and Goetz, K. (2014) Introduction: time, temporality and timescapes in administration and policy. *International Review of Administrative Sciences*, 80(3): 477–92.

Hutter, G. and Wiechmann, T. (2022) Time, temporality, and planning – comments on the state of art in strategic spatial planning research. *Planning Theory & Practice*, 23(1): 157–64.

Inch, A. (2015) Ordinary citizens and the political cultures of planning: in search of the subject of a new democratic ethos. *Planning Theory*, 14(4): 404–24.

Inch, A. (2018) 'Opening for business'? Neoliberalism and the cultural politics of modernising planning in Scotland. *Urban Studies*, 55(5): 1076–92.

Innes, J. and Booher, D. (2010) *Planning with Complexity: An Introduction to Collaborative Rationality for Public Policy*. New York: Routledge.

References

Jackson, T. (2009) *Prosperity without Growth: Economics for a Finite Planet*. London: Routledge.

Jackson, T. (2021) *Post Growth: Life after Capitalism*. New York. John Wiley & Sons.

Jenrick, R. (2020) Speech given at the Creating Communities Conference, MHCLG, 23 September. Available at: www.gov.uk/government/speeches/robert-jenricks-speech-on-planning-for-the-future (accessed 1 November 2022).

Jensen, M., Galland, D. and Harrison, J. (forthcoming) The mistreatment of time in planning: Towards planning without the clock in a world increasingly out-of-sync. In M. Tewdwr-Jones, P. Allmendinger and M. Wargent (eds) *Critical Planning Futures: New Directions in Planning Theory*, 2nd edn. London: Routledge.

Johnson, B. (2020) PM economy speech: 30 June 2020. Available at: www.gov.uk/government/speeches/pm-economy-speech-30-june-2020 (accessed 17 February 2023).

Johnson, N. and Johnson, M. (2021) Time and the making of space in urban development, *Rhetoric Society Quarterly*, 51(3): 215–26.

Kahneman, D. (2011) *Thinking, Fast and Slow*. Harmondsworth: Penguin.

Keil, R. (2009) The urban politics of roll-with-it neoliberalization. *City*, 13(2–3): 230–45.

Killian, J. and Pretty, D. (2008) *The Killian Pretty Review, Planning Applications: A Faster and More Responsive System. Final Report*. London: Communities and Local Government.

Kinneavy, J. (1986) Kairos: a neglected concept in classical rhetoric. In J. Moss (ed) *Rhetoric and Praxis: The Contribution of Classical Rhetoric to Practical Reasoning*. Washington, DC: Catholic University of America Press, pp 79–105.

Klein, G., Ross, K., Moon, B., Klein, D., Hoffman, R. and Hollnagel, E. (2003) *Macrocognition*. IEEE Intelligent Systems.

Klein, N. (2007) *The Shock Doctrine: The Rise of Disaster Capitalism*. Basingstoke: Macmillan.

Klosterman, R. (1985) Arguments for and against planning. *Town Planning Review*, 56(1): 5–20.

Kurland, E. (2023) Council officers are having it tough under our troubled planning system. *Architects Journal*, 23 January. Available at: www.architectsjournal.co.uk/news/opinion/council-officers-are-having-it-tough-under-our-troubled-planning-system (accessed 3 April 2023).

Kwarteng, K. (2022) The Growth Plan 2022 speech. Delivered to the House of Commons on 23 September. UK Government. https://www.gov.uk/government/speeches/the-growth-plan-2022-speech

Landwehr, C. (2014) Facilitating deliberation: the role of impartial intermediaries in deliberative mini-publics. In K. Gronlund, A. Bachtiger and M. Setala (eds) *Deliberative Mini-Publics: Involving Citizens in the Democratic Process*. Colchester. ECPR Press, pp 77–92.

Lauermann, J. and Temenos, C. (eds) (2022) *The Urban Politics of Policy Failure*. London: Taylor & Francis.

Laurian, L. and Inch, A. (2019) On time and planning: opening futures by cultivating a 'sense of now'. *Journal of Planning Literature*, 34(3): 267–85.

Lazar, N. (2019) *Out of Joint: Power, Crisis and the Rhetoric of Time*. New Haven, CT: Yale University Press.

Legacy, C., Metzger, J., Steele, W. and Gualini, E. (2019) Beyond the post-political: exploring the relational and situated dynamics of consensus and conflict in planning. *Planning Theory*, 18(3): 273–81.

Lemke, T. (2001) 'The birth of bio-politics': Michel Foucault's lecture at the Collège de France on neo-liberal governmentality. *Economy and Society*, 30(2): 190–207.

Lennon, M. (2017) On 'the subject 'of planning's public interest. *Planning Theory*, 16(2): 150–68.

Lennon, M. and Tubridy, F. (2022) 'Time' as a focus for planning research: exploring temporalities of coastal change. *Journal of Environmental Policy & Planning*, 25(3): 301–13.

LGA (Local Government Association) (2020) Housing backlog – more than a million homes with planning permission not yet built. 20 February. Available at: www.local.gov.uk/about/news/housing-backlog-more-million-homes-planning-permission-not-yet-built (accessed 21 February 2023).

LGA (2021) LGA's position on the government's planning reforms. 29 July. Available at: www.local.gov.uk/parliament/briefings-and-responses/lgas-position-governments-planning-reforms (accessed 2 November 2022).

Lichfields (2023) Counting the cost of delay. Blog, 30 January. Available at: https://lichfields.uk/blog/2023/january/30/start-me-up-but-then-you-stopped-the-continuing-cost-of-local-plan-delays/ (accessed 20 February 2023).

Linz, J. (1998) Democracy's time constraints. *International Political Science Review*, 19(1): 19–37.

Lord, A. and O'Brien, P. (2017) What price planning? Reimagining planning as 'market maker'. *Planning Theory & Practice*, 18(2): 217–32.

Lord, A. and Tewdwr-Jones, M. (2014) Is planning 'under attack'? Chronicling the deregulation of urban and environmental planning in England. *European Planning Studies*, 22(2): 345–61.

MacAskill, W. (2022) *What We Owe the Future*. London: One World.

Mace, A. (2016) The suburbs as sites of 'within-planning' power relations. *Planning Theory*, 15(3): 239–54.

Mace, A. and Tewdwr-Jones, M. (2019) Neighborhood planning, participation, and rational choice. *Journal of Planning Education and Research*, 39(2): 184–93.

Madanipour, A. (2017) *Cities in Time: Temporary Urbanism and the Future of the City*. London: Bloomsbury.

Maidment, C. (2016) In the public interest? Planning in the Peak District National Park. *Planning Theory*, 15(4): 366–85.

Mansbridge, J. (1994) Using power/fighting power. *Constellations*, 1(1): 53–73.

Mansbridge, J., Bohman, J., Chambers, S., Christiano, T., Fung, A., Parkinson, J., Thompson, D. and Warren, M. (2012) A systemic approach to deliberative democracy. In J. Parkinson and J. Mansbridge (eds) *Deliberative Systems: Deliberative Democracy at the Large Scale*. Cambridge: Cambridge University Press, pp 1–26.

Martineau, J. (2016) *Time, Capitalism and Alienation: A Socio-Historical Inquiry into the Making of Modern Time*. Chicago, IL: Haymarket Books.

Maton, K. (2012) Habitus. In M. Grenfell (ed) *Pierre Bourdieu: Key Concepts*. London: Routledge, pp 49–65.

Matthews, P. (2014) Time belonging and development. In N. Gallent and D. Ciaffi (eds) *Community Action and Planning*. Bristol: Policy Press, pp 41–56.

Mattila, H. (2016) Can collaborative planning go beyond locally focused notions of the 'public interest'? The potential of Habermas' concept of 'generalizable interest' in pluralist and trans-scalar planning discourses. *Planning Theory*, 15(4): 344–65.

Mazzucato, M. (2018) *The Value of Everything: Making and Taking in the Global Economy*. London: Penguin.

McGuirk, P.M. (2001) Situating communicative planning theory: context, power, and knowledge. *Environment and Planning A*, 33(2): 195–217.

McLuhan, M. (1980) Living at the speed of light. *MacLean's Magazine*, 7 January, pp 32–3.

McNay, L. (2001) Meditations on *Pascalian Meditations*. *Economy and Society*, 30(1): 139–54.

MHCLG (Ministry of Housing, Communities and Local Government) (2020) *Planning for the Future*. London: MHCLG.

Miller, C. (2020) *Living under Post-democracy: Citizenship in Fleeting Democratic Times*. Abingdon: Routledge.

Miller, H. (2005) Necessary space–time conditions for human interaction. *Environment and Planning B: Planning and Design*, 32(3): 381–401.

Minteer, B. (2005) Environmental philosophy and the public interest: a pragmatic reconciliation. *Environmental Values*, 14(1): 37–60.

Moore-Cherry, N. and Bonnin, C. (2022) Playing with time in Moore Street, Dublin: urban redevelopment, temporal politics and the governance of space–time. In Lauermann, J. and Temenos, C. (eds) *The Urban Politics of Policy Failure*. London: Routledge.

Moroni, S. (2014) Towards a reconstruction of the public interest criterion. *Planning Theory*, 3(2): 151–71.

Mouffe, C. (2005) *The Return of the Political*. London: Verso.

Moulaert, F. and MacCullum, D. (2019) *Advanced Introduction to Social Innovation*. Cheltenham: Edward Elgar.

Moulaert, F., Jessop, B. and Mehmood, A. (2016) Agency, structure, institutions, discourse (ASID) in urban and regional development. *International Journal of Urban Sciences*, 20(2): 167–87.

Mumford, L. (1934) *Technics and Civilisation*. Chicago, IL: Chicago University Press.

Nowotny, H. (1994) *Time. The Modern and Postmodern Experience*. Oxford: Polity Press.

Nozick, R. (1974) *Anarchy, State, and Utopia*. New York: John Wiley & Sons.

NPPF (National Planning Policy Framework) (2023) National Planning Policy Framework. London: Department for Levelling Up, Housing and Communities, UK Government.

NPPG (National Planning Practice Guidance) (2019) Plan-making. Paragraph: 003 Reference ID: 61-003-20190315. UK Government. Available at: www.gov.uk/guidance/plan-making

Odell, J. (2023) *Saving Time: Discovering a Life beyond the Clock*. London: Bodley Head.

ODPM (Office of the Deputy Prime Minister) (2004) *Planning Policy Statement 12, Local Development Frameworks*. London: The Stationary Office.

OECD (Organisation for Economic Co-operation and Development) (2020) Innovative citizen participation and new democratic institutions. Available at: www.oecd.org/gov/open-government/innovative-citizen-participation-new-democratic-institutions-catching-the-deliberative-wave-highlights.pdf (accessed 12 February 2023).

O'Flynn, I. (2022) *Deliberative Democracy*. Cambridge: Polity Press.

Ottinger, G. (2013) Changing knowledge, local knowledge, and knowledge gaps: STS insights into procedural justice. *Science, Technology, & Human Values*, 38(2): 250–70.

Parker, G. and Dobson, M. (2023) 'Do the right thing': Planning at the intersection of the culture wars. *Town and Country Planning*, 92(6): 381–6.

Parker, G. and Dobson, M. (2024) Diagnosing delay in planning: Dobry at 50. *Town and Country Planning*, 93(2).

Parker, G. and Street, E. (2015) Planning at the neighbourhood scale: localism, dialogic politics, and the modulation of community action. *Environment and Planning C: Government and Policy*, 33(4): 794–810.

Parker, G. and Street, E. (eds) (2021) *Contemporary Planning Practice. Skills, Specialisms and Knowledge*. Basingstoke: Red Globe and Macmillan.

Parker, G., Salter, K. and Wargent, M. (2019) *Neighbourhood Planning in Practice*. London: Lund Humphries.

Parker, G., Dobson, M. and Lynn, T. (2022) Governmental logics in commercialised planning practices. The case of local authority pre-application negotiations in the English planning system. *Planning Theory & Practice*, 23(1): 60–80.

References

PAS (Planning Advisory Service) (2023a) *Land Supply*. London: Local Government Association.

PAS (Planning Advisory Service) (2023b) *Evidence Based Research on National Best Practice in Local Authority Approaches to Pre-application Discussions and Planning Performance Agreements (PPAs)*. London: PAS.

Peck, J. (2010) Zombie neoliberalism and the ambidextrous state. *Theoretical Criminology*, 14(1): 104–10.

Peck, J. (2013) Explaining (with) neoliberalism. *Territory, Politics, Governance*, 1(2): 132–57.

Peck, J. and Theodore, N. (2019) Still neoliberalism? *South Atlantic Quarterly*, 118(2): 245–65.

Pickles, E. (2011) Planning reforms boost local power and growth. Joint article by the Secretary of State and the Chancellor, presented on 2 September, DCLG. Available at: www.gov.uk/government/speeches/planning-reforms-boost-local-power-and-growth (accessed August 2023).

Pierson, P. (2004) *Politics in Time: History, Institutions, and Social Analysis*. Princeton, NJ: Princeton University Press.

Pilling, D. (2019) *The Growth Delusion: The Wealth and Well-Being of Nations*. London: Bloomsbury Publishing.

PINS (Planning Inspectorate) (2022) *Called-in Planning Applications: Procedural Guide*. Bristol: Planning Inspectorate.

Pollitt, G. (2008) *Time, Policy, Management: Governing with the Past*. Oxford: Oxford University Press.

Presthus, R. (1951) The Schuster Report: an interpretation. *Journal of the American Institute of Planners*, 17(1): 43–5.

Raco, M. (2005) Sustainable development, rolled-out neoliberalism and sustainable communities. *Antipode*, 37(2): 324–47.

Raco, M. (2016) *State-Led Privatisation and the Demise of the Democratic State: Welfare Reform and Localism in an Era of Regulatory Capitalism*. London: Routledge.

Raco, M., Durrant, D. and Livingstone, N. (2018) Slow cities, urban politics and the temporalities of planning: lessons from London. *Environment and Planning 'C'*, 36(7): 1176–94.

Rawls, J. (1997) The idea of public reason. In J. Bohman and W. Rehg (eds) *Deliberative Democracy: Essays on Reason and Politics*. Cambridge, MA: MIT Press, pp 108–14.

Raworth, K. (2017) *Doughnut Economics*. Vermont: Chelsea Green Publishing.

Raynsford, N. (2018) *Planning 2020. Raynsford Review of Planning in England. Final Report*. London: TCPA.

Rees, T. (2022) Planning chaos to cause 5pc slump in housebuilding next year: Whitehall regulation is 'stifling investment' in new developments. *The Telegraph*, 29 August. Available at: https://www.telegraph.co.uk/business/2022/08/29/planning-chaos-cause-5pc-slump-housebuilding-next-year/

Rifkin, J. (1987) *Time Wars: The Primary Conflict in Human History*. New York: Simon and Schuster.

Rittel, H. and Webber, M. (1973) Dilemmas in a general theory of planning. *Policy Sciences*, 4(2): 155–69.

Rosa, H. (2010) *High-Speed Society: Social Acceleration, Power, and Modernity*. Philadelphia, PA: Penn State Press.

Rosa, H. (2013) *Social Acceleration: A New Theory of Modernity*. New York: Columbia University Press.

Rose, N. and Miller, P. (1992) Political power beyond the state: problematics of government. *British Journal of Sociology*, 43: 173–205.

Rosling, H., Rosling-Ronnlund, A. and Rosling, O. (2018) *Factfulness: Ten Reasons We're Wrong about the World. And Why Things Are Better Than You Think*. New York: Flat Iron.

Roy, A. (2011) Urbanisms, worlding practices and the theory of planning. *Planning Theory*, 10(1): 6–15.

RTPI (Royal Town Planning Institute) and Arup (2018) *Investing in Delivery*. London: RTPI.

RTPI (Royal Town Planning Institute) (2020) Invest and prosper: a business case for investing in planning. Vivid Economics report for the Royal Town Planning Institute. London: RTPI.

Russel, D. and Kirsop-Taylor, N. (eds) (2022) *Handbook on the Governance of Sustainable Development*. Cheltenham: Edward Elgar Publishing.

Rydin, Y. (2013) *The Future of Planning: Beyond Growth Dependence*. Bristol: Policy Press.

Sager, T. (2011) Neo-liberal urban planning policies: a literature survey 1990–2010. *Progress in Planning*, 76(4): 147–99.

Sager, T. (2013) *Reviving Critical Planning Theory: Dealing with Pressure, Neo-liberalism, and Responsibility in Communicative Planning*. London: Routledge.

Salter, K., Parker, G. and Wargent, M. (2023) Localism and the will to housing: neighbourhood development plans and their role in local housing site delivery in England. *Planning Practice & Research*, 38(2), pp 253–73.

Sandercock, L. (1998). *Making the Invisible Visible: A Multicultural Planning History*. Berkeley, CA: University of California Press.

Savini, F., Ferreira, A. and von Schönfeld, K.C. (2022) *Post-growth Planning: Cities beyond the Market Economy*. London: Routledge.

Scharpf, F. (1997) *Games Real Actors Play. Actor-Centered Institutionalism in Policy Research*. Boulder, CO: Westview.

Schon, D. (1982) Some of what a planner knows: a case study of knowing-in-practice. *Journal of the American Planning Association*, 48(3): 351–64.

Schon, D. (1983) *The Reflective Practitioner: How Professionals Think in Action*. New York: Routledge.

References

Schoneboom, A., Slade, J., Tait, M. and Vigar, G. (2022) *What Town Planners Do: Exploring Planning Practices and the Public Interest through Workplace Ethnographies.* Bristol: Policy Press.

Schwanen, T. and Kwan, M. (2012) Critical space–time geographies. *Environment and Planning A*, 44(9): 2043–8.

Shenkin, M. and Coulson, A. (2007) Accountability through activism: learning from Bourdieu. *Accounting, Auditing & Accountability Journal*, 20(2): 297–317.

Shepherd, E., McAllister, P. and Wyatt, P. (2022) State regulation of land financialisation: land promoters, planning risk and the land market in England. *Housing Studies*, DOI: 10.1080/02673037.2022.2149705

Shin, Y. (2013) Bourdieu and urban politics: conceptualizing a Bourdieusian relational framework for urban politics research. *Planning Theory*, 12(3): 267–89.

Slade, D., Gunn, S. and Schoneboom, A. (2019) *Serving the Public Interest? the Reorganisation of UK Planning Services in an Era of Reluctant Outsourcing.* London: RTPI.

Slow Movement (2017) Slow cities and the slow movement. Available at: www.slowmovement.com/slow_cities.php (accessed 5 August 2022).

Smith, G. (2003) *Deliberative Democracy and the Environment.* London: Routledge.

Smith, N. (2008) Neoliberalism is dead, dominant, defeatable – then what? *Human Geography*, 1(2): 1–3.

Sorensen, A. (2015) Taking path dependence seriously: an historical institutionalist research agenda in planning history. *Planning Perspectives*, 30(1): 17–38.

Southerton, D. (2003) Squeezing time, allocating practices, coordinating networks and scheduling society. *Time & Society*, 12(1): 5–25.

Southerton, D. and Tomlinson, M. (2005) 'Pressed for time': the differential impacts of a 'time squeeze'. *The Sociological Review*, 53(2): 215–39.

Standing, G. (2023) *The Politics of Time: Gaining Control in the Age of Uncertainty.* London: Pelican Books.

Stanley, J. and Hansen, R. (2020) People love the idea of 20-minute neighbourhoods. So why isn't it top of the agenda? *The Conversation.* Available at: https://theconversation.com/people-love-the-idea-of-20-minute-neighbourhoods-so-why-isnt-it-top-of-the-agenda-131193 (accessed 4 February 2023).

Stiglitz, J. (2019) The end of neoliberalism and the rebirth of history. *Project Syndicate*, 4(11): 1–2.

Strassheim, H. (2016) Knowing the future: theories of time in policy analysis. *European Policy Analysis*, 2(1): 150–67.

Surrey Heath Borough Council (2023) Surrey Heath Borough Council planning service is piloting a new 'fast track' service, and launching an improved pre-application service from 1 April 2023.

Swyngedouw, E., Moulaert, F. and Rodriguez, A. (2002) Neoliberal urbanization in Europe: large–scale urban development projects and the new urban policy. *Antipode*, 34(3): 542–77.

Tait, M., Chapman, K. and Inch, A. (2020) Is the planning system broken? In TCPA (ed) *The Wrong Answers to the Wrong Questions: Countering the Misconceptions Driving the Government's Planning Reform Agenda*. London: TCPA.

Taylor, Z. (2013) Rethinking planning culture: a new institutionalist approach. *Town Planning Review*, 84(6): 683–702.

TCPA (Town and Country Planning Association) (2020a) *The Wrong Answers to the Wrong Questions: Countering the Misconceptions Driving the Government's Planning Reform Agenda*. London: TCPA.

TCPA (2020b) *The Right Answers to the Right Questions?* London: TCPA.

TCPA (2021) Levelling Up: The Role of Planning. London: TCPA. Available at: https://www.tcpa.org.uk/resources/levelling-up-the-role-of-planning/

Tewdwr-Jones, M. (2017) *Spatial Planning and Governance: Understanding UK Planning*. London: Bloomsbury.

Thompson, E.P. (1993) *Customs in Common*. Harmondsworth: Penguin.

Thomson, P. (2012) Field. In M. Grenfell (ed) *Pierre Bourdieu: Key Concepts*. London: Routledge, pp 67–86.

Thousand, J., Villa, R. and Nevin, A. (2006) The many faces of collaborative planning and teaching. *Theory into Practice*, 45(3): 239–48.

Toffler, A. (1970) *Future Shock*. New York: Bantam.

Tomaney, J., Blackman, M., Natarajan, L., Panayotopoulos-Tsiros, D., Sutcliffe-Braithwaite, F. and Taylor, M. (2023) Social infrastructure and 'left-behind places'. *Regional Studies*, DOI: 10.1080/00343404.2023.2224828

Truss, L. (2022) Conservative Party Conference speech. Birmingham, 5 October. Available at: https://www.conservatives.com/news/2022/prime-minister-liz-truss-s-speech-to-conservative-party-conference-2022

Turner, B. (1990) Outline of a theory of citizenship. *Sociology*, 24(2): 189–217.

Turnhout, E., Metze, T., Wyborn, C., Klenk, N. and Louder, E. (2020) The politics of co-production: participation, power, and transformation. *Current Opinion in Environmental Sustainability*, 42: 15–21.

UN (United Nations) (2022) A world of 8 billion, Future of the World Policy Brief No. 140, October, Department of Economic & Social Affairs.

Uttlesford District Council (2021) Who are the Community Stakeholder Forum? Available at: www.uttlesford.gov.uk/CSF-Who (accessed 15 February 2023).

Virilio, P. (1986) *Speed and Politics: An Essay on Dromology*. New York: Semiotext(e).

Wajcman, J. (2015) *Pressed for Time: The Acceleration of Life in Digital Capitalism*. Chicago, IL: University of Chicago Press.

Wallis, G.W. (1970) Chronopolitics: the impact of time perspectives on the dynamics of change. *Social Forces*, 49(1): 102–8.

References

Walzer, M. (1999) Deliberation, and what else? In S. Macedo (ed) *Deliberative Politics: Essays on Democracy and Disagreement*. Oxford: Oxford University Press, pp 58–69.

Wargent, M. (2021) Localism, governmentality and failing technologies: the case of neighbourhood planning in England. *Territory, Politics, Governance*, 9(4): 571–91.

Wargent, M. and Parker, G. (2018) Re-imagining neighbourhood governance: the future of neighbourhood planning in England. *Town Planning Review*, 89(4): 379–403.

Watson, V. (2014) Co-production and collaboration in planning – the difference. *Planning Theory & Practice*, 15(1): 62–76.

Weber, M. (1904) *The Protestant Ethic and the Spirit of Capitalism*. London: Allen & Unwin.

Weber, R. (2015) *From Boom to Bubble*. Chicago, IL: Chicago University Press.

Widin, J. (2010) *Illegitimate Practices: Global English Language Education*. Bristol: Multilingual Matters.

Wilson, A., Vigar, G. and Tewdwr-Jones, M. (2020) Can technology create a faster and more participatory planning system? In Town and Country Planning Association (ed) *The Wrong Answers to the Wrong Questions: Countering the Misconceptions Driving the Government's Planning Reform Agenda*. London: TCPA, pp 42–46.

Wright, G., Cairns, G., O'Brien, F. and Goodwin, P. (2019) Scenario analysis to support decision making in addressing wicked problems: pitfalls and potential. *European Journal of Operational Research*, 278(1): 3–19.

Wycombe District Council (no date) Public speaking at Planning Committee. Advice note.

Young, I. (2002) *Inclusion and Democracy*. Oxford: Oxford University Press.

Zahariadis, N. (2013) Leading reform amidst transboundary crises: lessons from Greece. *Public Administration*, 91(3): 648–62.

Zielonka, J. (2023) *The Lost Future: And How to Reclaim It*. London: Yale University Press.

Index

Note: References to figures appear in *italic* type; those in **bold** type refer to tables. References to footnotes show both the page number and the note number (16n1).

A

Abram, S. 10, 51, 153
accessibility 86
accountability, of planners 81
Adam, B. 13, 17, 27, 46, 50, 96, 108, 145
  application of ideas to planning **47**
  on control of time 112
  on time and capitalism 30–40
Adkins, L. 42
Albrechts, L. 131
Alexander, E. 121
Allmendinger, P. 117, 142
annual position statements 62
Arnstein, S.R. 86
Atkinson, R. 86
Atkinson, W. 28
authenticity, in deliberative democracy 128
Authority Monitoring Report (AMR) (formerly annual monitoring report) 62

B

Bain, A. 87
Ball, M. 135
Bastian, M. 46
Beebeejaun, Y. 86
Berlin, Isaiah 126
blue tape 53, 113
Bonnin, C. 148
Booth, P. 72
Bourdieu, P. 13, 17, 38, 46, 48, 85, 112
  application of ideas to planning **47**
  doxa, *illusio* and hysteresis concepts 26–7
  habitus, field and capital concepts 23–6
  on time and practice 18–30
Briassoulis, H. 50, 78
Bristow, A. 97
Brownill, S. 114

C

calendars 31, **32**, 44
Cameron, David 97
Campaign for Better Planning (CBP) 110
Campbell, H. 121
capital **21**
  cultural **21**
  economic **21**
  social **21**
  symbolic **21**

capitalism 108
  time and 30–40, 94
Carney, M. 108, 135
Centre for Cities, *Planning for the Future* report 102
certainty 53, 99–105
Chilvers, J. 129, 130
chronos 41–2
chrono-synchronisation 14
chrono-technologies 4, 42, 112
citizen assemblies 131
citizen juries 131
citizenship 123
  rights of 125
Clegg, S. **22**
clepsydra 64
  application to planning decision making 72
Clifford, B. 72, 84
clock time 26, 30–1, **32**, 37, 39
  application of 29
  creation of conditions for 33–5
  regulation of time through 38
clocks 31, 44
coeval rhetorical temporalities 41
Cohen, E.F. 124
Colenutt, B. 144
collaborative planning theory 117
communicative theory 121
community, limits on involvement in planning 75
community engagement 54
community planning weekends 133
Community Stakeholder Forum 133
community-led and neighbourhood planning **74**, 76–7
Connelly, S. 86
consciousness 28
consequentiality, in deliberative democracy 128
consultation periods **74**, 76
control 153
co-production 131, 132
culture wars 6
Curato, N. 127–8

D

Daily Telegraph 112
Datta, A. 147
Davoudi, S. 86

Index

deadlines 29, 37, 40, 83, 97, 124, 134
  imposed on LPAs to determine planning applications **67**, 70–3
Dean, M. 41
decision making 7, 8, 45, 72, 75, 76, 88
  exclusion and 86
  fast-paced 144
  individualist process 78, 79
  political time and 111
  speed of 11, 152
  time frames for 73, 135
deferrals 30
delays 61
  and deliberation 134–6
  intentional 46
  in planning 63, 154
deliberation 8, 36
  and delays 134–6
  factors for **137**
  in planning 132–4
deliberative democracy 25
  authenticity in 128
  consequentiality in 128
  planning time for 127–36
  revisability of decisions made by 143
  see also democracy
deliberative planning
  normative principles and 136–9
  see also planning
deliberative polls 131
deliberative theory 25
democracy
  in planning 121–7
  public trust in 124
  see also deliberative democracy
democratic institutions, public trust in 124
democratic theory, and planning 123–7
deregulation 4, 53, 91, 113
developers 52–3
development, debates over times for 145
development management
  call-ins of planning cases by Secretary of State (SoS) **67**, 73–5
  fast-tracking planning service **67**, 69–70
  planning performance agreements (PPAs) **67**, 68–9
  planning timescapes 66, **67**
  pre-application advice (pre-apps) 66–8
  time limits imposed on **67**, 70–3
development management (DM)
  planners 51
discretion 99–105
dispositions **21**, 24
diversity 122
Dobry Report (1975) 72, 135
'doughnut economics' approach 106–7
doxa **20**, 26–7
Dunning–Kruger effect 99
Dunt, Ian 6

E

Eastleigh Borough Council, Hampshire, Local Development Scheme timetable **60**, 61, 62
economic growth
  challenges to 107
  indefinite continuation of 106
  planning as barrier to 153
Ellis, Hugh 100–1
England
  government department responsible for planning in 16n1
  planning timescape in 140
Enlightenment period 119
enterprise zones 96
environmental impact assessments 72
epistemology 118
esteem needs **82**
ethics 118
Ewing, D. 1, 2
exclusion 85, 86, 123
extensibility 86
'extensions of time' (EoTs) agreements 72–3

F

fast-track planning services **67**, 69–70, 71
Felt, U. 7, 124, 130, 143, 151
fields **19**, 23, 24 5
  field rhythm 28
Fletcher, Nick 54
Flyvbjerg, B. 78
Forester, J. 83, 85, **137**
Foye, C. 101
freeports 96
front-loading 133–4

G

Galuszka, J. 131
globalised markets 92
Goetz, K. 45, 87
governance, time-based/temporal 81
Graham, S. 87
Greater London Authority (GLA) 69
gross domestic product (GDP) 107, 109
growth, through speed, efficiency and certainty 9
Grube, D. 6
Guildford Borough, Surrey, housing delivery profile 64, 65

H

Habermas, J. 92
habitus **19**, 23–4, 25
Hall, Stuart 119
Hartmann, T. 9
Hassan, R. 98
Hayward, C. 25

Healey, P. 87
Hochschild, A. 29, 48, 77
Home Builders Federation (HBF) 112
housing
 back-ending delivery of **56**, 64–6
 drip-feeding supply of 144
Housing and Planning Act (2016) 98
housing crisis 102, 111, 144
Howe, E. 122
Howlett, M. 45, 87
hysteresis **21–2**, 24, 26–7

I

illusio **22**, 26–7
Inch, A. 11, 94, 127, 153
inclusivity 36, 83, 128
industrial time, '5Cs' of 32
institutions, alienation of actors from time 48–9

J

Jackson, T. 106
Jenrick, Robert 16, 57, 97
Johnson, Boris 16, 100, 102, 103
Johnson, M. 41
Johnson, N. 41

K

Kahneman, Daniel 7
kairos 40, 41, 42
Kearnes, M. 129, 130
Keil, R. 92
Killian, J. 68
Kinneavy, J. 42
Klosterman, R. 35
Kwan, M. 39, 87
Kwarteng, Kwasi 103

L

land developers, storage of land for future development 144
land supply requirement (over time) 62–4
Landau, F. 87
Laurian, L. 11, 153
Lazar, N. 4, 13, 17, 47, 102, 111
 application of ideas to planning **47**
 on time and politics 43–6
learned behaviour 24
'left-behind places' agenda 93
Lennon, M. 49
Levelling Up agenda 105
Levelling Up and Regeneration Act (LURA) (2023) 105
Levelling Up, Housing and Communities, Department of 72–3
Levelling Up the United Kingdom (2022) (White Paper) 104
Linz, J. 44
local communities 54–5

local development scheme (LDS) 59–62
Local Government Association (LGA) 59, 109
local planning authorities (LPAs) 55, 57–8, 63, 125
local plans 58
 time frames for 62
Localism Act (2011) 77, 124
London Borough of Barnet, fast-track planning service 70, *71*
Lord, A. 91, 93, 109
love and belonging needs **82**
Luhmann, Niklas 3

M

Madanipour, A. 4
Maidment, C. 123
Mansbridge, J. 128
market value 109
Marshall, R. 121
Maslow, hierarchy of needs 81, 82
Maton, K. **19**
Matthews, P. 2
McGuirk, P.M. 84
Meyer-Sahling, J.-H. 45
Miller, C. 86, 125
mini-publics 131
Ministry of Housing, Communities and Local Government (MHCLG) 16, 97
minority groups, exclusion in participatory planning 86
modern capitalism, relationship between time and 94
modern planning practice 84
money, relationship between time and 33
Moore-Cherry, N. 148
Mumford, Lewis 3

N

National Planning Policy Framework (NPPF) 62, 111
neighbourhood forum 77
neighbourhood planning 76–7, 124, 141, 148
Nellthorp, J. 97
neoliberal principles, normative and 140–5
neoliberal spatial governance strategy 142
neoliberal temporal governance 113, 142
neoliberal-informed policy 4
neoliberalism
 definition of 91
 laissez faire and state-led 92
 and planning 90–4
 and project speed 100
 'roll-back' and 'roll-out' 92
 slow 145
New Public Management (NPM) 34
normative principles
 and deliberative planning 136–9
 neoliberal and 140–5

Index

Nowotny, H. 13, 17, 47, 50, 113, 120, 150
  application of ideas to planning 47
  chrono-technologies 4, 42, 112
  on tendency for institutional power to alienate actors from time 48
  on time and power 40–3

O

O'Brien, P. 91, 109
Odell, J. 35
O'Flynn, I. 128, 138
orrery 146–7
outcomes, measurement of 129
Outline of a Theory of Practice (Bourdieu) 23

P

Parker, G. 46
participation 88, 143
  conceptualisations of **129**, 130
  models and normativities of **129**
  of professional planners 143
Peck, J. 91, 113
performance measures 52
permission in principle (PiP) 98
permitted development rights (PDRs) 96
phronesis, in planning 77–8
phronimos 78, 81, 130
physiological needs **82**
Pierson, P. 44
place-making 87
planning
  as a barrier to economic growth 153
  defined in terms of scope 142
  democratic theory and 123–7
  exclusion in and of 86–9
  fast and slow 143–5
  growth-dependent model for 142
  modernist and postmodernist 116–21
  multidimensional nature of 8
  neoliberal critique of 140
  pace of 83
  participation in 50–5, 77–85
  people and time in 77–85
  post-democratic theory and 123–7
  purpose of 103–4, 148
  relationship between time and 140, 154
  rights to participate in 125
  risk and development 53
  as temporal and spatial activity 155
  temporal politics of planning and growth 105–11
  time and deliberation in 116–39
  time effects/affects in 85–9
  see also deliberative planning
Planning 2020 (Raynsford Review of Planning in England) 103
Planning Act (1932) 72
Planning Advisory Service (PAS) 63, 72

planning applications, determination times for 70–3
planning cases 72
  call-ins of planning cases by Secretary of State (SoS) **67**, 73–5
planning committees, speaking rights at **74**, 75–6
planning delays 63, 109, 154
  cost to the economy 97
Planning for the Future (2020) (White Paper) 57, 100, 102, 104, 134
Planning Inspectorate (PINS) 57–8, 73
planning performance 8
planning performance agreements (PPAs) 38, 68–9
planning permission process 84
planning practitioners, justification of slow planning 150
planning reforms 77, 134
planning system(s)
  'principle-based' 132
  purpose of 111
  reforms 100
planning time 99–105
  for deliberative democracy 127–36
  problematising 140–5
planning timescapes 3, 48, 140
  30-month local plan production **56**, 57–9
  back-ending housing delivery **56**, 64–6
  community-led and neighbourhood planning **74**, 76–7
  consultation periods **74**, 76
  land supply (five-year) **56**, 62–4
  plan monitoring and delivery **56**, 62
  plan start time **56**, 59–62
  in practice 55–77
  speaking rights at planning committees **74**, 75–6
  and temporalities in planning 46–9
plans
  framing of/lifespan 62
  monitoring and delivery 62
  and policymaking 55–7
  start times and the 'local development scheme' 59–62
pluralism 126
policies 146
Policy Exchange 101
policy initiatives, time-bound outputs and expectations 147
policy planners 51
political time 45–6, 47, 64, 146
  and neoliberal planning timescapes 111–15
politicians, national and local 53–4
politics 117
Politics in Time (Pierson) 44
Pollitt, G. 44, 46

population growth 107
post-democratic theory, and planning 123–7
power 50, 144, 153
  Foucauldian treatment of 28
practice **20**, 27, 88
  social fields of 24
  time and 18–30
practice squeeze 51
Pretty, D. 68
professional planners, education and training of 136
project speed 4, 6, 9, 13, 14, 94, 97, 140, 149
  developers and 52
  manipulation of time for 142
  market value and 109
  and planning reform 94
  as timescape 147–9
proper time 42, 46–7, 140, 150
  in social situations 40–1
psychological biasing 128
public interest 138
  in planning 121–7
  proper time in planning for 140
public participation, measurement of 129
public reason, between free and equal individuals 126
public sector planners 51–2
publics 122, **129**

R

Raco, M. 2, 136, 145, 153
Rawls, J. 126
Raworth, Kate 106
Raynsford Review of Planning in England 103, 132
'red tape' 4, 16, 53, 100
reflection 8
reflective planning and practice 14
reflexivity **22**, 24
resistance 30
revisability, of decisions made by deliberative democracy 133
Richardson, T. 86
Rosling, H. 7, 34, 114
Royal Town Planning Institute (RTPI) 35, 108, 135
  Invest and Prosper report 99
Rydin, Y. 142

S

safety needs **82**
Sager, T. 93, 130
Sandercock, L. 119
schedules 29
Schon, Donald 8
Schwanen, T. 39, 87
Secretary of State (SoS) 97

self-actualisation needs **82**
self-reflection 8
Shepherd, E. 109
Shin, Y. 22, 86
Shuster Report 8
slow planning
  in political and business discourses 153
  as timescape 149–50
slow urbanism 11
social fields 18, **19**, 24
social theory 48
  time and practice in 16–49
  treatment of time in 15
social time 17, 39
society
  theory of 18
  timings of 11
socio-economic inequality 93
solar system 146
solubility 81
Sorensen, A. 83
Southerton, D. 29, 40
space–time activity theory 86
space–times 87
speaking rights, at planning committees **74**, 75–6
speed 40
  see also project speed
SPEED (swift, pragmatic, efficient, enhancement, delivery) 97
Standing, G. 44
statements of community involvement (SCIs) 125
Stiglitz, J. 107
Strassheim, H. 44, 46, 68
Street, E. 46
Surrey Heath Borough Council, fast-tracking planning service 70
sustainable development 104, 106, 110–11, 152
Swyngedouw, E. 92
systems theory 131

T

Tait, M. 96, 109
temporal power 23
temporal strategy 29
temporality 39–40
tempo(s) 40, 83
Tewdwr-Jones, M. 93
Thatcher, Margaret 77
Thinking, Fast and Slow (Kahneman) 7
Thomson, E.P. 31
Thousand, J. 51, 87
Threshold Approach 69–70
time
  5Cs of 32, 38, 39
  apportionment, regulation and management in planning 151

Index

calendar based **32**
clock based **32**
colonisation of and with 37–8
commodification of 35–6
compression of 36–7
conceptions of **32**
control of 11, 38–40
diachronic **32**
effects/affects on planning 85–9, 152
as a framework for planning 16–18
governance of 4
historical perspective on 3–7
linear **32**
markers in 29
measurement of 80
in a neoliberalised policy environment 14
in participatory planning 133
and planners 154
in planning 1–3, 121–7, 133
and politics 43–6
and power 40–3
as practice 17, 40, 80
-practice relationships 88
quantitative **32**
rational and collaborative 116–21
reflexiveness of 80
relational view of 4–5
relationship between money and 33
as a research agenda 152–5
as a resource 87
set time **32**
as a social construct and a technology of power 13
in social theory 15, 16–49, 140
and space 54
and speed 80
structural features of 39–40
target based **32**
trust and 3
Time, Policy, Management (Pollitt) 44
time binds 29
time consciousness 28
time economy 30
time shaping practice 7
time squeezes 29, 51, 85, 124
and planners 154
time talk 43, 44–5, 112
timekeeping 30
timescapes 14, 33, 48–9, 77, 78, 125, 132, 139
control through 96
multiple temporalities and 146–7

planning timescapes for the future 145–52
project speed as 147–9
slow planning as 149–50
timing 40
Toffler, A. 27–8, 150
Tomlinson, M. 40
Town and Country Planning Act (1947) 102
Town and Country Planning Association (TCPA) 100, 104, 105, 132
transport policy 97
Truss, Liz 105–6
trust
in democracy and democratic institutions 124
and time 3
Tubridy, F. 49
Turnhout, E. 133

U

uchronia (idealised perfect time) 42–3, 113, 118
United Kingdom
housing crisis 111
planning system in 2007 101
United Nations Sustainable Development Goals (SDGs) 111
urban redevelopment 148
usury 33
Uttlesford community forums 133

V

value pluralism 126
values 45, 126, 135
time and democracy 118

W

Wallis, G.W. 43
Walzer, Michael 127
Wargent, M. 92
Watson, V. 131
Weber, M. 3
Weber, R. 11
Weszkalnys, G. 10
Widin, J. 26
Wilson, A. 114
Wycombe District, Buckinghamshire, speaking rights at planning committees 75

Z

Zahariadis, N. 46
Zielonka, J. 45, 112, 139, 143

www.ingramcontent.com/pod-product-compliance
Lightning Source LLC
Chambersburg PA
CBHW051548020426
42333CB00016B/2157